THE AA GUIDE TO

Cornwall

D1628149

About the author

Laura Dixon has been entranced with the idea of Cornwall since reading stories of smugglers as a child. With an English degree from Oxford and a post-graduate in Journalism behind her, she left the corporate world to become a full-time travel writer in 2001 and has never looked back.

She has regularly contributed to national newspapers, glossy style magazines and leading websites about travel and lifestyle issues, and currently works as the Communications Director of Kid & Coe, where her role is to help make family travel around the world easier. She can think of nowhere better to take kids than Cornwall.

Living in the southwest, she loves to surf, swim and play along Cornwall's coast. Hiking isn't her strong point but local culture, shopping and water-based activities are. Her favourite places are Mawgan Porth, The Lizard Peninsula and St Ives.

Published by AA Publishing (a trading name of AA Media Limited, whose registered office is Fanum House, Basing View, Basingstoke, Hampshire RG21 4EA; registered number 06112600)
© AA Media Limited 2014

Maps contain data from openstreetmap.org
© OpenStreetMap contributors Ordnance Survey data © Crown copyright and database right 2014.

A CIP catalogue record for this book is available from the British Library.

ISBN: 978-0-7495-7594-6
ISBN (SS): 978-0-7495-7630-1

Cartography provided by the Mapping Services Department of AA Publishing

Printed and bound in the UK by Butler, Tanner & Dennis

A05140

Every effort has been made to trace the copyright holders, and we apologise in advance for any accidental errors. We would be happy to apply the corrections in the following edition of this publication.

The contents of this book are believed correct at the time of printing. Nevertheless, the publishers cannot be held responsible for any errors or omissions or for changes in the details given in this book or for the consequences of any reliance on the information it provides. This does not affect your statutory rights. We have tried to ensure accuracy in this book, but things do change and we would be grateful if readers would advise us of any inaccuracies they may encounter by emailing travelguides@theaa.com.

Visit AA Publishing at theAA.com/shop

▶ Finding your way

Use the maps below together with the atlas section and the town plans throughout the guide to explore Cornwall. The A–Z section lists the best of the region, followed by recommended attractions, activities and places to eat or drink. The Places Nearby section then lists other points of interest within a short travelling distance to help you explore a little further.

Many of the restaurants that we've included carry an AA Rosette rating, which recognises cooking at different levels nationwide, from the very best in the local area to the very best in the UK. Pubs have been selected for their great atmosphere and good food. You can find more Rosette-rated places to eat at theAA.com.

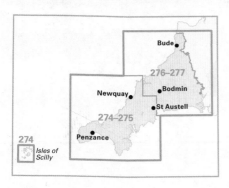

AA

THE AA GUIDE TO

Cornwall

WE KNOW BRITAIN

CONTENTS

We're guessing you probably have your accommodation sorted already, but for those who like to play it by ear, we've recommended a few campsites to help you out (see page 52). Caravan and campsites carry the AA's Pennant rating, with the very best receiving the coveted gold Pennant award. If your tastes run more to luxury then theAA.com also lists AA-rated hotels and B&Bs.

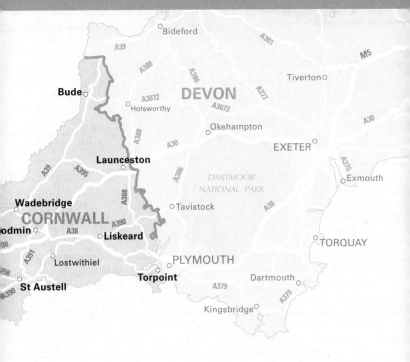

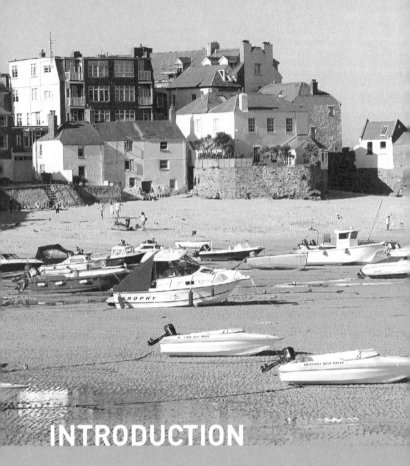

INTRODUCTION

The stereotypical image of Cornwall is captivating enough: craggy cliffs, smugglers' coves and surfers hanging ten off shore. But peek behind the nautical bunting, past the rows of ceramic campervan-shaped moneyboxes and the sunburned tourists on the beach and you'll discover the real Cornwall – a compelling land of myth, legend, dramatic scenery and rich culture.

This county has independence, as well as tin, in its veins; a land once held to be a nation apart from England that still retains the right to veto any English laws it chooses. Its people are quirky and interesting: fishermen who fish by day, sing in fishermen's choirs by night and host gig-racing championships at the weekend; former fashion designers turned boutique caravan owners and guesthouse owners dying to spill the local secrets; gardeners who travel the world in search of exotic seeds to plant in the Cornish soil of their grand sub-tropical estates. There's an enormous pride in being Cornish and you can't disagree with that impulse – this is a place where giants have walked, King Arthur ruled and

smugglers made fortunes overnight. It has a mythical edge unlike anywhere else.

You don't need to be told why people visit Cornwall. From bucket and spade resorts to wild, windswept beaches, regular ridges heralding a great day of surf and fantastic clifftop walking paths with views of schools of breaching dolphins, the sea's the thing. You're never far from it and you can reach either the north or south coast, sometimes both, in under an hour from most places. The unique environment inland – a patchwork of dairy fields, ancient woodlands, misty moors and headlands dotted with Bronze Age remains – is a haven for wildlife and walkers. With multiple Sites of Special Scientific Interest (SSSIs) and Areas of Outstanding Natural Beauty (AONBs), their appeal is undeniable. And the unique climate owing to this county occupying the southernmost and westernmost parts of the UK means that you can see astonishing floral displays, whales and sharks in the sea, and an array of migratory birds not seen anywhere else in the country.

There's also something that you can't pin down about the county. It's in the air, in the sea and in the light, something indefinably free-spirited and distinct from the rest of the mainland UK. Stand by Tate St Ives and look at the sea: that turquoise-blue colour is unique to Cornwall, and deserves its own Pantone reference.

Before you fall in love with Cornwall, as you almost certainly will, heed some words of warning. It's a treacherous place to desire, with a head-spinning number of places to stay and ruinously expensive homes to buy, not to mention a dearth of jobs. Travelling here by car every year will make your blood pressure rise, especially when stuck behind a tractor on a long, slow, sunken road. Make a mental note to look into other, more eco-sound options. Camping, though friendlier on the pocket, can be a depressing experience with a leaky tent on the top of a windy hill. Fish and chips, pasties, clotted cream and ice creams will add inches to your waistline that a gentle daily swim in the sea can't take off. And you'll never be a local, unless you can count your family back ten generations in the same village.

Those foolhardy enough to throw off these words of caution will already be contemplating how they can move down here, run a craft business, cream tea cafe or B&B, and spend their days eating fresh local produce, surfing, walking the dog on a blustery hilltop and sheltering from the rain in an ancient wood-beamed pub, dodging the odd ghost of a smuggler or two. It's hard not to.

Cornwall is an addictive place, and whether you come for a week or a weekend, you'll be back, for sure. Getting here's the easy bit; persuading yourself to holiday in any other part of the UK in the future is the struggle.

TOP ATTRACTIONS

▲ Get lost in the gardens

Cornwall's climate means that the gardens here can cultivate plants and trees you'd never otherwise see in the UK. And the lush country estates of Cornwall revel in it: not just at the Lost Gardens of Heligan (see page 168), but in more than 50 properties around the county, from Trebah (see page 102) to Tresco's Abbey Garden (see page 254).

▼ Visit Eden

Tim Smit's mega tourist attraction near St Austell (see page 89) is a monument to what Cornwall has achieved: a china clay quarry turned eco-centre with rainforests and jungles inside unique biomes. It's the county's top rainy day spot for families and always has something interesting and educational on show.

◄ Reach Land's End

The most southwesterly point of mainland Britain hosts a shopping village and plenty of family attractions (see page 120), as well as the famous Land's End signpost and beautiful clifftop scenery. Something for everyone.

▶ Go underground at Geevor

Winner of three awards at the 2013 Cornwall Tourism Awards, dramatically situated Geevor Tin Mine (see page 197) has a museum, visitor centre, underground tour and even mineral panning, so you can learn all about Cornwall's mining heritage – whilst keeping out of the rain.

◄ Book seats at the Minack

This incomparable open-air theatre near Land's End (see page 215) was originally made for *The Tempest*, with the wild, raging waters of the Atlantic as a backdrop. Created in the 1930s, it's just as good today, with a summer programme of classics, proms and children's shows, and sub-tropical gardens surrounding it.

◀ Check out the National Maritime Museum

Half museum, half interactive experience, the National Maritime Museum Cornwall (see page 96) is right on the waterfront. Watch the tides turn from the safety of an underwater viewing gallery, or learn to sail a model boat in artificial winds.

▶ Be the king of the castle at St Michael's Mount

Walk across the causeway and beside rocks strewn with bladderwrack at low tide to reach this unique island topped with sub-tropical gardens and a castle (see page 159). The modern-day home of the St Aubyn family is a real a one-off, and is the former home of the mythical giant Cormoran, so the legends say.

◀ Visit the other Tate

Artists are drawn to St Ives for the quality of the light; less talented visitors can appreciate the fruit of their labours at the fourth Tate (the others are in London and Liverpool), Tate St Ives (see page 237), which hosts ever-changing exhibitions of contemporary art, frequently including the work of leading local artists of the 'St Ives School'.

▲ Explore King Arthur's Tintagel

Perched on a cliff edge, with Merlin's cave down below, legend combines with landscape at the ruins of Tintagel Castle (see page 261). Visit on a wet, moody day for added drama.

HISTORY OF CORNWALL

People living in Devon were already visiting Cornwall as far back as the Palaeolithic period, around 400,000–200,000 BC. Archaeologists have found flint axes and blades which show that modern humans travelled through the southwest, but, so far as we know, none settled in Cornwall. By 10,000 BC, hunter-gatherers had started to settle around Cornwall's coastline, and from the New Stone Age or Neolithic period (4000–2400 BC), they farmed the lands, creating hedges and building settlements.

Tin mining brought great prosperity to the county in more modern times; but it was a great boon in these early days too. In the Early Bronze Age period, metalworking in bronze began, using the natural resources of tin and copper. Many of the stone circles, menhirs and barrows standing today commemorate this period: Cornwall has the second largest number of prehistoric remains in the UK, after Wiltshire.

The Celts arrived in Britain around 600 BC and the Iron Age began. In Cornwall, weapons and farming tools were made from

◀ Iron Age Village, Chysauster

iron and people started to live in settlements. Economic and social centres were established on hilltops and headlands, such as Trevelgue Head near Newquay.

According to the Ancient Greeks and Romans, at this time the southwest tip of Britain was named Belerion or Bolerium and the Cornovii tribe was based here. This tribe may have given its name to the Cornish word for the area, *Kernow* or *Curnow*, later mixed with the Anglo-Saxon word *Wealas* for Welshman or foreigner to make *Curnow-wealas*: Cornwall.

Roman times: tin trading with Gaul
Cornwall was far enough west to escape most of the Roman dominance of Britain and was a place of refuge for many Celts. Roman roads did make it to the peninsula but there are only a few Roman sites in the county; Tregear, near Nanstallon, Restormel Castle, and a fort near St Andrew's Church in Calstock included. Likewise, only a few Roman road milestones have been found – and it looks likely that in Roman times the sea was more important than roads, forming trading routes between other parts of the British Isles and Gaul.

The Chysauster, Scilly Isles and Carn Euny archaeological sites date from this period, showing uniquely Cornish-style stone courtyard houses. Under Roman influence, rural life was largely unchanged in the county. Cornwall notably traded in tin at this time with other places, including Ireland, Wales and Brittany, which grew to influence its development, language and culture.

Post-Roman times: the Arthurian period
From around AD 500, Celtic kings ruled Cornwall, and lovers of legend say that the real King Arthur ruled in Tintagel during this period. The Saxons began to advance through the West, destroying Roman civilisation and bringing Roman Christianity to England. In 710, Ina, the King of the West Saxons, attempted to destroy the kingdom of Dumnonia, as Cornwall was known. There were battles for the next 50 years, until the Vikings visited the Wessex coasts in 807 and formed an alliance with the Cornish against the Saxons.

Over the next few hundred years, Cornwall was contested by the Saxons, Vikings and resident Cornish tribes. King Athelstan, grandson of King Alfred, fixed the boundary of Wessex and Cornwall as the east bank of the Tamar River.

Medieval times: church building and an independent nation
In the later Medieval period, Cornwall showed great signs of development. After the Norman Conquest, the Earl of Cornwall

built a castle at Launceston. The Domesday Book recorded markets and fairs in various points in the northern part of the county, reflecting the rural and trading development of the area which continued for the next 100 or so years, with more and more markets granted legal status.

Like Wales, Cornwall was still held to be a nation apart from the rest of England. Cornish was the most widely spoken tongue. Men worked in the mines, in the fields and on the sea. Churches were built and rebuilt, according to the wishes of the Bishop of Exeter, and in 1284, the King of England's claim to jurisdiction over Cornwall was rebuffed. In 1338, Edward the Black Prince was created the first Duke of Cornwall, and in 1346, Cornish archers, who had longbows and a reputation for sharp shooting, distinguished themselves at the Battle of Crécy (4,000 French knights were killed, among many others).

The Black Death then swept through Cornwall, killing half the populations of Truro and Bodmin. During the next 100 years, almost every Cornish church was altered or enlarged.

Tudor and Stuart times: sea forts and the English tongue
This period was distinguished by a gradual erosion of Cornwall's status as an independent nation as the English language became widely introduced.

This greater interaction and enslavement to the king began with Henry VII demanding taxation from the Cornish to pay for his war against the Scots – previously they had been exempt. Despite a spirited uprising, the Cornish failed and their leaders were

▼ Lanyon Quoit

executed. In 1508, Henry VII issued the Charter of Pardon to the county allowing the Cornish Stannary Parliament to veto English legislation – a law that still exists today.

In this period, Henry VIII built fortifications along the south coast of Cornwall, including Pendennis Castle in Falmouth and its twin, St Mawes Castle, across the estuary from it.

The introduction of the *Book of Common Prayer* in English into Cornwall in 1549 heralded the end of the Cornish tongue and the county's independent status. The Cornish rebelled against it, preferring Latin over English as a language that was more widely understood in church, but were put down. Some 150 years later, only 5,000 people were still able to speak Cornish, most of whom lived at the furthest reaches of the county.

While Elizabeth I ruled, Cornwall came under repeated attacks from the Spanish, who attempt to burn Penryn and landed in Mount's Bay, attacking Mousehole, Newlyn, Penzance and Paul.

Small tin mines were worked at St Agnes, later to become a large source of wealth and jobs during Queen Victoria's reign.

17th–19th centuries: tin mining and a tsunami
Through the 17th century, country estates were built in Cornwall and the Cornish played a role in the English Civil War as a Royalist enclave in the largely Parliamentarian Southwest. Cornwall's deepest and most significant tin mines were built as the industrial revolution hit Cornwall, and china clay was quarried in locations including St Austell – the future site of the Eden Project.

▼ Restormel Castle

▲ Wheal Coates Tin Mine, St Agnes

In 1755, an earthquake in Lisbon triggered a tsunami that reached Cornwall, causing great loss of life and property. In 1777, Dolly Pentreath, said at the time to be the last speaker of Cornish, died. In fact, Cornish was still spoken in part until the 19th century, but this shows how dramatically the language was overtaken by English. English was the compulsory language for teaching in schools in the 18th century.

Mining and china clay quarrying continued to build a prosperous Cornwall through the 18th and 19th centuries, and various canals, horse-drawn rail links and railways were mooted and developed as ways to transport the raw materials. In the 1860s, Great Wheal Vor was described as probably the richest tin mine in the world. Copper ore was also mined in much of Cornwall at this time.

From the 1830s onwards, the great Cornish migration began as Cornish mining skills were highly sought abroad, especially in the silver mines of Mexico and the iron mines of Canada. The migration continued following the decline of the mines in Cornwall as emigrants sought a better life elsewhere. It is said that the Cornish diaspora exported rugby union around the world and helped to develop the game in Australia, New Zealand and South Africa.

The flag of St Piran – a white cross on a black background, also known today as the Cornish flag – was first mentioned as such in 1838.

In legal arguments running through the mid-19th century, there was much debate about whether Cornwall was part of England and under the rule of the Crown, or independent and semi-autonomous. The Crown was defeated: Cornwall still had a degree of independence.

▲ The Eden Project

20th and 21st centuries: tourism and a revival of the language

Some mines continued until the 1980s in Cornwall, but most dwindled and closed in the early part of the 20th century. China clay is still excavated and exported today, but Cornwall's industrial glory days were drawing to a close and the mines gave up their last.

In the 1950s, attempts were made to support greater self-government of the county by the political party Mebyon Kernow, to no success; Cornish pride has however been fostered by the party's use of the flag of St Piran, which can be seen in many places today.

The 1990s saw Cornwall divided: an increasing population plus decreasing job prospects meant that the county had high levels of poverty, with three times more people unemployed than in 1961. At the same time, tourism was growing, bringing wealth to some, along with wealthy second homeowners from the rest of the UK. The division still exists.

The Eden Project opened in 2000 in a 160-year-old exhausted china clay quarry near St Austell, heralding a move towards environmental sustainability.

In 2001, inhabitants of Cornwall were allowed to record their ethnicity as Cornish on the national census and Cornish culture was growing. Cornish is spoken in a number of places and is encouraged in select schools today. The people of Cornwall are rightly proud of their heritage, and are fully intent on continuing into the future with their unique culture and customs going from strength to strength.

BACK TO NATURE

The story of Cornwall as told by its landscape starts 400 million years ago, with rocks containing veins of tin and copper being twisted and carved by the last Ice Age. Erosion, weathering and man have shaped this mass of rocks, with granite at their heart, to create a county surrounded on three sides by the sea and with views, nature and habitats seen nowhere else in the country.

From the coastal villages and sandy beaches to windswept moors, green fields and grazing pastures, estuary valleys and dramatic cliffs, Cornwall's landscape is dazzling and diverse. Sustainable tourism is essential to preserve the unique characteristics of the Cornish landscape. That means obeying local bylaws, the Countryside Code and common sense; it also means going out of your way to enjoy the scenery and wildlife as far as you can, and contributing to the conservation economy where possible.

There are 12 AONBs in Cornwall, 167 SSSIs and many local nature reserves. If you're interested in wildlife, geography and the landscape, the Cornwall Wildlife Trust runs events and guided walks and has downloadable walks on its website, cornwallwildlifetrust.org.uk.

▲ Golitha Falls; Cheesewring

These are a few of the most notable areas:

Bodmin Moor
Bodmin Moor is the ancient heart of Cornwall. What makes it so special is its wild quality – the fens, bogs, wetlands and moor here are remote and unsettled in most parts, and some of the moor has never been tamed or enclosed. It includes valuable wildlife habitats and the remains of Neolithic tors, Bronze Age roundhouses, barrows and standing stones, plus Brown Willy, the highest point in Cornwall. There are stacks of eroded rocks on the tors, such as Cheesewring, one of the iconic views of the Cornish moorland, and rivers flow from the moor to the north and south coasts.

The Lizard Peninsula
Geologists go crazy for this peninsula, the most southerly tip of England, which is formed mostly from a unique rock, serpentine, found nowhere else in the rest of Cornwall or the UK. This rock is a part of the Earth's mantle normally found tens of kilometres underground, but here it was thrust up to the surface as the continents shifted, many millions of years ago. The Lizard's churches typically have fonts, lecterns and bible stands made from shaped and polished serpentine. The peninsula is also home to some of the oldest rocks in Cornwall.

Hartland Peninsula

This part of north coast Cornwall, an AONB which is shared across the border with Devon, has remarkable creased and distorted cliffs with ridges of folded rock strata visible on the beach at low tide in corduroy-like lines. The views are dramatic. Away from the sea, the peninsula gives way to dairy farms, green fields and small hamlets.

St Agnes

For an example of Cornwall's mining heritage, visit St Agnes on the north coast. Known for its sandy surf beach, you don't have to look far along the headland to see engine houses, chimneys and shafts, along with rocky, bare patches of ground stained by iron ore. There are mining tracks across the fields and heathland, and small former mining villages all around the area.

Wildlife

With all these distinctive habitats comes a unique array of bird, mammal and sea life. It wouldn't be silly season in the UK press without a story suggesting that there are great white sharks cruising the sea around Cornwall waiting to pick off surfers – the truth is that there are sharks in the sea but none of them want to eat you.

▼ Basking shark

Cornwall's largest creature, excepting occasional visits from migratory minke whales, is the basking shark, which can often be seen from Land's End. While you're there, look out for dolphins too: Risso's dolphins and bottlenose dolphins are the most commonly seen, not just here, but from many beaches and cliffs in the county. Grey seals are also residents; Mutton Cove near Godrevy is a good places to see them, as well as nesting seabirds in the cliffs.

Inland, Cornwall's woods provide a fantastic habitat for native bird species. Tehidy Woods, the largest woodland area in Cornwall, is a good stop for birders, where you might see robins, blue tits, jays, nuthatches and green woodpeckers, and also squirrels.

Migrant waders, gulls and terns are seen in the Hayle Estuary, and Stithians Reservoir plays host to unusual diving birds such as pochard and golden eye; and there are buzzards and sparrowhawks in the surrounding farmland. There's a hide there too.

Several animal centres focus on local wildlife, including the Cornish Birds of Prey Centre at St Columb Major and the Cornish Seal Sanctuary in Gweek. But you don't have to make a special trip anywhere to see Cornish wildlife. You could see peregrine falcons nesting on Truro Cathedral, wildflowers growing in cracks in the pavement, seals bobbing in pretty fishing village harbours and buzzards perched on pylons. It's that kind of place.

▼ Dozmary Pool, Bodmin Moor

LORE OF THE LAND

The ancient lore of Cornwall is as wild as its scenery, reflecting a history of Celts driven west by invaders. They brought with them tales of giants, gods and fairies. Among the fiercest of Cornwall's giants was Bolster, so tall that he could plant one foot on Carn Brae, near Camborne, and the other at St Agnes 6 miles away. This place is named for the saint who, as a young lass, destroyed Bolster (who was already married) when he fell in love with her. Tasked by the beautiful Agnes to prove his love by filling a hole in the cliff at Chapel Porth with his own blood, he failed in his mission because the hole is bottomless, leading directly to the ocean, and he bled to death in the attempt.

Cornish little folk, still invoked today as tourist traps for the unwary with money to spend, come in many guises. The Piskies, who live on the moorlands and can come into homes to help around the house, are thought to be the souls of the dead. Also indoors are the ever-helpful Brownies. Underground, Knockers inhabit the old tin mines and, by tradition, miners always left food out to placate them

◀ King Arthur and his round table (a medieval fake)

and insure against fatalities. In old ruins and barrows, treasure is guarded by the Spriggans who, because they are purported to swell themselves to huge sizes, are believed to be giants' ghosts.

The king of legend

Arthur gets star billing in Cornwall's folklore. Atop the windswept crags of north Cornwall stands Tintagel Castle, believed to be the hero's birthplace. It was here in an ancient fortress that Uther Pendragon, assisted by the magician Merlin, disguised himself as the husband of the beautiful Igerna, wife of Gorlois, the Duke of Cornwall. Igerna was indeed seduced and gave birth to the future king.

The home of Merlin, the young Arthur's teacher and guide, was the massive cave hollowed out by the waves below the fortress. According to the most popular version (there are several, and not just in Cornwall), the infant Arthur was found here by Merlin, plucked from the mighty waves and carried to safety. In the cave's echoing vaults, the wizard's ghost is still believed to wander, holding aloft Arthur's magical sword Excalibur to light his way.

Across the county episodes from the Arthurian legends can be found at every turn. Arthur is reputed to have held court in the city of Celliwig, believed to be the modern Castle Killibury, an ancient hill fort so high up that it was said that from here Arthur's protectors could 'shoot an arrow through the legs of a wren in Ireland'. The still and brooding Dozmary Pool, just south of Bolventor – said to be bottomless – is allegedly where Excalibur was returned to the Lady of the Lake by Sir Bedivere after Arthur had been defeated by Mordred, his evil nephew, and was dying of his wounds. The Cornish chough, a now rare bird with an explosive, onomatopoeic voice, is said to embody Arthur's soul, its red bill and legs symbolising the king's bloody end.

Tragic lovers

The doomed lovers Tristan and Iseult (Isolde) featured in Cornish lore long before Wagner publicised them in an opera. Their demise is commemorated by the starkly simple Tristan Stone near Fowey. Tristan, nephew of King Mark of Cornwall, reached Ireland's shores having been wounded by a poisoned spear. There he was nursed to health by the beautiful Iseult before returning to Cornwall.

In time, Tristan was in Ireland once again, at the request of King Mark, on a mission to return with Iseult, who was destined to be the king's bride. But on the journey back, the pair accidentally drank the love potion intended for the wedding night. They fled into the Cornish countryside, but eventually the royal marriage went ahead. On the way to their wedding, however, Mark and Iseult met a leper – actually Tristan in disguise – who carried her across a ford. At the ceremony she was then able to swear that apart from Mark and the leper no other man had ever touched her. On his deathbed Tristan sent a ship to fetch his love so that she could heal him, instructing a messenger to hoist white sails if she was on board when the ship returned. But only black sails were flown and Tristan died of his grief. A cross at Castle Dore, Mark's redoubt, stakes out Tristan's last resting place.

Healing powers

All over Cornwall, the rocks and stones that dot the landscape are believed to have magical or healing powers. Near Madron, 2.5 miles from Penzance, is Men-an-Tol, an alignment that includes the enigmatic circular 'holed stone'. At dawn, sick children were passed naked through the hole towards the sun to effect cures; for rickets the child needed to pass through nine times. Adults with rheumatism would also crawl through nine times while facing the sun, presuming their joints were not too stiff to make the moves. To ensure their fertility women who had recently taken up with a new partner would also pass through the holes. And long before *Mastermind*, it was traditional to place a pair of brass nails across each other within the hole in the belief that the stone would then answer any question put to it.

Out on the moor

Even on the windiest night on Bodmin Moor – and there are many – the desperate cries of a dark spirit can be heard ringing out. This is the speaking soul of Jan Tregeagle, a man doomed to wander the moor as recompense for the sin of murdering his wife and children. He is said to have returned from the grave to bear witness in court in a case of fraud. As a reward his soul was saved but cruel spells were cast on him, such as requiring him to empty Dozmary Pool using a limpet shell with holes in it. But on a wild and windy night Tregeagle escaped onto the moor, away from the power that bound him, where his screams persist.

More mysterious yet is the Beast of Bodmin, possibly an escaped big cat, which has been held responsible for killing sheep. While it has not yet been identified, stories of the creature persist; perhaps it's more than just a shaggy cat story...

Woman power

Cornwall is witch country. At Trewa, in the rugged landscape near Zennor, was a rock where all the witches of the west were believed to meet on Midsummer's Eve to light fires. To touch the rock nine times at midnight – at any time of year – was a sure way of dispelling misfortune. Among the most notorious of these evil women was Madgy Figgey, leader of a gang of witches who were notorious wreckers. From her 'seat of storms' near Raftra, the hag whipped up the seas and led sailors to their doom. What's more, when the bodies were washed ashore they were stripped of their valuables and the jewels presented to local girls.

She may not have been a witch, but Sarah Polgrain of Mount's Bay had powers from beyond the grave. Sarah was the lover of Yorkshire Jack, and was hanged for the murder of her husband. On the scaffold Sarah and Jack exchanged wedding vows, and after her death sightings of her ghost – bearing tell-tale black bruises on her neck – were widely reported. Jack went off to sea, but he was swept from the ship's deck in a terrifying storm. The last sight to reach his eyes was Sarah and the Devil screaming at him.

Mysteries of the sea
It's not just the land that's awash with myth and legend: phantom ships sail off the Cornish coast. Typical is the story of the vessel that was once seen approaching land between Penzance and Land's End. The night was clear, with a gentle breeze, but the ship appeared to be heading for the rocks. However, instead of crashing to its doom, it mounted the land from the waves and 'sailed' on to the village of Porthcurno, where it vanished for good.

And of course mermaids, or 'merry maids', swim in Cornish waters. Zennor (see page 271) has one famous legend, while at Doom Bar, Padstow, the sand that blocks the entrance to the harbour is said to have been put there as a curse by a mermaid: she used to guide ships safely into the harbour, but a man with a gun took a pot shot at her while she was bathing. The sand bar was her dying curse; something to remember if you overhear someone going into a pub saying, 'I'm dying for a Doom Bar...'

SMUGGLING IN CORNWALL

In the 18th and 19th centuries, Cornwall's coastline was awash with smugglers and wreckers evading the King's men and their excise duty, and hiding rum, tea and lace in caves and tunnels along the coast while the locals turned their eyes to the wall so they could say they had seen nothing.

At a time when high taxes were sought to finance wars, fishermen and packet ship crews needed to smuggle to survive. Miners too at this time experienced ruinous conditions: some were laid off in summer due to a lack of water to complete their tasks, leaving them penniless for months. Smuggling was a way of life for many people and was not so much romantic as desperate and steeped in poverty.

Cornish smuggling was also buoyed by a lack of prevention. Customs officers were not as plentiful in the county as elsewhere, and with so many coves and inlets to cover, they were stretched to their limit. With sympathies to their fellow men, Cornish juries were said to rarely convict any smugglers in the dock. And customs officers were often easy to bribe, too.

'Harvesting from the sea', or wrecking, was a key Cornish activity. There's no suggestion that the people of the coastal communities actually lured ships on to the rocks, killed their sailors and took their loot, as fictional accounts would have it, but ships wrecked on rocks were regularly ransacked for their cargo as their helpless crew looked on. Again evading the customs officers, hundreds of local villagers would run towards the site of a wounded ship at shore, stripping it of every last valuable item.

Smuggling and wrecking brought enormous wealth to some parts of Cornwall. Variously bringing in brandy, rum, gin, tea and spices from the Indies and untaxed Guernsey, and selling it on upcountry, gangs of smugglers saw gold coins beyond their wildest dreams. They had inventive ways to evade the customs officers, from filling hearses with contraband to tying bladders full of spirits under the full skirts of local women and hiding goods under carts filled with seaweed. Stories of tunnels from the beaches to local houses and churches are the most evocative of this time, but while stories and documents mention pubs, churches and country houses with these passages, fewer than you'd think still exist today.

If you want to explore Cornwall's smuggling history, start on the south coast. Its gently shelving sandy beaches were more popular than those of the north shore, which were more exposed with heavy waves. Looe has a particularly strong smuggling history, with caves used to store goods and Looe Island as a strategic outpost. A farmer is said to

▲ Jamaica Inn

have ridden his white horse along Looe beach to alert those on the island to customs raids. Ye Olde Jolly Sailor Inn in Looe itself is a well-known smugglers' pub.

Pretty Polperro just down the coast has a strong smuggling history too: lace, brandy and tea were brought in. The ghost of a smuggler, Battling Billy, shot while desperately trying to escape from the customs and excise men with goods in the back of a horse-drawn hearse, can apparently still be seen on its cobbled streets.

Further south, the beaches near St Michael's Mount were some of the most famed for their smuggling gangs. Pisky Cove, Bessy's Cove and King's Cove were regularly used, with secret passages to nearby houses, cliff paths, caves and a secluded harbour where boats could slip in and out unnoticed.

More risky locations on the north coast included Sennen, St Ives and Hayle, where tunnels from the beach to nearby houses have been found. There are caves in the cliff at Porthcowan where goods were stored, and Pepper Cove is so named because pepper and spices were regularly brought in to this perfect smugglers' cove, where ships were hidden from view by the high cliffs.

Clovelly, just over the Devon border, is associated with perhaps the most grisly smuggling history. Locals whispered of cannibals keeping tubs of salted human flesh in the caves along the coast as a way to keep visitors away from their secret smuggling stash. If you walk east along the shore from the harbour you can see the smugglers' cave today.

If you want to find out more about smuggling in Cornwall, there is a museum about it at Jamaica Inn on Bodmin Moor (see page 66). The inn dates from the 1760s and is the famed location for Daphne du Maurier's novel about a group of murderous wreckers. The inn itself was a staging post between the coast and Devon, and smugglers and traders regularly passed through it with their goods. As Rudyard Kipling's *Smuggler's Song* goes, 'Watch the wall my darling while the Gentlemen go by.'

THE AA GUIDE TO

Cornwall

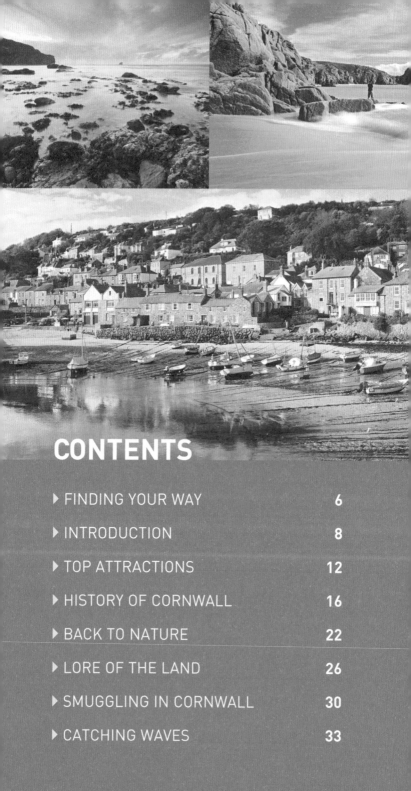

CONTENTS

▶ Finding your way

Use the maps below together with the atlas section and the
town plans throughout the guide to explore Cornwall. The A–Z
section lists the best of the region, followed by recommended
attractions, activities and places to eat or drink. The Places
Nearby section then lists other points of interest within a short
travelling distance to help you explore a little further.

Many of the restaurants that we've included carry an AA
Rosette rating, which recognises cooking at different
levels nationwide, from the very best in the local area to the
very best in the UK. Pubs have been selected for their great
atmosphere and good food. You can find more Rosette-rated
places to eat at theAA.com.

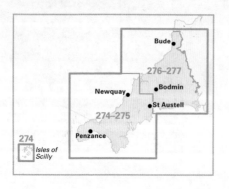

CATCHING WAVES

It's hard to describe how exhilarating and addictive surfing can be unless you've tried it – after spilling off your board into cold water time and time again, gaining the balance to stand, and finally carving through bigger and bigger waves, you can feel as if you're in harmony with the water and landscape around you, and get a huge adrenaline rush at the same time.

It's enough to make serious fans travel for five hours each way at weekends to keep up the habit, or ditch jobs in the city and move to Cornwall, just so they can surf every morning before work. All this, and it's good for you, too. Cornwall's status as the UK's top surf destination was born in the 1960s, when surfing reached the UK and early pioneers realised that the waves of the North Atlantic combined with the beach breaks of Cornwall were ripe for the picking. Newquay was then, and is now, the surf capital of the county, with Fistral Beach one of the best beach breaks in

Cornwall. It hosts the annual Boardmasters festival, an international music festival which encompasses the surfing contest that has been running for more than 30 years and which has a huge surf industry around it, including the O'Neill and Quiksilver surf schools, countless surf shops, and hotels and B&Bs geared up for surfing. Altogether, the sport brings £64 million to the county every year and provides 1,600 jobs.

Beyond the beach, surf lifestyle is a big deal, and certainly where the money is made. Huge VW transporters, hoodies and surf-style beach bars prop up the look: it's all about being carefree, trying hard to look as if you're not trying too hard and being cool. You don't need to surf to look the part, after all.

If you are keen to get in on the action, there are many ways to do it. Just about every beach you visit will have a VW van advertising surf lessons; the more established hubs of Watergate Bay, Harlyn and Newquay are obvious spots. The north coast is considered better than the south coast, which is too sheltered for big waves aside from a few select beaches. Summer is a time to be avoided if you're a keen surfer, though: while there may be surf schools open for business everywhere, the beaches are crowded, weather patterns mean that swell is small, and it's likely to be a fairly frustrating experience. The spring and autumn are better, while winter brings an occasional monster wave, the Cribbar, in the sea off Newquay. It's not uncommon to see serious surfers in the sea at Christmas and on New Year's Day.

◀ Porthmeor Beach, St Ives ▼ Surfboards

▲ Surfers riding a wave

The best advice for beginners is to start small. Shy away from the crowded beaches of Newquay and Watergate Bay – however famous they are, it's not fun to be hit by other people's surfboards in the sea, and there will be a lot of other learners there. Try Gwithian, Hayle, Polzeath, Perranporth or Towan Head for starters, all safe beaches for beginners.

Having lessons is essential – the last thing you want is to annoy local surfers by taking their waves, or to find yourself in a rip current. Lifeguards aren't on every beach, especially out of season. Surf camps where you spend a week having lessons – one lesson is rarely enough – and staying in accommodation with other surfers tend to be clustered around Newquay; Harlyn Surf School near Padstow is an exception to the rule. There are also various women-only surf camps.

One thing you'll learn very early on is that surfing is dependent on the weather, and not just the local weather either. Surfers check forecasts and learn to read weather patterns all across the globe to determine what the wave patterns on their shores will be. Learning

about wave patterns, geography, wind directions and coastal directions is just the start of becoming a full-blown surfer: you need a degree in oceanography to get your head round some of the finer details – so much for the reputation of surfers as laid-back stoners. You could also use a shortcut and check magicseaweed. com for local surf forecasts.

The other unpublicised side to surfing is that it's not all about point breaks, aggressive short boards, fist pumping and shouting 'Gnarly!' after you've been 'barreled'. Surfing has a competitive edge, but at its best it's a soul-soothing sport, where you can be cruising along on a wave, looking out at the Cornish cliffs or hanging out in the line-up watching dolphins on the horizon as you wait for a set to come in. It's an uncommercial experience – despite all the labels flung around, once you're zipping along a wave, it doesn't matter what brand your board is, what car you drive or what type of wetsuit you're wearing. Well – as long as your wetsuit's black you'll be taken seriously, anyway.

A MINI CORNISH PRIMER

Cornwall's language looks strange to an outsider, with unusual collections of syllables and more Zs than you'd expect outside a bedroom. It's far from a comedy turn, though; the history of the Cornish language is the history of the Cornish people, fighting to maintain their independence and unique culture.

Cornish was the main language of Cornwall until Tudor times, when law dictated that church services should be conducted in English. Its unique language, up to this point, meant that Cornwall was held to be a nation apart from the rest of the country; as soon as English became widespread in the county, it was rapidly accepted as part of England. Having nearly died out in the 19th century, Cornish is now taught in some local schools and is one of the fastest-growing languages in the world.

In 2009, Cornwall Council adopted a policy encouraging its departments to use Cornish, including installing bilingual street

Some common components of Cornish words:

Bod –   a home or dwelling, as in Bodmin

Bos –   a homestead, house, as in Boscastle

Chy –   a house, as in Chy-an-Mor

Pen –   the end of something, for example a headland, as in Penryn, Penzance, Pentire

Perran –   named after St Piran, the patron saint of Cornwall, as in Perranporth, Perranzabuloe, Perranuthnoe

Pol –   a pool or inlet, as in Polbathic, Polzeath, Polruan

Porth –   a port or landing place, as in Porthtowan, Perranporth

Ros –   a moor, heath or promontory, as in Roseland, Roskear

Tre –   a house, settlement or farmstead, as in Trerice, Trebarwith, Trelissick

Wheal –   a mine or shaft, as in Wheal Kitty, East Wheal Rose.

signs. By no means a way to learn Cornish, it's still an accessible way to get to know Kernow's distinct Celtic language and culture.

The components of Cornish largely reflect the landscape and history of Cornwall, with ports and mines named alongside villages, headlands and pools. Religion also plays a large role in place names. In Cornwall, this means that you'll find plenty of towns called St something – St Erth, St Austell, St Agnes – which refer to church parishes. There are also references to Irish saints in place names – some less obvious than others – for example St Senan, as in Sennen, and St Senara, which has become Zennor. Padstow doesn't mean 'the seat of Rick Stein' but in fact reflects St Petroc, the local saint, in combination with the Anglo Saxon word for place, stow. Over time, Petrocstow has become Padstow; one of Mr Stein's restaurants is called St Petroc's in the saint's memory.

Demelza, now used as a girl's name, is in Cornish *Dyn Malsa*, or Maelda's fort in translation. Puffin Island in the Scillies has clearly had some bright-beaked visitors in the past; Chacewater near Redruth means 'stream in the hunting grounds', suggesting a vision of medieval pageantry and hunting in ancient forests more than the small village in a valley that exists today. The village of Rock needs no explanation, while Calenick, meaning 'holly bushes' in Cornish, gives a clear indication of what you would have found there in the past.

Some places sound more interesting in translation and hint at Cornwall's tapestry of myths and legends. Praa Sands, *Poll an Wragh* in Cornish, means 'witch cove' in translation. The village is the site of Pengersick Castle, said to be one of the most haunted buildings in the UK. Hessenford – *Rys an Gwraghes* in Cornish – means 'hag's ford' and, maybe by coincidence, the Copley Arms in Hessenford is haunted by two ghosts, Matthew and The Lady.

Indian Queens has a lovely story behind it – and it's not what you think. Records show that there was a coach house on that spot called the Indian Queen, with an inscription on the porch telling the story of a Portuguese princess who landed in Falmouth and slept a night there on her way to London. Her dark appearance made locals think she was an Indian. Locals would like to link the story or visitor to Pocahontas, but no historian has yet found the proof.

While all these place names bring together items of topological and cultural information about Cornwall's places, there's no doubt that the things that jump out to a non-Cornish speaker are the funny ones. The name of the tor Brown Willy, far from meaning anything rude, actually means 'hill of swallows', from the Cornish *Bronn Wennili*. Mousehole, pronounced 'mouzel', is named after the tiny harbour entrance while Lostwithiel has nothing to do with getting lost. The Cornish name, *lostwydhyel*, means 'tail of a wooded area'.

LOCAL SPECIALITIES

'Local specialities' in Cornwall tends to mean food. This part of the UK is home to several Michelin-starred and TV chefs who do wonders with the produce grown here. While you might find a number of these delights elsewhere in the country, nothing beats eating this traditional food in its homeland.

FOOD AND DRINK

Cider
It's not a real West Country holiday if you don't get some cider inside yer. Healey's is the main producer, but you'll do well to knock on the door of any farm advertising its own version of Old Rosie. Watch out – it can get very messy very quickly.

Clotted cream
Dairy farmers in the Southwest specialise in this delicacy, made by heating full-cream cow's milk until the clots of cream rise to the top. Rodda's, based in Redruth, is the best-known brand name; don't tell your cardiologist, but the minimum fat content is 55%.

Cornish fairings
These round ginger biscuits have been sold in Cornwall since before the 1800s and were given as a treat to children or by men to their sweethearts. These days, they're a good gift to take home to your work colleagues or housesitter.

Cornish pasty
The daddy of Cornish food is a semicircle of pastry with a crimped edge, filled with meat, vegetables and seasoning. All manner of varieties are available in most local bakeries, including vegetarian pasties.

Cornish yarg
This is a creamy, crumbly semi-hard cheese made from Friesian cow's milk and is often sold round or heart-shaped and wrapped in nettle leaves. It's very pretty.

Cream tea
A traditional Cornish cream tea consists of two buttered scones spread with strawberry jam and topped with clotted cream,

served with a pot of tea. The best are served fresh with a sea view. Dodge any outlet trying to serve you a scone in a plastic wrapper – freshly baked scones are the only way to do it.

Hevva cake

Hevva is a type of fruit cake baked in a slab with a criss-cross pattern on the top. The name relates to the word the fishermen would shout when they saw shoals of pilchards in the sea; the pattern resembles a fishing net.

Ice cream

With all that lovely grass to munch, it's no wonder that Cornwall's cows produce such fantastic dairy products. Ice cream is a real treat here – Roskilly's is one of the bigger producers, but local independents such as Moomaid of Zennor are also well worth seeking out.

Real ale

Real ale is brewed down in these parts, with Sharp's, Skinner's and St Austell breweries being the producers of note. Cornish Knocker, Heligan Honey and Doom Bar are some of the more intriguing names to look out for.

Stargazey pie

This classic Cornish dish is a pie containing pilchards. It is thought that the name comes from the fact that the fish heads protrude from the pastry, looking up at the sky. Cooking them like this means that the oil from the fish drains back into the pie and keeps it moist.

Wine

As the warmest county in the UK, Cornwall has a few vineyards. English wine has had a bad rap but some of these – in particular Camel Valley wines – stand up to scrutiny. Being boutique vineyards, the wine does tend to cost more than imports from France and New Zealand.

A few other notable things made in Cornwall:

ART

Dame Barbara Hepworth

The godmother of Modernist sculpture, Dame Barbara Hepworth is best known for her bronze abstract sculptures and for heading the St Ives School. The Barbara Hepworth museum in St Ives includes her former workshop and is well worth a visit.

Ben Nicholson

Barbara Hepworth's husband, Ben Nicholson, painted abstract still lives and landscapes in St Ives and is closely associated with the town. Some of his work can be seen at Tate St Ives.

MADE IN CORNWALL

Finisterre

This Cornwall-based surf label sells wetsuits, beanies, hoodies and just about everything you need for the lifestyle as a cold-water surfer down in Cornwall.

Seasalt

One of the modern classics to come out of Cornwall, Seasalt is a fashion label with dresses inspired by the Lost Gardens of Heligan, sporty deck shoes and a good range of quality rainwear.

NOT FROM CORNWALL

Cornishware

This distinctive blue and white-banded pottery has been made since the 1920s and the original egg cups, jars and crockery are highly prized by collectors. It was actually made in Derbyshire, not Cornwall; the name came about as an employee thought that the blue bands looked like the Cornish sky, and the white the white-capped waves. So now you know!

▼ St Ives

BEFORE YOU GO

THINGS TO READ

Get in the mood for a Cornish holiday with these dramatic tales featuring windswept cliffs, stormy moors and long-lost family estates.

Rebecca – Daphne du Maurier

'Last night I dreamt I went to Manderley again...' This gothic novel set in a rambling West Country estate has never been out of print and is du Maurier's best known work. She lived and wrote in Kilmarth, near Par, and is Cornwall's foremost literary figure. *The House on the Strand*, *Jamaica Inn* and *Frenchman's Creek* also feature Cornwall.

The Poldark series – Winston Graham

Following the Poldark family in Cornwall during the last half of the 18th century, these 12 novels are full of suspense, family feuds, tin miners and smugglers, bringing this period of Cornwall's history alive.

The Camomile Lawn – Mary Wesley

The lawn in question belongs to a house on the Cornish cliffs where an extended family gathers to have an annual holiday in 1939, prior to the outbreak of war.

The Forgotten Garden – Kate Morton

A 4-year-old girl is found alone on a ship to Australia on the eve of World War I...and as the story unfolds, an inheritance, an estate and a forgotten garden in Cornwall become a key part of the story.

John Betjeman

Poet Laureate John Betjeman had a lifetime love of Cornwall and was buried at St Enodoc Church, Trebetherick, north Cornwall. Many of his poems are about Cornwall, featuring sea campion, gorse and crashing surf.

Thomas Hardy

Hardy was working as an architect near Boscastle in north Cornwall when he met his first wife, Emma. Several of his poems about her, their meeting and their marriage have Cornwall as a backdrop.

The Lost Gardens of Heligan – Tim Smit

If you even have a passing interest in gardens and heritage, this will pique your interest. Until World War I, the gardens of the Heligan Estate were among the finest in Cornwall. When Tim Smit discovered them decades later, they were wild and overgrown. This is the story of his reinvention of the gardens.

The Levelling Sea – Philip Marsden

This highly rated historical story follows the town of Falmouth from the 16th to the19th century as it grows from a single house to a significant Atlantic village. It's not just about the sea, but also about our relationship with it and how it has captured our imagination over time.

THINGS TO WATCH

Get inspired and prepared for a trip to the far Southwest with these TV shows and films.

Coast

This long-running BBC series has chased up and down every patch of sand and every cliff top around the UK now, and remains a great point of reference for interesting stories about biology, history, marine life and living by the sea. The sections on Cornwall are without doubt worth looking out.

Doc Martin

Martin Clunes stars in this long-running ITV series about a grumpy urban surgeon with a fear of blood who moves to Cornwall to become a GP. It's a gentle comedy with love stories, strange maladies and peculiar

▼ Fistral Beach

people, and was filmed in Port Isaac. The sixth and possibly final series of the show aired on British TV in 2013, though fans are hoping for a seventh.

Saving Grace

This 2000 film is set in Port Isaac and follows the story of recently widowed Grace Trevethyn – Brenda Blethyn – as she discovers her husband's secret debt problem and turns to gardening, specifically the hydroponic cultivation of marijuana, to make ends meet. It's a gentle Cornish take on the drugs industry – with limited sex and violence – and features Martin Clunes as the local doctor, another Martin, in his pre-*Doc Martin* days.

Wild West

Dawn French and Catherine Tate starred in this 2002–4 sitcom set in a shop in St Gweep (really Portloe). It's a dark comedy where the two

main characters meddle in people's lives as strange things happen: Tupperware washes up in a shipwreck; a bungee jump is set up in town and there are swingers parties at the pub. Probably not Cornish tourist board approved.

The Witches

The Headland Hotel in Newquay is the site of the big witches' conference in this 1990 adaptation of Roald Dahl's children's book. These days, the transformations seem a bit dated – it's all pre-CGI – but it's fun nevertheless.

Wycliffe

Jack Shepherd played Detective Superintendent Wycliffe in the TV adaptation of the novels by W J Burley. It's worth a mention because Cornwall is as big a character as any of the others, and because the lifestyles portrayed reflect real life – well, real life but with more murders.

▼ *Saving Grace* (2000)

▲ Coastal path towards Millook, Widemouth Bay

One episode is about the Beast of Bodmin. The series ran from 1994–8 and you can buy them as a DVD box set.

THINGS TO KNOW

You're going to find facts and figures and peculiar myths and legends dotted through this guide – Cornwall is full of wonderful places and incredible, unbelievable stories. Here's just a taster of what's to come.

The Beast of Bodmin

More than 60 people claim to have seen the Beast of Bodmin, a large, black, cat-like creature that preys on local wildlife. Nobody knows for sure that there's a big cat living on the moor; one theory is that a panther escaped from a private zoo and it or its descendants are roaming the moor today.

Authentic pasties

The Cornish pasty really does taste better in Cornwall. It also now has EU Protected Geographical Indication status, so only pasties made in Cornwall can be called Cornish pasties. But did you know that it's only an authentic pasty if it has beef, potato and swede in it, and that it's been around since at least 1300?

Mutiny on the Bounty

Before we even mention pirates, Cornwall's most well-known seafarer is probably William Bligh, the captain of the *Bounty*. He's best remembered for the mutiny on his ship, bound for Tahiti, which led to many of the mutineers colonising Pitcairn Island.

Celebrity visitors

Cornwall's a bit of a magnet for famous types. David Cameron spends holidays down near Rock; Richard and Judy live near Polperro and Madonna has allegedly bought a mansion near Falmouth.

Beware the Bucca

Cornwall has its own version of a leprechaun, a Bucca, which is 2ft tall, wears Cornish tin-mining gear and is always up to mischief. Blame the traffic jams and disappearing tent pegs on him.

Local pride

Cornish people are rightly proud of their unique heritage and landscape. They display their own flag, the white cross on a black background of St Piran or Perran, and St Piran's Day, 5 March, is celebrated as the national day of Cornwall.

Speaking Cornish

The Cornish language, which nearly died out in recent times, has been revived and is now taught in some nurseries, primary and secondary schools in the county.

Let's talk statistics

Cornwall has the longest coastline of any county in Great Britain, running to nearly 435 miles. The Lizard is the southernmost promontory in Great Britain, and Land's End is one of the UK's most westerly points. The Isles of Scilly are the kingdom's farthest outcrop to the south. And the largest biome in the Eden Project is taller than the Tower of London.

How to eat a cream tea in Cornwall

In Cornwall, a cream tea consists of two buttered scones slathered with strawberry jam and topped with clotted cream, while over the border in Devon, you put the cream on first and then add the jam.

Waving, not drowning

The county's biggest wave is the Cribbar, also called the Widow Maker, a wave off the Towan Headland in Newquay that can top 32ft.

THINGS TO PACK

Don't set off for Cornwall without these essentials:

Swimming kit

A towel and a swimming costume or trunks are the absolute first thing you should put into your bag if you're visiting this county, surrounded on three sides by the sea.

Warm clothes for the winter

You'll need a warm jumper, waterproofs, jeans and a few layers to stay warm in the biting winter wind. Plus gloves and a woolly hat.

Warm clothes for the summer

You'll need a warm jumper, waterproofs, jeans and a few layers to stay warm in the biting summer wind. Plus a sunhat and some suncream.

Forgiving clothes
Pack these because it's easy to eat an ice cream, a pasty and two scones with cream every day of your stay in Cornwall, and loose, forgiving clothes will help to hide your weight gain.

Comfy shoes
Cornwall is not the place for high heels or power dressing, unless you're staying at the Scarlet in Newquay, and probably not even then. If you're taking coastal walks, visiting pretty cobbled villages or larking about on the beach, you'll want to be wearing something comfortable.

A cameraphone
The best use for your phone in Cornwall is as a camera – reception is patchy and being cut off from the world helps you to appreciate how lovely it is. Plus there are great things to photograph, from the views to your loved ones falling off a surfboard or being buried up to their necks in the sand.

Fishing gear
Bring a rod, a net and a bucket and try fishing for your supper. Crabbing is a popular pastime off Cornwall's piers – bacon makes good bait – and the whole family can join in fishing tiny blennies and starfish out of rock pools too.

A wetsuit
Even in the height of summer, most of the people in the sea will be wearing wetsuits, whether they're surfing, bodyboarding or swimming.

A dog
What better excuse do you need to get out and explore Cornwall's rural lanes and coastal routes? Dogs are welcome in most of the county's pubs and in select places to stay, and make your holiday even better.

Cash
Useful to have in the event that you're staying somewhere a drive from a cash point. Most businesses in Cornwall will take a card, of course, but honesty food stalls by the side of the road, selling eggs and local produce, just have a box for coins.

National Trust and/or English Heritage membership
If you've got it, bring it with you: the National Trust and English Heritage look after a number of properties and places around Cornwall, including Tintagel Castle and Bedruthan Steps, and membership gives you free entry and free parking in plenty of beautiful spots.

Patience
Needed for the A30 and the summer traffic.

▸ Whipsiddery, Newquay

FESTIVALS & EVENTS

Most of the county's key events take place in the summertime; dates given are for 2014. For more information, see the 'What's on' page of visitcornwall.com.

MAY

▶ **Padstow May Day**
Padstow, 1 May
May Day is celebrated all over Cornwall with parades and fairs. It's a particularly popular celebration in Padstow, when residents and former residents gather for a day of merriment.

▶ **World Pilot Gig Championships**
St Mary's, Scilly Isles, 2–5 May
Crews compete to be the world champions in a colourful, energetic and friendly event, racing from St Mary's Quay to St Agnes or Nut Rock and back.

▶ **St Ives Literature Festival**
St Ives, 10–17 May
This popular literary festival includes book launches, readings, live music and comedy. Join locals and visitors for creative writing workshops and informative events aimed to kick-start your writing career.

▶ **St Ives Food and Drink Festival**
St Ives, 17–18 May
Porthminster Beach plays host to the region's finest food and drink producers and chefs for this two-day festival. Centred on the highly regarded Porthminster Beach Cafe, it's possibly the UK's only beach-based food and drink festival.

▶ **Polo on the Beach**
Watergate Bay, Newquay, 17–18 May
This Veuve Clicquot-sponsored annual event includes horse displays, kite surfing, fantastic food and Champagne alongside polo games and tuition.

JUNE

▶ **The Royal Cornwall Show**
Wadebridge, 5–7 June
A fascinating glimpse into Cornish rural life, this county show includes flower arranging, show jumping, a hunt relay and livestock judging.

▶ **Falmouth International Sea Shanty Festival**
Falmouth, 13–15 June
Get into the groove of Falmouth's seafaring past with maritime music, close harmony singers and a few bottles of rum. The festival supports the town and also the vital work of the RNLI.

▶ **Rock Oyster Festival**
Dinham House, Wadebridge, 20–22 June
A celebration of the Camel Estuary's fabled oysters in the 17th-century Dinham House overlooking it, the Rock Oyster Festival is a midsummer festival of music, food and art.

JULY

▶ **Port Eliot Festival**
St Germans, 24–27 July
A glamorous, offbeat literary festival in Port Eliot house with speakers, wild swimming, silent discos and creativity. Previous speakers have included Caitlin Moran and Dominic West.

▶ **St Endellion Summer Music Festival**
Port Isaac, 29 July–8 August
This internationally famous music festival includes classical music concerts, Broadway show tunes and brass band music. There is also an Easter music festival in the same location, running 12–20 April.

AUGUST

▶ **Newquay Boardmasters**
Newquay, 6–10 August
The UK's biggest surf festival has a pro-surf competition as well as live summer music from some of the best names around, from The Vaccines to Razorlight and James Blunt.

▶ **Fowey Royal Regatta and Carnival Week**
Fowey, 18–24 August
This premier sailing event also draws families for its carnival, stalls and entertainment. The Red Arrows do a fly past and locals parade in fancy dress.

▶ **Newlyn Fish Festival**
Newlyn, 26 August
This fish festival aims to raise money for the Royal National Mission to Deep Sea Fishermen and celebrates the town's most famous produce with plenty of food and drink.

▶ **The Electric Beach Festival**
Newquay, 31 August
A music festival newcomer, this Watergate Bay festival has had headliners including Soul II Soul and De La Soul.

SEPTEMBER

▶ **Cornish Pasty Festival**
Redruth, 6–8 September
This celebration of the Cornish pasty revels in the history of the former mining town of Redruth. The three-day event is free and the streets of Redruth are lined with pasty stalls.

▶ **Newquay Fish Festival**
Newquay, 6–8 September
Newquay isn't exactly famed for its harbour, but in this local food festival it's the centrepiece. The local chefs show how to make a fish dish to be proud of.

▶ **World Bellyboard Championships**
St Agnes, 8 September
A fun celebration of surfing using old-style wooden boards. Expect to see plenty of vintage gear, a competition for the best swimming hat, and fancy dress. No wetsuits allowed.

▶ **St Ives September Festival**
St Ives, 14–28 September
This 14-day programme of events, talks, concerts, theatre and much more takes place in Cornwall's most creative town Previous performers have included The Wurzels.

DECEMBER

▶ **Montol Festival**
Penzance, 16–21 December
This historic six-day festival celebrates the Midwinter solstice and Cornish traditions of the past. It culminates in beacons being lit around the town on 21 December.

▶ **Mousehole Christmas Lights**
Mousehole, 14 December–4 January
Thousands of people come every year to see the Christmas lights floating in Mousehole harbour. The pretty town also holds a Christmas market.

CAMPSITES

For more information on these and other campsites, visit theaa.com/self-catering-and-campsites

Carnon Downs Caravan & Camping Park ▶▶▶▶▶

carnon-downs-caravanpark.co.uk
Carnon Downs, Truro, TR3 6JJ
01872 862283 | Open all year
This is a beautifully mature park set in meadowland and woodland close to the village of Carnon Downs. An extensive landscaping programme has been carried out to give more spacious pitch sizes, and there is an exciting children's playground with modern equipment, plus a football pitch. Great for families.

Carvynick Country Club ▶▶▶▶

carvynick.co.uk
Summercourt, TR8 5AF
01872 510716 | Open all year
Set within the gardens of an attractive country estate, this spacious, dedicated American RV Park (also home to the 'Itchy Feet' retail company) provides full facility pitches on hardstandings. The on-site amenities include an indoor leisure area with swimming pool, fitness suite, badminton court and a bar and restaurant.

Gwithian Farm Campsite ▶▶▶▶

gwithianfarm.co.uk
Gwithian Farm, Gwithian, TR27 5BX | 01736 753127
Open 31 Mar-1 Oct
Gwithian Farm is an unspoilt site located behind the sand dunes of Gwithian's golden beach, which can be reached by footpath directly from the site, making this an ideal location for surfers. If you don't have your own gear, they'll rent you surf boards and wet-suits.

Padstow Touring Park ▶▶▶▶▶

padstowtouringpark.co.uk
Padstow, PL28 8LE | 01841 532061
Open all year
This popular park is set in open countryside above the quaint (and fashionable) fishing town of Padstow. It is divided into paddocks by maturing bushes and hedges that create a peaceful and relaxing holiday atmosphere.

Polmanter Touring Park
▶▶▶▶▶

polmanter.com
Halsetown, St Ives, TR26 3LX
01736 795640 | Open Spring
BH-10 Sep
A well-developed touring park
on high ground, Polmanter has
been tastefully landscaped, and
includes a field with pitches for
motorhomes. The fishing port
and beaches of St Ives are just a
mile and a half away, and there
is a bus service in high season.

Porthtowan Tourist Park ▶▶▶▶
porthtowantouristpark.co.uk
Mile Hill, Porthtowan, TR4 8TY
01209 890256 | Open Apr-Sep
This neat, level grassy site is on
high ground above Porthtowan,
with plenty of shelter provided
by mature trees and shrubs.
The park is almost midway
between the small seaside
resorts of Portreath and
Porthtowan, with their beaches
and surfing.

St Mabyn Holiday Park ▶▶▶▶
stmabynholidaypark.co.uk
Longstone Rd, St Mabyn, Wadebride,
PL30 3BY | 01208 841677
Open 15 Mar-Oct
St Mabyn is a family-run site
close to the picturesque market
town of Wadebridge and within
easy reach of Bodmin; it's
centrally located for exploring
both the north and south coasts
of Cornwall. The park is in a
country setting and provides
plenty of on-site activities
including a swimming pool,
small petting zoo, and
children's play areas.

Seaview International
Holiday Park ▶▶▶▶▶
seaviewinternational.com
Boswinger, Mevagissey, PL26 6LL
01726 843425 | Open Mar-end Sep
Seaview International is an
attractive holiday park set
in a beautiful landscaped
environment overlooking
Veryan Bay. The beach is
just half a mile away. There
is also an 'off the lead' dog
walk, and a 'ring and ride'
bus service to Truro, St Austell
and Plymouth.

Trethem Mill Touring Park
▶▶▶▶▶

trethem.com
St Just-in-Roseland, TR2 5JF
01872 580504 | Open Apr-mid Oct
Trethern Mill is a quality park
in all areas, with plenty of
amenities. It's in a lovely rural
setting, with spacious pitches
separated by young trees and
shrubs. The very keen family
who own the site are
continually looking for ways
to enhance its facilities.

Wooda Farm Holiday Park
▶▶▶▶▶

wooda.co.uk
Poughill, Bude, EX23 9HJ
01288 352069 | Open Apr-Oct
Wooda Farm is an attractive
park overlooking Bude Bay,
with lovely sea views. A variety
of activities are provided by
way of the large sports hall
and hard tennis court, and
there's a super children's
playground. You can also try
your hand at clay pigeon
shooting or coarse fishing.

A–Z of Cornwall

VISIT THE MUSEUMS | GET OUTDOORS | EXPLORE BY BIKE | GO BACK IN TIME | TAKE A TRAIN RIDE | MEET THE WILDLIFE
TAKE IN SOME HISTORY | HIT THE BEACH | EAT AND DRINK | GET INDUSTRIAL | VISIT THE GALLERIES | GO CANOEING
TRY HORSE-RIDING | PLACES NEARBY | CATCH A PERFORMANCE | GO ROUND THE GARDENS | TAKE A BOAT TRIP

▲ Bedruthan Steps

▶ **Bedruthan Steps**

nationaltrust.org.uk

Bedruthan, St Eval, PL27 7UW | Open all year for cliff walks;
cliff staircase closed 4 Nov–mid-Feb

Cornwall has more than its fair share of ancient myths and
legends, but it turns out that the tale of the giant Bedruthan
who used the weathered rock stacks here – Queen Bess,
Samaritan Island and Diggory's Island among them – as a
shortcut across the sandy beach isn't one of them. This
dramatic north coast beach, much loved by photographers, is a
National Trust site, along with the mine of Carnewas on the
cliff top overlooking it, and was a popular holiday spot for the
Victorians, along with Newquay down the coast. An enterprising
storyteller seems to have created the tale of a giant for tourism
purposes around this time – there are no older references to it.
But myth-busting aside, it's a gorgeous beach to visit, and the
clifftop path is perfect on a blustery day. Watch out if you're on
the beach – there are dangerous currents and nearby Mawgan
Porth (see page 164) is a better and safer bet for swimming.

EAT AND DRINK
Carnewas Cafe
nationaltrust.org.uk
Bedruthan, St Eval, PL27 7UW
01637 860701
Carnewas mine didn't yield up a vast fortune for its owners but it did leave behind some interesting buildings, repurposed today as the National Trust cafe and shop at Bedruthan Steps. The cafe serves cream teas and is a good stop after a blustery coastal walk.

▶ Bodmin

Bodmin might look like any other middle-sized town in mid-Cornwall, but its history shows it punching above its weight, often quite literally. As the site of both the Cornish rebellion of 1497 and the Cornish uprising of 1549 when the Cornish people fought against the compulsory introduction of the *Book of Common Prayer* in English, it was always an important place for Cornishmen to gather and defend their heritage. During the mining boom of the 18th and 19th centuries, it was an important trading town and many of the impressive buildings of the town date to this period. It was also the former administrative centre of Cornwall. The church of St Petroc, in the centre of Bodmin, is the largest church in Cornwall. It's not pretty, wave-lapped or strewn with nautical bunting, but if you're looking for the heart of Cornish history and culture, it's here rather than in the surf beaches and tea rooms.

The town has some unique ways of leveraging its history – all of which make largely entertaining rainy day activities too. First of all, you can participate in a trial in the old courthouse, where a Victorian-era murder case runs for visitors. Then meet ghosts and hear chilling stories at Bodmin Jail, dating from 1779, as featured on TV's *Most Haunted*. There's also a light infantry museum, the town museum, which tells tales of life in Bodmin through to the post-war period, and a steam railway, which takes you out 6.5 miles beyond the town in a cloud of steam to the River Camel or the River Fowey.

Activity lovers may well find time to hire bikes and cycle to the coast on the largely flat Camel Trail. It's a 22-mile cycle from Bodmin to Wadebridge then along the coast to Padstow. Bodmin is not the prettiest town in Cornwall but there's plenty going on and there is good access from here to the north and south coasts and most major attractions.

VISIT THE MUSEUMS AND GALLERIES

Bodmin Jail

bodminjail.org
Berrycoombe Road, PL31 2NR
01208 76292 | Open all year 9.30–5

This spook-filled jail held murderers, cow stealers and petty criminals from its opening in 1779 and is now a popular tourist attraction with a wine bar, a restaurant and scary nighttime ghost walks. The ghost of a priest has been seen in the chapel and plenty of visitors have said they've felt hot, cold or followed around during their visits.

Bodmin Museum

museumsincornwall.org.uk
Mount Folly Square, PL31 2DB
01208 77067 | Open Easter–end Sep
Mon–Fri 10.30–4.30, Sat 10.30–2.30, Oct Mon–Sat 10.30–2.30

In the site of the town's former Franciscan friary, this county museum holds exhibits about life in Bodmin, including materials on trade and transport, rocks and minerals, mining in the area and blacksmiths of the parish. The story of Bodmin through World War II is shown, and there's also a quiz for children.

Cornwall's Regimental Museum

cornwalls-regimentalmuseum.org
The Keep, Lostwithiel Road,
PL31 1EG | 01208 72810
Open all year Mon–Fri 9–5

Atten–shun! This military museum, in a former Victorian barracks building, offers an insight into military life and the history of the Cornish Regiment. Expect to see stirring displays of uniforms, weapons, medals and more. There's also an extensive reference library and the largest single section of the Berlin Wall in the UK.

Shire Hall

bodminlive.com
Mount Folly, PL31 2DQ
01208 76616 | Court is in session hourly Mar–end May Mon–Fri 11–3, Jun–end Sep Mon–Sat 11–4, Oct–end Feb Mon–Fri 11–1

In 1844, the body of local girl Charlotte Dymond was found on Rough Tor on Bodmin Moor. This 45-minute courtroom experience takes visitors through the trial of Matthew Weeks, accused of her murder. Will he be put to death, sent to Australia or sentenced to hard labour, or will he walk out a free man?

GET OUTDOORS

Cardinham Woods

forestry.gov.uk
Bodmin | 01208 72577
Open all year

This Forestry Commission-managed woodlands area has four different marked trails. There is a 7-mile Bodmin Beast blue-graded trail and two red-graded trails for mountain bikers, along with lovely scenery, and a river with a stone bridge. Some routes are wheelchair and pushchair friendly. There's also a cafe with a play area for young children beside it.

TAKE A TRAIN RIDE
Bodmin & Wenford Railway
bodminrailway.co.uk
Bodmin General Station,
PL31 1AQ | 01208 73555
Open daily 20 May–5 Oct
The Bodmin & Wenford Railway runs steam trains along a delightful 6.5-mile rural line, from Bodmin to Bodmin Parkway Station on the main Paddington to Penzance line. The views are lovely and there are tea rooms at or near the final destination stations in both directions. Check the website for precise train times and routes.

EXPLORE BY BIKE
Bodmin Bikes
bodminbikes.co.uk
Hamley Court, Dennison Road,
PL31 2LL | 01208 73192
Open Mon–Sat 9–5
What a choice: the Camel Trail, leading from Bodmin to Wadebridge and Padstow, or the peaceful network of narrow lanes that link the villages of Helland, Helland Bridge, Blisland, St Breward, St Tudy and St Mabyn in a circular tour. Brave the steep hills and reward yourself with a pub lunch or cream tea.

EAT AND DRINK
The Crown Inn
wagtailinns.com
Lanlivery, PL30 5BT | 01208 872707
One of the oldest pubs in Cornwall, this 12th-century longhouse with rooms is on the historic Saints Way. In winter, the low-beamed, cosy bar is perfect for a pint of Doom Bar beside the fire. Changing menus include fresh Fowey fish, crab salad, and steak and ale pie.

Woods Cafe
woodscafecornwall.co.uk
Cardinham Woods,
PL30 4AL | 01208 78111
Whether you're keen to ramble in the woods or just want somewhere pretty to stop for a while, this cafe in a woodsman's cottage is worth a visit and is rated as one of Cornwall's best places for a cream tea. They don't just serve the standard jam-and-clotted-cream treats, though – they also serve savoury cheese scones served with cream cheese and onion relish.

▶ PLACES NEARBY
Close to Bodmin you'll find Cornwall's top winery the Camel Valley vineyard, and the Georgian house and estate Pencarrow (see page 83), known for its gardens, along with Lanhydrock, a stunning Victorian house and estate.

Camel Valley Vineyard
camelvalley.com
Nanstallon, PL30 5LG
01208 77959 | Guided tours
Apr–end Sep Mon–Fri 2.30
Cornwall's most successful vineyard, Camel Valley has won plenty of awards for its still and sparkling fine wines grown in this boutique vineyard, including double international gold medals in 2012. Stop by for

a drink and a tour in the summer, or just visit the wine bar/shop out of season.

Lanhydrock

nationaltrust.org.uk
Bodmin, PL30 5AD | 01208 265950
Gardens open all year daily 10–6;
house open Mar–early Nov 11–5.30,
closed Mon outside peak season

This magnificent Victorian estate and house, 2.5 miles north of Lostwithiel and reached from Bodmin on the A30, offers a glimpse of above-stairs elegance and below-stairs endeavours, along with a 1,000-acre garden. On first sight, the house gives every impression of being wholly Tudor, but in fact all that remains of the original house, built between 1630 and 1642 for wealthy Truro merchant Sir Richard Robartes, are the gatehouse, entrance porch and north wing. The east wing was removed and the rest fell victim to a terrible fire in 1881, but the house was rebuilt to match the surviving part.

The interiors are very grand, notably the Long Gallery, and there are lavish furnishings throughout the house. Of all the 50 rooms that are open, visitors tend to find the below-stairs sections the most interesting part, including the kitchen, larders, bakehouse, dairy, cellars and servants' quarters. In August and September there are Up and Under tours (free) exploring some of the history and workings of the Victorian-era house, and all year you can try out being a servant. The costumed volunteer team demonstrate how to lay a table setting and fold a napkin and invite you to join in. A lot of effort has been put into creating an experience rather than a static museum to visit.

▼ Lanhydrock

Lanhydrock is surrounded by beautiful grounds, with a glorious bluebell wood in late spring and camellias, rhododendrons and magnolias in the higher garden. There is also a modern sculpture trail in the higher garden. Adjoining the house are formal gardens with clipped yews and bronze urns, and there's an adventure playground for children. Family events, particularly in evidence in the summer months, include trails and craft activities. Check the website for up-to-date details on events.

The house also holds gardening workshops and has a plant centre for those inspired by its estate, along with a second-hand bookshop. There is a restaurant in the old servants' hall and a cafe in the former stables serving lovely Cornish ice cream and cream teas.

Pinsla Garden
pinslagarden.net
Pinsla Lodge, Glynn, Bodmin, PL30 4AY | 01208 821339
Open daily 23 Feb–end Oct 9–5.30
On a far smaller scale than Pencarrow or Lanhydrock, which are the draw for many, the 2-acre Pinsla Garden and Nursery is bursting with colour and beautiful plants, all set around a fairytale cottage in the woods where the owners live. It's beautifully thought out, unconventional, wild and romantic, all at the same

10 rainy day ideas

▶ Visit the Eden Project near St Austell
page 89

▶ Visit the National Maritime Museum in Falmouth
page 96

▶ Have some fishy fun at the Blue Reef Aquarium, Newquay
page 180

▶ Go coasteering or surfing – so what, you're wet anyway!

▶ Go swimming – either in the sea or in one of Cornwall's great indoor pools. Try Penzance (page 198), Falmouth (page 93) or Bude (page 70)

▶ Browse art and eat ice cream at Roskilly's Farm on the Lizard Peninsula
page 180

▶ Spend a morning at Tate St Ives
page 237

▶ Visit one of Cornwall's historic houses, such as Port Eliot (page 116) or Prideaux Place (page 190)

▶ Meet rescued seals at the Cornish Seal Sanctuary in Gweek
page 188

▶ Hunker down in a local pub until it stops

time. Dogs are welcome (and might make it on to the 'Dog blog' part of their website) and it's a flat, easy walk around the garden with the option of a cream tea or homemade cake at the end.

▶ Bodmin Moor

▲ Rough Tor

Dominated by granite tors, peppered with Bronze Age relics and coloured by myths and legends going back to the time of King Arthur, Bodmin Moor is an essential part of the Cornish experience. It feels larger than its boundaries, just 10 miles by 10 miles, perhaps because of its barren landscape and its height – Brown Willy, the highest point in Cornwall at 1,377ft, is on its western side along with Rough Tor. Gaping holes in the ground left by the mining and quarrying industries, such as Cheesewring Quarry and Phoenix United Mine, add to the drama.

But let's start with the stories. The Beast of Bodmin is the moor's best-known inhabitant, a big, black, puma-like cat that has been spotted more than 60 times since 1983 and investigated by multiple agencies, but to no avail. Nobody has actually verified that there is a big cat living on the moor. Like many similar sightings across the West Country, the suggestion is that it is the descendant of a panther or similar big cat escaped from a private zoo in the 1970s. Catch it on camera if you can.

Going back to King Arthur, who reputedly lived at Tintagel Castle on the coast, the story goes that on his deathbed he ordered his sword Excalibur to be cast into a lake. Locals say that Dozmary Pool is the home of Excalibur and the Lady of the Lake. It's also the site of the myth or legend of Jan Tregeagle, a disgruntled spirit condemned by the Devil to complete Sisyphean tasks, such as baling out Dozmary Pool with a holed shell. The Tregeagles were a powerful local family between the 16th and 18th centuries, and were notorious for their brutality and dishonesty.

More recent history swirls around Rough Tor: Charlotte Dymond, a local lass, was found murdered here in 1844. There is a monument to her at the foot of the tor and her ghost has apparently been seen in the area, a figure in a gown and a silver bonnet.

Unverifiable tales aside, the moor is great walking territory, with plenty to see. The remarkable layered granite formations at Cheesewring – named because they look like the part of a cider press used to squeeze the 'cheese' or juice from apples – are one of the defining images of the moorland. The Hurlers and the Pipers, a collection of early Bronze Age stone circles near Minions village, inspired a song by West Country folk singer Seth Lakeman. According to tradition, a group of hurlers (men playing Cornish hurling) were turned to stone for playing on a Sunday; likewise, a group of pipers played on the Sabbath and suffered the same fate. Rillaton Barrow and Trethevy Quoit, an entrance grave from the Neolithic period, stand nearby.

Craddock Moor to the west is also peppered with burial mounds from the Bronze Age, hut circles of the Iron Age and medieval field systems. There's quite some history here in the landscape. North of Minions is Twelve Men's Moor and the rocky ridges of Kilmar Tor and Bearah Tor.

▼ Twelve Men's Moor

Walking up the two most significant peaks is fairly straightforward. Brown Willy can be reached from a starting point in Camelford, while Rough Tor is reached via various paths across the open moorland and via Camelford too. Both offer views of the ancient landscape at its best, showing off the Bronze Age remains, wind-sculpted rocks, barren heath and mining history. Bodmin Moor is one of Cornwall's 12 AONBs and provides habitats for many unique species, including 23 species of butterfly, golden plovers, otters, bats, cows, sheep and wild ponies. It is the last world site of Cornish path moss. For this reason, dogs are not allowed off the lead.

What to do when visiting Bodmin Moor? Bring your walking boots and a picnic and explore, whatever the weather. Along with the obvious landscape-related sights, Jamaica Inn is an evocative and famed place, a pub on the through route for smugglers taking contraband upcountry and the setting for Daphne du Maurier's novel of the same name about murderous wreckers. Today it contains a museum of smuggling. To find out more about the human history of the moor, and the landscape, the Minions Heritage Centre is a good bet. The small villages dotted around the moorland also hold some interesting sights.

▼ The Cheesewring

EXPLORE THE MOOR

Brown Willy and Rough Tor

Approach from Camelford on
the A39. Head southeast on a
minor road to Poldue Downs;
there is car parking at the end
of the road

Cornwall's highest point can be
reached in a couple of hours
along a clear path. Rough Tor,
pronounced 'Row tor', is the
first peak, with a scramble of
rocks at the top, rough Neolithic
stone walls and the foundations
of a medieval chapel; Brown
Willy is less dramatic but has
great views. Adders have been
seen in the area.

Cheesewring

Stowe's Hill, 4 miles north of
Liskeard. A 4-mile walk, taking in
the Hurlers as well, starts at the
Hurlers Car Park in Minions

The weathered formation
of layered granite gave its
name to the quarry next to
it. Granite from the quarry
was used to build Devonport
Dockyard, Birkenhead Docks
and part of Copenhagen
Harbour, and was included
in the materials used in the
Thames Embankment
and Westminster and
Tower Bridges.

Daniel Gumb's Cave

Southwest edge of Cheesewring
Quarry; access via Hurlers Car Park
in Minions as before

Back in the 18th century,
stonecutter Daniel Gumb lived
in a cave here with his family to
avoid paying tax. Known as the
'mountain philosopher', he

carved one of Euclid's
theorems in the roof of his
cave, still visible today. The
cave has been partly
reconstructed, as much was
destroyed when the quarry
was extended in the 1870s.

Dozmary Pool

On the A30, 1.3 miles south
of Bolventor

This small lake is the only
freshwater inland lake in the
Southwest Peninsula. Look out
for the Lady in the Lake and
Jan Tregeagle's ghost (see page
62). It's a lovely spot for a
woodland/lakeside walk and is
calm and peaceful. The name
means 'drop of sea'.

Golitha Falls

St Neot, Lanreath. Approximately
5 miles southeast of Colliford Lake.
Car park

These cascades in the River
Fowey as it drains from
Bodmin Moor towards the
south coast make for a
beautiful walk in the ancient
oak and beech woods. Otters
have been seen, as have
kingfishers in the stepped
waterfalls. Good for a dog
walk; some of the woodland
is pushchair and wheelchair
accessible.

VISIT THE MUSEUMS AND GALLERIES

Minions Heritage Centre

cornish-mining.org.uk
Close to the car park in Minions
Open all year

This heritage centre in the
Houseman's Shaft engine

house of South Phoenix Mine has displays on the history of the landscape from the Stone Age, through 18th- and 19th-century mining up until today. It's a great introduction to the moor and the archaeology, ecology and mining heritage of the Caradon Hill area.

Smugglers Museum

jamaicainn.co.uk
Jamaica Inn, Bolventor, PL15 7TS
01566 86250 | Open Apr–end Oct
10–5, mid-Jul–end Aug 10–6; closed
Nov–Easter

Jamaica Inn was made famous by Daphne du Maurier; this small museum explores the connection, with artefacts and period costumes. Best if you've read the book first or have a particular interest in smuggling in the local area around Bodmin and Bolventor.

GET OUTDOORS
Colliford Lake Park

swlakestrust.org.uk
Bolventor | 01409 211514
Open all year

Cornwall's second largest lake is easily accessed via the A30 and has an 8.5-mile perimeter walk and picnic areas. Watersports are not allowed on the lake: it's a peaceful spot for a walk and has an important nature reserve for overwintering wildfowl. Permits for fly-fishing for brown trout can be arranged through Jamaica Inn.

SEE A LOCAL CHURCH
Cathedral of the Moors

Altarnun, around 4.5 miles west of
Launceston; there's a car park just off
the A30 within walking distance of
the village

In this small village on the edge of Bodmin Moor, the 'Cathedral of the Moors', the village church, which has a decorated Norman font and some beautiful carved bench ends inside, is the literal and figurative high point. Also known as St Nonna's Church, it's a beautiful, tranquil spot. It features in Daphne du Maurier's *Jamaica Inn*.

EAT AND DRINK
Jamaica Inn

jamaicainn.co.uk
Jamaica Inn, Bolventor,
PL15 7TS | 01566 86250

This 18th-century inn stands high on Bodmin Moor and has plenty of history, as detailed above, along with beamed ceilings, roaring fires and a children's play area. A tourist attraction in its own right rather than a gourmet destination, they serve breakfast, lunch, bar snacks and dinner.

The Rising Sun Inn

therisingsuninn.co.uk
Altarnun, PL15 7SN
01566 86636

It's still fine to arrive by horse at this inviting 16th-century moorland inn – there's a hitching post in the car park. Lunch and dinner dishes include Fowey River mussels with fries, and Cornish ham with free-range eggs, washed down with local Cornish Orchards cider or Skinner's Betty Stogs ale.

▶ PLACES NEARBY

Close to Bodmin Moor there's an interesting church at Laneast with medieval touches and a memorial to the man who discovered Neptune, and a family-friendly water park.

St Sidwell and St Gulvat's Church
Off the A935, Laneast, PL15 8PN
Set at the head of a wooded valley, Laneast's church has an almost complete and very well preserved set of medieval benches and bench ends, a well preserved rood screen, and a prayer desk from the beginning of the 16th century. In the church is a memorial to astronomer John Couch Adams, who discovered the planet Neptune in 1846.

Siblyback Water Park
swlakestrust.org.uk
Siblyback Water Park, near Liskeard, PL14 6ER
Ranger Tel: 01579 346522
Open all year
This water park on the edge of Bodmin Moor offers plenty of watersports, from family rowing-boat hire to sailing, windsurfing and canoeing, alongside the more gentle pursuit of rainbow trout fishing (permits are available from the centre on site). There's also a

10 mythical beings of Cornwall

▶ The Beast of Bodmin
page 62

▶ The giant Bedruthan
page 56

▶ The giant Cormoran of St Michael's Mount
page 159

▶ The Whooper of Sennen Cove
page 256

▶ Joan the Wad
Queen of the Piskies, associated with the elements fire and water and sometimes said to be married to Jack-o'-lantern

▶ The Bucca
page 47

▶ The Owlman of Mawnan
A mysterious winged creature first spotted in 1976 and reported to be as big as a man

▶ The Spriggans of West Penwith
page 26

▶ The Cornish Knocker
page 26

▶ Morveren, the mermaid of Zennor
page 271

cycle centre with child seats and trailers as well as adult and child bikes, and Segways available to hire for an unusual way to get around the lake's edge. There are miles of walks, a small campsite and a cafe overlooking the water, open Easter–end Oct 11–5, to round it off.

▶ Boscastle

The dramatic natural harbour of Boscastle makes it part of a foursome of must-see north coast villages together with Crackington Haven (see page 85), Port Isaac (see page 211) and Tintagel (see page 257). It provides the dramatic scenery that inspired Thomas Hardy while he was working as an architect on the nearby St Juliot's church tower; he also met his first wife, Emma, here. Today, the sea surges in and out of the National Trust-owned harbour in a menacing way between the slate and shale cliffs. The town made the national news when extreme flooding in 2004 nearly washed away the village, sending at least 84 cars into the harbour and leaving 155 people clinging to trees and rooftops.

You're not likely to get washed away today, of course, and the National Trust and local businesses have done a lot to restore the vitality of the village and make it a lovely place to visit. Back in the 19th century, Boscastle was an important commercial port, with up to 200 ships a year carrying goods in and china clay and slate away, until the railway arrived in the 1890s. So while it's a quiet place now, the fine old buildings that remain tell of a more prosperous, busy period in its history.

Walks along the coast are fantastic. To the right, you'll reach Pentargon Waterfall, while to the left the blowhole in Penhally Point, the headland on the northern side of the harbour entrance, erupts water an hour before and after low tide. It is also known as the Devil's Bellows. To the south of Boscastle you can see 'the Stitches' on Forrabury Common, a pattern of Iron Age land tenure where long, narrow strips of land were cultivated and farmed, now preserved by the National Trust.

VISIT THE MUSEUMS AND GALLERIES

Boscastle Pottery and Mochaware
Boscastle, PL35 0HE
01840 250291
This unique little pottery reproduces the Victorian art of Mochaware, selling hand-thrown pots, cups and teapots with the characteristic cloud, tree and fern patterns on a painted background. Visitors to the shop can meet the potter and watch him at work.

Museum of Witchcraft
museumofwitchcraft.com
The Harbour, PL35 0HD
01840 250111 | Open 29 Mar–3 Nov Mon–Sat 10.30–6, Sun 11.30–6
This popular and highly rated museum, which opened in the 1960s, has the world's largest collection of witchcraft-related bits and bobs, from sickles used to gather medicinal herbs to mysterious stones carved with maze patterns and information on wise women, curses, charms and sacred sites. Local

legends and folktales tell of witches changing into cats, hares and owls. Fascinating, but perhaps not for sensitive children.

Pilchard Palace
nationaltrust.org.uk
The Harbour | 01840 250353
The National Trust visitor centre, shop and cafe are all in a light and airy renovated pilchard-packing building, where pilchards were previously salted, pressed and packed for export. You can get details of circular walks, children's trails and great cream teas in the building. WiFi access; dogs welcome.

SADDLE UP
Tredole Trekking
Trevalga, PL35 0ED
01840 250495
Horse and pony trekking along the north Cornwall coast for all abilities and a wide variety of interests, from those seeking riding holidays to others wanting to hitch up a pony to ride them to a local pub. Sunset rides are particularly beautiful.

EAT AND DRINK
The Cobweb Inn
cobwebinn.co.uk
The Bridge, PL35 0HE
01840 250278
Once a warehouse where customs agents guarded taxable imported goods, it's now a pub with a whitewashed restaurant serving pasties, seafood, steaks and more. Rumour has it that the beamed,

flag-floored back room drew illicit drinkers; today Cornwall-brewed real ales and farm ciders can be ordered without subterfuge.

Harbour Light Tea Garden
The Harbour, PL35 0HD
01840 250953
A whitewashed building on the quayside contains one of Boscastle's hidden gems: this tea room serving brunch and snacks, including locally caught crab in delicious sandwiches, and freshly baked scones with lashings of clotted cream, all with a warm, friendly welcome.

Helsett Farm Cornish Ice Cream
helsettfarm.com
Helsett Farm, Lesnewth, PL35 0HP | 01840 261207
A happy herd of Ayrshire cows produces thick organic milk to create this much-loved ice cream, sold in Waitrose, Harrods and Selfridges, which comes in delightfully named flavours such as Charlie's Chocolate. Drop into the farm – which has cottages to rent – or look out this brand in local shops.

Wellington Hotel ⓐⓐ
wellingtonhotelboscastle.com
The Harbour, PL35 0AQ
01840 250202
A local landmark with a castellated tower overlooking the harbour, the Wellington also dates from the 16th century, and has soothing

Georgian charm and ambitious cooking. Expect the likes of pressed rabbit confit, halibut with oxtail, and blackberry and orange Arctic roll using local hedgerow berries.

▶ Bossiney

Bossiney, a short distance from busy Tintagel, is a quiet relief from too much Arthurian legend. Much of the coast at Bossiney is in the care of the National Trust. The beach below the cliffs at Bossiney Haven is reached by a steep path where donkeys once carried seaweed up from the beach to be used as fertiliser on neighbouring fields.

A short distance to the east lies Rocky Valley, where the river cuts through a final rock barrier into the sea. At the heart of the valley are the ruins of an old woollen mill. Within the ruins are small maze carvings on natural rock, most likely to be Victorian. Rocky Valley's river can be followed inland through the wooded St Nectan's Glen to St Nectan's Kieve, where a 60ft waterfall plunges down a dark, mist-shrouded ravine. A fee is payable to view the falls and there is a tea garden above. The site can be reached by public footpath, which starts behind the Rocky Valley Centre at Trethevy on the B3263, a mile northeast of Bossiney.

▶ Bryher

see **Isles of Scilly**, page 248

▶ Bude

Bude is without doubt one of the best and most popular beach destinations in the county. With two beaches in the town itself plus several more along the coast, plenty of holiday accommodation nearby and a friendly small town at its centre, it's a great place to be based.

Summerleaze Beach is the more attractive of the two, a long, sandy beach where the River Neet runs into the sea and an open-air sea pool nestles against the cliffs; topped up twice daily by the Atlantic, it's a safe place for people to swim, particularly when the sea is choppy. Campaigns are often under way to save it – it's a unique place, half manmade and half formed from the natural shape of the rocks. Local children swap wild tales about the day a shark was caught in it; that has almost certainly never happened.

The other main Bude beach is called Crooklets, and has more appeal for surfers than families. Nearby are Widemouth

Bay, a long, sandy stretch for both surfers and families; Northcott Mouth, good for rock pooling; National Trust-owned Sandymouth, which has a cafe and a waterfall; plus Duckpool, Millook Haven, the Strangles and Crackington Haven.

Bude town centre has two main shopping streets, the Strand and Belle Vue. The former fishing port was a hub for commerce through the 19th century but tourism has certainly taken over today. You'll find souvenir shops, surf and activity shops, supermarkets, clothes shops and toy shops as you stroll through.

There are pleasant walks around the cliff top on level, close-cropped grassland, and also inland along the Bude Canal, a popular place to go boating, walking and wildlife watching. In the 19th century this canal transported sand to inland farms, where it enriched the soil. It reaches nearly to Launceston.

Hartland is a stunning AONB just over the Devon border with wild, dramatic beaches. You can also visit Morwenstow nearby (see page 170), home of an interesting Victorian-era preacher, whose life is recounted in Bude's Castle Heritage Centre.

VISIT THE MUSEUM
Castle Heritage Centre
thecastlebude.org.uk
Lower Wharf, EX23 8LG
01288 357300 | Open Easter–end Oct Sun–Fri 10–4, Nov–Easter Mon–Fri 10–4
This local history centre covers the natural history and geology of the north Cornish coast, the area's industrial history and the famous wreck of the *Bencoolen* on Summerleaze Beach, overlooked by the centre. Local character Reverend Robert Hawker, vicar of Morwenstow, is also depicted recounting his horror of watching shipwrecks from storm-lashed cliffs.

HIT THE BEACH
Both Crooklets and Summerleaze Beach have lifeguards May–end Sep, beach cafes, surf tuition and car parks. Crooklets is famed for having one of Britain's first Surf Life Saving Clubs, while Summerleaze has candy-coloured beach huts for hire and a tidal pool, much used by triathletes and children. There is a clifftop path between the two beaches.

TAKE A BOAT TRIP
Bude Canal Boat Hire
Lower Wharf, Bude Canal, EX23 8LE | 07968 688782
Rowing boats, pedalos and canoes are available for hire on Bude Canal. Bude Marshes, beside the canal, are designated a Local Nature Reserve, and are home to otters, swans, bats, herons, kingfishers and grass snakes. The canal runs from Petherwicks Mill to

Helebridge. Canal boats often pass through too.

GO COASTEERING
Outdoor Adventure
outdooradventure.co.uk
Atlantic Court, Widemouth Bay,
EX23 0DF | 01288 362900
Coasteering trips and surfing lessons are provided by Outdoor Adventure, an activity centre based at Widemouth Bay. Coaches take you out to explore Cornwall from the sea, jumping off cliffs, riding waves and climbing barnacle-covered ledges. It's all a big adrenaline rush. Residential courses are on offer alongside one-off sessions, and the team caters for families and stag and hen parties – separately, of course.

EXPLORE BY BIKE
Bude Bike Hire
budebikehire.co.uk
Pethericks Mill, EX23 8TF
01288 353748 | Open Mon–Sat
9.30–5.30

Circular routes from Bude link to Widemouth Bay in the south, Northcott Mouth beach in the north and across inland to Marhamchurch and Stratton. Bude Bikes has a good range of bikes and suggested downloadable cycling routes for all the family, with tagalongs, bike seats and electric bikes. Book ahead during school holidays.

GO FISHING
Bude Canal
EX23 8LE
Coarse fishing in Bude's canal is an option for a relaxing day. The 2-mile stretch has carp, roach, rudd, dace, perch, tench and more. To fish, an Environment Agency rod licence from any Post Office, plus a day permit from the Crescent Post Office – next to the canal – are required. Additional fishing options include Hele Barton Fishery, Lower Lynstone Lakes and the Tamar Lakes.

▼ Bude

SADDLE UP
Broomhill Manor Stables
broomhill-manor-stables.co.uk
Poughill, EX23 9HA
07796 470625 | Open all year
Individual tuition, group rides
and hacks along the north
Cornish countryside and
beaches, for all ages and
experiences. There are plenty
of country lanes and bridleways
in the nearby area to explore
on horseback; this stables also
has its own sand school and
can run family lessons and
taster sessions. Call for
further details.

GO SURFING
Big Blue Surf School
bigbluesurfschool.co.uk
12 Summerleaze Crescent,
EX23 8HH | 01288 331764
Lessons Apr–end Oct
Bude's beaches are for more
than just picnics. Join the
surfers with lessons or a
week-long course with Big
Blue Surf. They also offer surf
hire, as do several shops in the
centre of Bude, and vans in
season at both beaches. This
surf school has BSA
accreditation and a low
pupil-to-teacher ratio.

PLAY A ROUND
Bude and North
Cornwall Golf Club,
budegolf.co.uk
Burn View, EX23 8DA
01288 352006 | Open all year
The traditional links course
at Bude and North Cornwall
Golf Club, dating from 1891, is
in the centre of Bude with
magnificent views of the sea.
It's known as a challenging
course with super greens and
excellent drainage, making the
course playable throughout
the year off regular tees
and greens.

EAT AND DRINK
Bay View Inn
bayviewinn.co.uk
Marine Drive, Widemouth Bay,
EX23 0AW | 01288 361273
Dating back around 100 years,
this welcoming, family-run
pub has fabulous views of the
rolling Atlantic from its
restaurant and the large
raised decking area outside.
The menu includes a signature
dish of fish pie, and plenty
of variety for meat eaters
and vegetarians.

Life's a Beach
lifesabeach.info
Summerleaze Beach,
EX23 8HN | 01288 355222
The best place to eat out in
Bude is this stylish cafe with a
view of the beach, which serves
beachgoers during the day,
cafe-style, and a more
sophisticated clientele from
7pm, with some of the best
seafood in the town. It also has
an ice cream parlour and a
beach shop.

Margaret's Rustic Tea Room
Northcott Mouth, EX23 9EG
01288 355241
In a field in Northcott Mouth,
this tea room is one of
Cornwall's finest and is a sight
for sore walkers' eyes – or

should that be feet? Margaret serves up teatime treats, including a classic cream tea, in her open-air lounge with a bridge and stream running through it, just as her mother did since the 1940s.

The Weir

weir-restaurant-bude.co.uk
Whalesborough, Marhamchurch,
EX23 0JD | 01288 362234

This little treasure of a place inland from Bude is surrounded by a children's playground, a lake and a woodland nature reserve. Great locally sourced food and good coffee are on offer in this restaurant and wildlife centre. Ploughman's lunches, jacket potatoes, cream teas, sandwiches and local drinks are served inside and on the terrace overlooking the water.

▶ PLACES NEARBY

There are a number of places to visit from Bude itself, including the remains of a moated manor house, the pretty town of Stratton, neighbouring villages with interesting churches and Widemouth Bay, where you can learn to surf or go coasteering.

Penhallam Manor

english-heritage.org.uk
Week St Mary, south of
Widemouth Bay | 0870 333 1181
Check website for opening times

Not another Cornish country estate, but a low, grass-covered and complete ground plan of a 13th-century moated manor house surrounded by woods. Built by Andrew de Cardinham, it's a rare example of a moated manor house in the Southwest – they are mainly found in Central and Eastern England. It's an interesting place to wander around if you're staying nearby – the full medieval ground plan has survived unaltered after the property was abandoned in the 14th century. Dogs on leads are welcome.

Stratton

The nearby market town of Stratton, inland from Bude, is also a lovely place to visit, all narrow streets and ancient through routes. The town is reached by turning off onto the Holsworthy road from the A39, just east of Bude. The Tree Inn, on Fore Street, was once the home of Antony Payne, aka the Cornish Giant, who grew to 7ft 4in. When he died in 1691, his coffin had to be lowered through the ceiling as it was too big for the stairs. Colebrook Farm near the town offers Pick Your Own gooseberries, raspberries and strawberries in season. There is a car park at Howells Bridge on the eastern edge of Stratton. From the car park, walk up Spicer's Lane to the church and from there into the centre of the town.

St Olaf's Church

Off Poughill Road, Poughill,
EX23 9ER

The 16th-century woodwork and wall paintings are the

main reasons for visiting here. St Olaf's has two wall paintings of St Christopher, a medieval south door and roof bosses dating from the 1530s. Records show that in the 1520s the church had at least five guilds, including one to St Christopher and another to St Olaf, a Scandinavian saint.

St Winwaloe's Church
Off Vicarage Lane, Poundstock, EX23 0AX
St Winwaloe's is set in a wooded hollow and has features from many ages, including a Norman font, a 16th-century chest and an early 17th-century pulpit. Most notable are the wall paintings, including one with the message 'Don't work on Sundays' and another of the Seven Deadly Sins. Parts of the rood screen survive, as does a symbol of St Luke in a panel of medieval stained glass.

Widemouth Bay
Marine Drive, Widemouth Bay, EX23 0DF
Pronounced 'Wid-muth', this wide surf beach 3 miles or so south of Bude is great for families and has a lifeguard during the summer season. At low tide there are rock pools, and you'll find plenty of surf schools touting for business in peak season – it's a great place to learn, especially because it's uncrowded and has beach and reef breaks. A seasonal ban on dogs applies to the northern part of the beach but they are welcome all year at the south part, called Black Rock locally. There's free parking at the north and south ends of the beach.

Cadgwith
see **The Lizard**, page 165

Calstock
On the banks of the River Tamar, Calstock is on the boundary with Devon and today is known for an eclectic mix of festivals, including those of the bike, rock and art varieties. In the shadow of the huge viaduct carrying trains into Cornwall from Plymouth, it is one of those hidden spots in the county where you can traverse the river by canoe, buy local produce from roadside stalls and walk in the woods. In the summer, there's a ferry running from Calstock Quay to Cotehele House, a National Trust-run Tudor mansion with extensive gardens that attracts most of the area's visitors. Occasional passenger boats from Plymouth also come to Calstock, known locally for its pubs, restaurants, shops and galleries. It's funny to imagine full-masted schooners, steam-powered coasters, barges and

paddle steamers taking tin, copper and granite along the river back when Calstock was an important quay, before the railway made its way into Cornwall.

TAKE IN SOME HISTORY

Cotehele

nationaltrust.org.uk
St Dominick, PL12 6TA, between
Tavistock and Callington. Turn off
the A390 at St. Ann's Chapel, signed
2.5 miles south of junction
01579 351346/352736 (info)
Garden open all year, 10–dusk;
house open mid-Mar–end Oct,
limited opening Nov–Dec

One of Cornwall's great gardens and finest Tudor houses, Cotehele is tucked away in a huge estate in the Tamar Valley. Visitors have marvelled at the Great Hall with its armour and arched timber roof since the 18th century. The layout owes much to the medieval period, with three internal courtyards, a fine old kitchen, ancient furniture and tapestries on the walls. Later additions include a tower built in the 1620s and a splendid bedroom where Charles I was said to have spent a night in a four-poster bed.

Step into the garden and you'll be blown away. It's not so much a case of stepping back in time as stepping into another world, with enormous ferns and a garden tunnel leading from the formal East Garden into the wild Valley Garden, planted with azaleas and rhododendrons. There's also a tiny Chapel in the Wood, a thatched Victorian summerhouse, and a medieval stew pond and dovecote.

Cotehele Quay – part of the wider Cotehele estate, which is 1,300 acres in total – has an onsite Discovery Centre in the former stone lime kiln buildings telling the story of the Tamar. You'll find the restored sailing barge, Shamrock, built in 1899 and used to carry cargo, including manure, coal and limestone, up and down the river. She's in the port every day and the hold is open for explorers from 1–4 on Sundays. There are also

10 sub-tropical gardens

fantastic walks around the estate from here, with river views, secret woods and glimpses of the riverside wildlife. You can download walking trails from the National Trust website.

MEET THE WILDLIFE
Tamar Wildlife
tamarwildlife.co.uk
01756 829163

Birding cruises run from Cremyll, Saltash and Plymouth Hoe with specialist 3-hour boat trips following ospreys along the estuaries. Avocet and spoonbill cruises are also available; consult the website for sailing details which are on specific dates once or twice a month. All boat trips are commentated by a local naturalist.

TAKE A TRAIN RIDE
Tamar Valley Line
www.greatscenicrailways.com
Gunnislake–Plymouth, via Calstock
08457 484950 | Check website for timetable

Known as one of England's loveliest country branch lines, this particular stretch of the Cornwall–Devon border can be traversed on a main-line train over Brunel's Royal Albert Bridge and along the Bere Peninsula. Stop at local village stations for a cream tea. It takes approximately 40 minutes to reach Plymouth from Gunnislake and vice versa, through a largely hidden and lesser-visited part of the county.

▲ St Germans Viaduct

CANOE THE TAMAR
Canoe Tamar
canoetamar.co.uk
Cotehele Quay | 0845 430 1208
Trips run Apr–end Sep

Join experienced river guides on a Canadian canoe trip taking in the best parts of the river from Cotehele Quay to Calstock. Each 3-hour trip takes in beautiful scenery, including old quays, mine chimneys, farms and boatyards, and offers the chance to spot bird life, seals and otters.

PLAY A ROUND
St Mellion International Resort
st-mellion.co.uk
St Mellion, PL12 6SD
01579 351351 | Open all year

Set in 450 acres of glorious Cornish countryside, St Mellion is heralded as the premier golf and country club in the Southwest. The Kernow Course is perfect for golfers of all abilities. The spectacularly sculptured fairways and carpet greens of the Jack Nicklaus Course are a challenge and an inspiration to all golfers. There is another course, plus a spa and fitness centre, at the China Fleet Country Club in Saltash (china-fleet.co.uk).

EAT AND DRINK
The Edgcumbe
nationaltrust.org.uk
Cotehele, Saltash, PL12 6TA
01579 35271
Set in Cotehele Bay, the Edgcumbe's dining room nestles beside the river with lovely views, and serves hearty Cornish cream teas. Choose from nine types of tea to accompany your sandwiches, cakes and scones with jam and cream. Book ahead if you're bringing a large lunch party.

▶ **PLACES NEARBY**
Not far from Calstock and Cotehele, you'll find a couple more historical sights, plus a country park, a donkey sanctuary and the wonderful Port Eliot (see page 116).

Cotehele Mill
nationaltrust.org.uk
St Dominick, near Saltash,
PL12 6TA | 01579 351346
Open all year
More than just a 19th-century watermill, Cotehele Mill next to the Morden Stream in the Tamar Valley is a working mill selling wholemeal flour. As well as outbuildings

providing a historical insight into the wheelwright's, saddler's and blacksmith's workshops, there is a traditional furniture maker, a potter and a hydro-electric scheme bringing everything bang up to date.

Dupath Well
english-heritage.org.uk
Callington | Open all year
In the medieval period, holy wells were held in high regard, and this pretty stone-built well-house standing over an ancient stream is a good example. It was believed to cure whooping cough when sufferers were immersed in the pool, and was built by the Augustinian canons of St Germans Priory in around 1500. Entry is free.

Kit Hill Country Park
Callington | 01579 370030
The magnificent granite dome of Kit Hill rises to just over 1,000ft above the town of Callington, about 4 miles northwest of Calstock. It stands in splendid isolation between the granite masses of Bodmin Moor to the west and Dartmoor to the east. For centuries Kit Hill was quarried for stone and mined for tin, copper, zinc, lead and even silver, but it is now a country park. The hill is topped by an 80ft chimneystack built in 1858 as part of the engine house of the Kithill Consols mine. There's a waymarked walking trail as well as a heritage trail.

Saltash Heritage Museum

saltash-heritage.co.uk
17 Lower Fore Street, Saltash,
PL12 6JQ | 01752 848466
Open Apr–end Jun and Oct–Nov
Wed 2–4, Sat 10–4, Jul–end Sep
Wed 2–4, Fri 10.30–12.30 and
2–4, Sat 10–4

This small local museum
celebrates the history and
heritage of Saltash, covering
anything from wartime life in
the area to the impact of
Isambard Kingdom Brunel in
the southeast district of
Cornwall. There is also a
heritage trail around Saltash,
including a stop at Mary
Newman's cottage, a historic
preserved site where Francis
Drake's wife reputedly lived.

Tamar Valley Donkey Park

donkeypark.com
St Ann's Chapel, Gunnislake,
PL18 9HW | 01822 834072
Open 29 Mar–end Sep daily 10.30–5
(Jul–end Aug 10–5), Oct Thu–Sun
10.30–4, at most other times
weekends only 10.30–4

A great option for small
children if it's raining, this
donkey sanctuary includes a
small petting zoo/farm with
guinea pigs, goats, sheep,
rabbits, pigs and of course
donkeys, plus a large indoor
play barn with a soft play area
and cafe. The highlight of the
day is the chance to take a
donkey for a walk.

▶ Camborne

Camborne – 'crooked hill' in Cornish – is not a beauty spot
and is part of the largest conurbation in the county. This was
once one of the richest tin-mining areas in the world and
famed for its mines; the Camborne and Redruth Mining District
with Wheal Peevor and Portreath Harbour are now designated
as World Heritage Sites by UNESCO. Today the mining spirit
lives on – although all its mines have fallen silent – at Pool,
midway between Camborne and Redruth, where the National
Trust has restored two great steam engines used for pumping
water and winding men and ore up and down deep mine shafts.

The town's most famous son, Richard Trevithick (1771–
1833), was an early steam engine inventor who invented a
steam threshing machine, an early road vehicle and the first
railway engine. A special Trevithick Day is held in his honour in
April, when the town remembers his achievements.

Beyond the industrial heritage, there are two key areas of
countryside to visit: Tehidy Country Park, with leafy walks,
streams and ornamental lakes, and Tuckingmill Valley Park, an
area of award-winning parkland near Camborne and Redruth
that has conservation at its heart.

GET INDUSTRIAL
East Pool Mine
nationaltrust.org.uk
and cornish-mining.org.uk
Illogan Highway, Pool, near Redruth,
TR15 3ED | 01209 315027
Open Apr–end Jun and Sep–end Oct
Sun–Mon, Wed–Fri 11–5, Jul–end
Aug Wed–Mon 11–5
This former Cornish mine
and World Heritage Site has
two great beam engines at
its centre, preserved in
towering engine houses that
were originally powered by
high-pressure steam boilers
invented by local lad Richard
Trevithick. The restored
winding engine is in action
every day, and there are
family trails and plenty of
displays about the industrial
mining past in Cornwall.

GET OUTDOORS
Tehidy Country Park
TR14 0HA
01209 610094
This, the largest area
of woodland in West
Cornwall, is a great place
to go birding or lose yourself
in the woods. With more
than 9 miles of paths and
250 acres of woods and lakes
to discover, plus a picnic area
and cafe, you can wander
freely. The woodlands were
formerly owned by the
Basset family, one of the
four most powerful families
in Cornwall.

▼ An engine house near Camborne

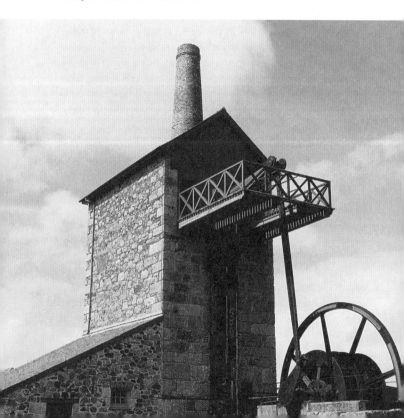

Tuckingmill Valley Park
tcv.org.uk
Just a mile east of Camborne, this country park has won awards for its conservation work and is a great place for families, with a bespoke skate park, walking trails, playgrounds, picnic areas and art installations. You can't miss the mining history, with chimneystacks on the hill and the Red River that runs through it, so named for the colour it ran because of the minerals from the mines. Cornish wildlife is now flourishing here, including gorse and unusual species of dragonfly.

PLAY A ROUND
Tehidy Park Golf Club
tehidyparkgolfclub.co.uk
TR14 0HH | 01209 842208
Open all year
This well-maintained parkland course is a good bet for holiday golf and offers a challenge for golfers of all abilities. With views over the Cornish countryside, it also has a well-stocked professional shop and offers lessons.

Camelford

Legend has it that King Arthur died at the hands of Mordred, his nephew, near to Camelford at the village of Slaughterbridge. There, you can find 'Arthur's tomb', marked by an inscribed stone dating back 1,500 years, at the Arthurian Centre. The strong local Arthurian connection begs the question: does the old market town Camelford have a strong connection with Camelot? Could it actually *be* Camelot?

Sadly, no evidence has been found to suggest that the name of Camelford relates to Camelot rather than an ancient Cornish place name, but the town is pretty close to some key Arthurian sights, including Tintagel Castle (see page 261) and the Slaughterbridge Arthurian Centre, so it's a good place to visit if it all appeals to you.

The historic market town of Camelford is 6 miles inland and around 10 miles north of Bodmin, overlooked by Rough Tor on the edge of Bodmin Moor, and is well placed for exploring the north coast of Cornwall. Port Isaac (see page 211) is a short drive away, as are many north coast surf beaches. Some decent walks up Rough Tor and Brown Willy start in Camelford's car parks (see Bodmin Moor, page 62); both of the town's car parks are free.

There are other things to see nearby too – including the Delabole Slate Quarry (see page 88), which runs guided tours.

VISIT THE MUSEUMS AND GALLERIES

Arthurian Centre

arthur-online.co.uk
Slaughterbridge,
PL32 9TT | 01840 212450
Open Easter–early Nov daily 10–5

Walk through the fields where King Arthur and Mordred supposedly had their final battle; look at the 6th-century stone by 'Arthur's tomb' and find out more about the legends of King Arthur at the Arthurian Centre. Archeological digs are sometimes going on in the 20 acres of property here. One such dig in 2005 uncovered a secret garden dating from the 18th century, now called Lady Falmouth's Secret Garden. If that's not enough for the children, there's brass rubbing, a play castle and more.

North Cornwall Museum and Gallery

bodminmoor.co.uk
The Clease, PL32 9PL
01840 212954 | Open Apr–end Sep
Mon–Sat 10–5

This small private museum about life in Cornwall covers the last 100 years or so and principally examines farming life. It includes a reconstructed moorland cottage with a section on tools, an exhibition on lace bonnets and a collection of Cornish and Devonshire pottery as well as an unusual collection of early vacuum cleaners.

GO FISHING

Crowdy Reservoir

swlakestrust.org.uk
near Camelford | 01566 771930
Open for fishing 15 Mar–12 Oct

Within Bodmin Moor's SSSI, Crowdy Reservoir offers free trout fishing in its 115 acres for Environment Agency rod licence holders in season – buy online at environment-agency.gov.uk. The moorland lake attracts a lot of birders, and no other activities, beyond walking and fishing, are allowed in the area.

SADDLE UP

Lakefield Equestrian Centre

chycor.co.uk
Lower Pendavy Farm,
PL32 9TX | 01840 213279

This equestrian centre on a local farm caters for all abilities, from lessons in the sand school right through to show jumping. Short rides around the farm are great for beginners; off-road hacks for the more experienced are also available. There's also a tea room, the Lakeside Teapot, which serves cream teas and cakes to waiting parents.

PLAY A ROUND

Bowood Park Hotel and Golf Course

bowoodpark.com
Lanteglos, PL32 9RF | 01840 213017
Open all year

This hotel and golf course in Lanteglos near Camelford are set in 230 acres of ancient deer park once owned by Edward the Black Prince. The rolling parkland course has 27 lakes and ponds and is a haven for wildlife. Summer golf breaks in the 3-star hotel are good value; there's also a fine dining restaurant on site.

▶ PLACES NEARBY

The Georgian estate of Pencarrow, south of Camelford, is known for its gardens.

Pencarrow
pencarrow.co.uk
Washaway, PL30 3AG
01208 841369 | House open end
Mar–end Sep Sun–Thu 11–3;
gardens Mar–Oct daily 10–5.30;
cafe, shop and plants end Mar–early
Oct Sun–Thu 11–5

Still a family home, this Georgian house has a superb collection of pictures, furniture and porcelain. The 50 acres of formal and woodland gardens include a Victorian rockery, a lake, more than 600 varieties of rhododendron and an acclaimed conifer collection. There is also a children's play area. There are special events throughout the year – visit the website for details.

▶ Cawsand
see **Kingsand and Cawsand**, page 113

▶ Charlestown

Gorgeous Georgian Charlestown, on the south coast of Cornwall just beyond St Austell, is a sight to behold. With two tall ships in its harbour, it feels like something from *Treasure Island* or Cornwall's glorious past, when pirates roamed the high seas and the local sailors travelled the world. Once you've had your fill of the beautiful ships, you can wander down to two shingle and sand beaches and the rest of the harbour, where modern fishing boats bob about. It's a peaceful spot.

The port was created by a local entrepreneur, Charles Rashleigh, in the late 18th century and is named after him. Before that, it was known as West Polmear and was a modest fishing cove. Rashleigh's ambitions are also behind the broad, tree-lined streets on the way into Charlestown, which have a grand feel. At time of writing, the harbour has been up for sale and the future of the town is in question – if the new owner decides he wants to use the harbour for other reasons, it may look less appealing. But if not, it's a lovely place to visit, with cream tea cafes, a handful of pretty interiors shops, a pub overlooking the beach and a Shipwreck and Heritage Centre to visit with the children, where you can see items from shipwrecks, including the *Titanic*.

10 top museums

VISIT THE MUSEUM

**Charlestown Shipwreck
and Heritage Centre**
www.shipwreckcharlestown.com
Quay Road, PL25 3NJ
01726 69897
Open Mar–end Oct 10–5
This family-friendly museum is
the largest private collection of
shipwreck items on display in
Europe and includes unique
items from local shipwrecks as
well as a large exhibit on the
Titanic. There's an audio-visual
theatre that tells you the history
of Charlestown harbour.

Children under 10 go free and
there's a good selection of
pocket-money treats in the
museum shop. Outside, you can
examine a lifeboat and a 1920s
German diving suit.

HIT THE BEACH

Crinnis Beach & Carlyon Bay
As well as the two beaches
in Charlestown, a short hop
down the coast will take you
to Carlyon Bay, a wide,
white-sand beach. It's not
all as pretty as it sounds, as
development plans mean that
some of it is marred by fences
and steel; head to Crinnis
Beach, as the westerly end of it
is called, for the easiest access.
There are no facilities here and
dogs are not allowed; it gets
very popular in season.

PLAY A ROUND

**Carlyon Bay Hotel
Golf Course**
carlyonbay.com
Beach Road, Carlyon Bay,
PL25 3RD | 01726 814228
Open all year
The Carlyon Bay Hotel course
is a championship-length, cliff
top parkland course, running
east to west and back again
– uphill and down. The fairways
stay in excellent condition all
year, as they have since the
course was laid down in 1925.
Enjoy the magnificent views
from the course across St
Austell Bay; particularly from
the 9th green, where an
approach shot remotely to
the right will plummet over
the cliff edge.

EAT AND DRINK

Austells ◉◉
austells.co.uk
10 Beach Road, Carlyon Bay,
PL25 3PH | 01726 813888

A 10-minute walk from Charlestown, this modern, stylish bistro is open plan so you can see the chefs at work, and serves such delights as baked Cornish pollock and lemon and raspberry cheesecake verrine, plus a great Sunday lunch and a pot-luck Sunday dinner.

Charlie's Coffee House
79 Charlestown Road, PL25 3NL
01726 67421

A family-friendly, homely cafe in Charlestown's former Post Office, serving enormous sandwiches, delicious cakes, and great coffees and teas. The cafe's sister restaurant, Charlie's Boathouse, is worth checking out for something more substantial.

Tall Ships Creamery
The Harbour,
PL25 3AJ | 01726 654444

Rated as one of the finest ice cream shops in Cornwall, this delightful place has some interesting flavours and a host of intriguing names inspired by the town. Take your pick from Chocolate Booty, Peaches of Eight, Buccaneering Banoffee, Swashbuckling Strawberry or the inventive Bacon, Pancakes and Maple Syrup variety.

▶ PLACES NEARBY

Near to Charlestown, you'll find a large sandy beach, and a hotel and golf course. A short drive and you'll find yourself in St Austell (see page 229) and can visit some of the lovely fishing villages nearby, including Mevagissey (see page 165) and Fowey (see page 104).

Carlyon Bay Hotel ◉
carlyonbay.com
Sea Road, Carlyon Bay,
PL25 3RD | 01726 812304

Surveying the rugged Cornish coast from its clifftop perch above St Austell, the creeper-curtained Carlyon Bay Hotel is an imposing presence above the bay. Inside, the Bay View Restaurant is smartly turned out and serves a traditional menu including Cornish mussels, roast lamb and vanilla panacotta.

▶ Coverack
see **The Lizard,** page 168

▶ Crackington Haven
Between Boscastle and Bude on the north coast, the pretty cove of Crackington Haven has a small cafe and pub at its heart and a large, family-friendly beach with sand and rock pools at low tide.

Crackington Haven has given its name to a geological phenomenon, the Crackington Formation – fractured shale that has been shaped into incredibly twisted and contorted forms. On the sheared-off cliff faces of the area, you can see the great swirls and folds of this sedimentary rock that was metamorphosed by volcanic heat and contorted by the geological storms of millions of years ago. Even the name 'Crackington' derives from the Cornish word for sandstone, 'crak'.

There are some great walks on the dramatic cliffs nearby. The steep coast path leads north to Castle Point where there are the remnants of Iron Age embankments. A mile or so further on is Dizzard Point, where an old oak wood clings to the slopes.

South of Crackington Haven you'll find Strangles Beach, a secluded cove with Northern Door, a natural rock arch where the soft shale has been eroded by the waves. High Cliff, to the south, is the highest cliff in Cornwall at 731ft.

HIT THE BEACH
Crackington Haven beach
The beach is the thing to do in Crackington Haven, a stretch of rock and shingle beach giving way to deep rock pools and sand when the tide goes out. There's a pay-and-display car park at the top of the beach and there are lifeguards on duty in early Jun and Jul–end Sep. Dogs are only permitted Oct–Easter. Bring a bucket for rock pool finds and some money for ice creams from the nearby shop.

▼ Crackington Haven

WALK AROUND CRACKINGTON HAVEN

For clifftop walks, start at St Gennys Church nearby. You can see plenty of the drama of the coastline and geology from up high here without a need to plunge steeply down to the centre of the village.

The area above Strangles Beach is National Trust land and similarly dramatic. Park along the coast road south of Crackington if you want to explore it.

There is also a lovely walk from the National Trust farm at Trevigue, down through the wooded valley and into Crackington Haven.

Wherever you walk, watch your step. The whole area is affected by landslips and though the coast path is stable, don't stray from it.

EAT AND DRINK

Cabin Cafe
cabincafecrackington.co.uk
EX23 0JG
01840 230238
Whether you're looking for pasties, cream teas or ice creams, this cafe makes all its food on the premises and offers takeaway for the beach or dining in. It's also a farm shop, handy if you're self-catering nearby, and there's a beach shop and surf hire if you plan to spend your day on the beach.

The Coombe Barton Inn
thecoombebartoninn.co.uk
EX23 0JG
01840 230345
This hearty local pub with rooms serves breakfast, lunch and dinner. It's not a gourmet spot – expect Cornish-style pub grub with a view of the sea and plenty of family favourites. It overlooks the beach and has a beach cafe in front of it; local real ales are on tap.

▶ Crantock

It's hard to believe that such a pleasant stretch of sand could be so close to Newquay's heaving beaches. Just 2 miles south of the most popular beaches in Cornwall, Crantock stands beside the long, narrow estuary of the River Gannel. It's a good place to check out in the height of summer to remember why Cornwall is so special, if you're in the area.

Founded by Irish hermits in AD 460, Crantock has a strong religious history, with two holy wells, one in the centre and one on the road to the beach, and a church with 13th- and 14th-century features.

These days, the beach is the key pilgrimage site: a surf beach with lifeguards and a beach kiosk in season. It's backed by Rushy Green, an area of sand dunes.

To the west of Crantock is West Pentire, a headland bursting with wild flowers and plants that has been designated an SSSI. There's also a car park. From here you can take the zigzag track south to Porth Joke, also known as Polly Joke, an unspoilt sandy cove. There are some lovely coast path walks around the area.

HIT THE BEACH

The sandy beach at Crantock is manned by lifeguards in the summer season. It's a wide sandy beach with caves to explore at high tide. When the tide is out, to the left-hand side of the beach in one of the caves you can see a rock carved with a woman's face, a horse and a poem.

VISIT HOLYWELL BAY

This large sandy bay is great for families and popular with surfers. At low tide you can explore the Holywell cave – keep an eye on the tide, though, take a torch and don't go alone. At low tide you can also see a 70-year-old shipwreck. There are lifeguards in the bay during the summer.

▶ Delabole

Delabole's biggest claim to fame, once you've discounted the fact that it's en route to the tourist haven of Port Isaac, Doc Martin's town, is its slate. Back in medieval times, Delabole slate was being taken from this deep pit in the earth; at 500ft it's the deepest quarry in England and is still being quarried. The village itself is named after the quarry and is also the birthplace of the Cornwall Air Ambulance. There's not much to see, beyond the quarry and its visitor centre; every July it holds a week of events as part of its annual carnival.

About a mile north of Delabole, along the B3314, you can see Britain's first commercial wind farm. The 10 white towers and their whirling vanes generate electricity for 3,000 homes. Just south of Delabole is St Teath, a pretty village with an attractive church.

GET INDUSTRIAL
Delabole Slate Quarry
delaboleslate.co.uk
Pengelly, Delabole, PL33 9AZ
01840 212242 | Tours and presentations May–end Aug Mon–Fri 2pm
If you're keen to know more about slate quarrying, this is the place to get a first-hand look at it. With walkabout tours around the quarry plus access to the showroom, the quarry invites visitors to find out more about its operation. Small group tours can be organised on an individual basis, otherwise visit the website for precise tour information.

▶ The Eden Project

▲ BioDomes, Eden Project

edenproject.com
Bodelva, St Austell, PL24 2SG | 01726 811911 | Open all year daily 9–6;
closed 6 days in Jan; check website for details

Cornwall's blockbuster attraction near St Austell in the southeast of the county is a modern marvel, an eco-tourism site that aims to educate and entertain and, perhaps most importantly, somewhere that you can take the children for a whole day when you're camping and it's raining. Everything about it is good – even the obligatory gift shop, which is packed to the rafters with eco-friendly and ethical goodies. For those of you who want a refresher, here's a little background to how this Cornish super-garden was created.

How Eden was made
In the mid-1990s, Bodelva Quarry near St Austell was exhausted. Worked for more than 160 years, its china clay had run out and it seemed that it would stand ravaged and empty forever as the quarrymen moved on to a more fruitful site. But not so. Enter visionary businessman Tim Smit, architect Nicholas Grimshaw and a whole host of top-level building and engineering talent. After the success of the Lost Gardens of Heligan, Smit recognised that people were interested in the environment and that he could create something extraordinary, which he did by developing a series of biomes: dome-shaped structures like large glasshouses, housing plant life in unique hot-house environments.

The vision was not just that of a unique rainforest garden under cover in Cornwall, but of something much larger: a social foundation, education programmes, and a focus on biodiversity and climate change. It's so much more than an impressive display of plants and butterflies.

Eden opened in 2001 and counted its millionth visitor just three months later. It's been a runaway success and continues to develop its programmes and diversity today. One of the greatest things about the attraction is that it never stands still. Perhaps because it has multiple aims and public engagement at its heart, you can guarantee that every time you visit you'll see something new: maybe some of the 100,000 plants that you missed the first time, maybe a new seasonal event, maybe a whole area that you hadn't discovered before. Eden is huge and warrants at least a full day's attention.

The Rainforest Biome

This, the largest biome, includes the plants and products of West Africa, South East Asia, Amazonia, Malaysia and Oceania. It's a huge space, 164ft high, with the capacity to accommodate trees from tropical rainforests, and contains, as they put it, the largest rainforest in captivity. There are teak, mahogany and rubber trees interspersed with bamboo, a banana plantation and a host of intriguing tropical plants, all fed by the moisture from a cascading waterfall. The temperature is kept between 18°C and 35°C. Glasses wearers will realise that immediately as their specs fog up. What's missing are the larger animals that populate a rainforest in the wild – lizards, insects and butterflies are fun to spot, but you don't need to worry about chancing on anything with big teeth and a threatening growl.

The Mediterranean Biome

The temperature is cooler and the environment is a notch less exotic in the Mediterranean Biome, which replicates the habitats of Southern Africa, the Mediterranean and California, with hundreds of vividly coloured flowers intermingled with olive groves and vines. In these environments, plants thrive on drought and poor, thin soils. Summers are hot while winters are wet and cool. Plants in this zone include tobacco, grape vines, cotton and Mediterranean fruits. Tales are told through this area, as through the Rainforest Biome, to help you put the plants and environment in context, showing you which plants are used for food and medicine, construction and entertainment. The idea is that you start to see the way that

▶ The Mediterranean Biome

plant life supports our lives, and develop an understanding and appreciation of them and their importance to the world and the way we live.

Beyond the biomes

The walk down into the quarry takes you past sculptures and Eden's stunning outdoor gardens, which cover 30 acres and include the best West Country plants alongside those of the Himalayas, Chile and Australasia. It's fun to run and play here; there are outdoor stages set up in summer with events; theatre companies and local choirs put on performances, and the Eden Sessions, a short season of gigs and comedy shows, take place in the summer months and demand advance booking. Previous acts have included Tim Minchin, The Vaccines and Mumford and Sons. The music and comedy are as cutting edge and remarkable as the venue.

Seasonal events take place through the year, including an ice-skating rink and winter attractions, Easter egg hunts and an autumn harvest festival. There's always a reason to go and new things to see and do.

If you're visiting as a family, there is a cafe at Eden, serving local and seasonal dishes of course, or you can bring a picnic. While the ticket prices seem on the high side, there is an option to convert your ticket to an annual pass for no extra money (ask when you buy) and those arriving at the site by public transport, on foot or by bike get a discount. Buying online in advance is cheaper too.

▼ Red Heliconia, tropical biome

Beyond the visitor attraction, Eden is a social enterprise and charity and runs, among many things, the Big Lunch, an initiative seeking to get people talking to their neighbours and strengthening their communities by having lunch together in their street. It's another part of their mission – not just to get people talking and thinking about biodiversity and the future of the planet, but also to help us realise that we're all connected and all have a role to play in the future.

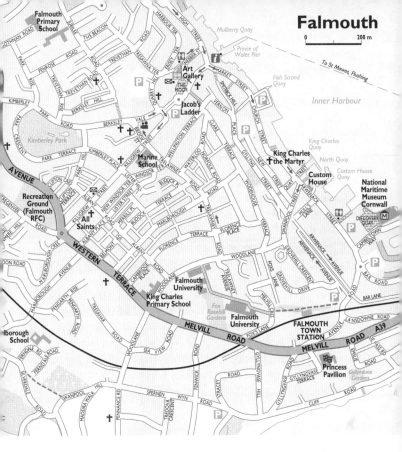

Falmouth

Cornwall's fifth-largest town has a distinctly different
atmosphere. Thanks to its renowned university, which serves
the arts, and its long history as a port, the sorts of people
you meet in Falmouth are exciting, flamboyant and diverse,
including boatbuilders, artists, musicians and chandlers.
This isn't a slur on the rest of Cornwall – really, it's not – but
it reflects the fact that this town is young and vibrant and used
to anyone and everyone, no matter how bizarre, washing up on
its shores. You can be sat in a pub at 3 in the afternoon in the
middle of the week when a wave of people in fancy dress runs
through it. While eyebrows would certainly be raised in the
more traditional villages of the county, nobody bats an eyelid
in Falmouth.

It's a town with diverse appeal as a result: if you like your
boats, the harbour, which is the third largest natural harbour
in the world, is the place to visit. It's been in use for hundreds
of years, and during the 17th century, gold and silver came in
and out of it on routes from the Americas, Indies and Spain.
Smuggling and privateering are key components of the town's

history, while today shipbuilding and yachting continue to contribute to the town's economy. This isn't a town that exists solely for tourists. Key sailing events take place in Falmouth each year, including Henri Lloyd Falmouth Week and the Pendennis Cup. For those in love with the sea and its daily rise and fall, Philip Marsden's excellent book *The Levelling Sea* recounts the tale of Falmouth from the very beginning. Take a stroll around Pendennis Head and you'll see yachts, fishing boats, and huge tankers and liners. The excellent National Maritime Museum is worth a visit for an in-depth look at boats; it's also great for children.

Pendennis Castle, built by Henry VIII at the same time as St Mawes Castle opposite (see page 244) to protect the Fal Estuary, can be visited and is looked after by English Heritage. You can explore inside to see barracks, cells and tunnels, and then enjoy a cream tea with a view of the sea on the terrace. There's a lovely walk around the headland to Gyllyngvase Beach, with a stretch taking you through rock pools at low tide.

Falmouth's beaches are great – as long as you're not a surfer. Being on the south coast and fairly sheltered, the town's beaches rarely get enough swell for surfing. Gyllyngvase Beach has one of the county's best beach cafes, and is sandy and safe for swimming.

▼ Falmouth Bay

Most of Cornwall's towns don't offer much in the way of shopping, but Falmouth bucks that trend too. Down its narrow streets you'll find vintage stores, independent shops, design shops and some high street shops nestled amid the usual surf shops, pubs and pasty vendors. Strolling the back streets and side streets is a pleasant way to spend an afternoon.

Falmouth's layout can make it hard to navigate. The town follows the riverside and has plenty of winding, linking streets. Offshoots from them take you to the town quays, where you can watch buskers, eat snacks from food wagons and stalls and watch the world go by. From The Moor, the 111-step Jacob's Ladder leads up the side of a steep hill and is named after its creator, a builder and property owner called Jacob Hamblen who needed access to his business. You may also spot a number of characterful 'opes' in the town, open passageways between the town's buildings which were used to give easy access to the sea.

As the streets are narrow and parking in town is expensive and limited, the best way to access Falmouth, especially in summer, is by using the Park-and-Float service, parking at Ponsharden on the edge of Falmouth. A 10-minute ferry ride takes you into the centre of the town. It runs Mon–Fri only.

TAKE IN SOME HISTORY

Pendennis Castle

english-heritage.org.uk
Pendennis Headland,
TR11 4LP | 01326 316594
Open Jul–Aug daily 10–6 (Sat 10–4),
Jun and Sep daily 10–5 (Sat 10–4),
Oct daily 10–4, weekends 10–4 rest
of year. Parts of castle may be closed
for private events

Together with St Mawes Castle, Pendennis forms the end of a chain of castles built by Henry VIII along the south coast as protection from attack from France. Journey through 450 years of history and discover the castle's wartime secrets, from Tudor guns to a World War I guardhouse and a World War II Experience. The cafe serves the usuals plus World War II-recipe homity pies.

VISIT THE MUSEUMS AND GALLERIES

Falmouth Art Gallery

falmouthartgallery.com
Municipal Buildings,
The Moor, TR11 2RT
01326 313863 | Open all year,
Mon–Sat 10–5

This free town art gallery is dynamic and innovative – like the town's art-school residents. With engagement programmes and workshops for children and the community, the idea is to get people involved, not just hang some dusty old oil paintings on the walls. The permanent collection includes works by Man Ray, John William Waterhouse and Laura Knight, and is considered one of the most important in Cornwall. There's a good gift shop too.

National Maritime Museum Cornwall

nmmc.co.uk
Discovery Quay, TR11 3QY | 01326 313388
Open all year daily 10–5

This award-winning museum offers something for everyone, from ever-changing exhibitions, hands-on family activities, talks, lectures, displays and events to crabbing and the opportunity to sail and see marine and bird life. Admire the views from the 95ft tower or descend the depths in one of only three natural underwater viewing galleries in the world. The purchase of a full-price individual ticket gives you free entry to the museum for a year.

National Maritime Museum Cornwall
See highlight panel opposite

MEET THE LOCAL SEALIFE
AK Wildlife Cruises
akwildlifecruises.co.uk
01326 753389 | Open all year
Join an AK sea adventures cruise where you might see seals, porpoises, pods of dolphins and even minke whales and leatherback turtles. It's an exciting prospect. As well as sea safaris, they run wildlife and birding trips around the Fal Estuary. Consult the website for precise trip information – some sailings are 4 hours long, some are 7, and all depend on the weather and tides.

HIT THE BEACH
There are four beaches to choose from in Falmouth:

Gyllyngvase Beach
Ten minutes' walk from the town centre, Gyllyngvase Beach is a wide arc of golden sand with lifeguard cover May–end Sep and some great facilities, including a stand-up paddleboard hut,an ice cream hut and an award-winning beach cafe. It's a sheltered and safe beach for children. Parking is on the road beside a landscaped garden or in the large car park nearby.

Castle Beach
Castle Beach is the most northerly beach, by Pendennis Point and overlooked, of course, by the castle. It's rocky and is a good beach at low tide for rock pooling. Divers and snorkellers love to visit too. There's a small beach cafe and parking is at Pendennis Point. At high tide the beach is submerged, so check your tide times before you lay out your towels.

Maenporth Beach
Only 2 miles from the town centre, Maenporth beach is a sheltered sandy cove with lovely views and good rock pooling. It's family friendly – although there are no lifeguards – with a cafe and toilets. There is also a kayak hire company, Arvor Sea Kayaking, based here offering lessons, guided trips and simple day hire. The car park is behind the beach.

Swanpool Beach
Further out of town, Swanpool Beach backs on to Swanpool Lake Nature Reserve, an SSSI, and has a decent watersports centre offering dinghy sailing, kayaking and windsurfing. There's also a beach cafe. The lake itself has plenty of resident swans, hence the name, as well as an extremely rare plant-like creature called the trembling sea mat.

TAKE A BOAT TRIP
Prince of Wales Pier
falriver.co.uk
TR11 3DF | 01326 741194
Easter–end Sep only
Enterprise boats run along
the Fal River between Truro,
Falmouth and St Mawes, and
various other river and sea
cruises are available from
Falmouth's Prince of Wales
Pier and from other boarding
points around the estuary.
Evening cruises on the
Fal are another option,
along with sea-angling trips.

GO DIVING
Cornish Diving School
cornwalldivers.co.uk
Marine Crescent, TR11 4BN
01326 311265 | Open all year
Mon–Sat 9–5.30
This top local dive centre
offers small group and
one-to-one tuition plus dive
trips, diver training, boat
charter and spear fishing.
There is a lot of shallow wreck
diving in the sea around
Falmouth and trips also go
as far as the Manacles,
Hayle, Penzance and Rock.
Contact them for lessons,
hire or trips.

GO FISHING
Argal Reservoir, Penryn
swlakestrust.org.uk
Falmouth | 01209 860301
There are beautiful walks
around this reservoir near
Falmouth and plenty of picnic
and barbecue areas. It's also a
well-stocked course fishery
with permits available from a

self-service unit in the barn
beside the lake.

PLAY A ROUND
Falmouth Golf Club
falmouthgolfclub.com
Swanpool Road, TR11 5BQ
01326 314296 | Open all year
Falmouth's par 72 golf course
dates from 1894 and has
great sea views over the
Cornish cliffs. There's a
modern clubhouse and the
website provides a set of top
tips for each hole – essential
reading. Golf lessons are
also available.

EAT AND DRINK
de Wynn's
55 Church Street,
TR11 3DS | 01326 319259
For a traditional Cornish
cream tea, de Wynn's is the
place. This traditional tea shop
in a historic listed building with
bow windows offers eight
different types of tea plus
sandwiches, scones and
cakes. It's justifiably popular,
with specialities including
Granny Nunn's bread pudding.
You may need to book in
advance in the summer.

Fal Falafel
falfalafel.com
Adjacent to The Moor (Oct–May)
and Prince of Wales Pier (Jun–Sep)
Quite delicious takeaway falafel
in pitta bread, drenched in
delicious sauces, from the
town's premier food cart. It's a
fresh Cornish take on the Israeli
delicacy and is a whole lot
better for you than fish and

chips or a pasty. Herb teas and Turkish coffees are served alongside them.

Falmouth Hotel ⊚

falmouthhotel.com

Castle Beach, TR11 4NZ

01326 312671

This commanding Victorian hotel overlooks Pendennis Castle, the sandy beaches and the sea and serves fine Cornish and West Country food in its Trelawney dining room. Expect the likes of Cornish seafood terrine with lemon and dill crème fraîche, followed by pan-fried cutlets and braised shoulder of lamb with rosemary mash, sweet red cabbage and broad bean jus, and local cheeses to finish.

The 'Front

Custom House Quay,

TR11 3JT | 01326 212168

CAMRA's pub of the year twice over, The 'Front is a bar on the quay with a hearty selection of real ales where customers are invited to bring their own food from the fish and chip shop nearby. It's small and cosy and is much loved by serious beer and cider fans.

Greenbank Hotel ⊚⊚

greenbank-hotel.co.uk

Harbourside, TR11 2SR

01326 312440

This waterfront hotel overlooks the Fal towards the marina. Its first-floor restaurant menu divides into Classics and Fusions, which could be a classic fish in Betty Stogs

beer batter with chunky chips, or a more unusual crispy beef tongue with celeriac remoulade in a port and orange glaze.

Gylly Beach Cafe

gyllybeach.com

Cliff Road, TR11 4PA

01326 312884

This superb modern beach cafe has won awards for its locally sourced food and has to be one of the best beach cafes in Cornwall. Young, friendly staff, beach views and a veranda sheltered from the wind get a thumbs up, as does the menu including nachos, Cornish mackerel sandwiches and burgers. Family friendly, and a fairly upmarket spot in the evening with music and a slightly more sophisticated menu.

Rick Stein's Fish

rickstein.com

Discovery Quay,

TR11 3XA | 01841 532700

Stein's successful outpost on the south coast of the county has classic fish and chips at the heart of its menu and has a takeaway in operation too so you can eat by the sea. Set lunches and family takeaway deals are good value.

Royal Duchy Hotel ⊚⊚

brend-hotels.co.uk

Cliff Road, TR11 4NX

01326 313042

This 4-star hotel's view across the bay towards

Pendennis Castle and out to sea is magnificent and if you're seated on the terrace, you've got the best seat in town. The dining room, with its rich red tones, crisp white linen-clad tables and chandeliers, is a reassuringly traditional setting for some gently contemporary cooking, including local fish and some great vegetarian options.

St Michael's Hotel and Spa ◉

stmichaelshotel.co.uk
Gyllyngvase Beach, TR11 4NB
01326 312707

St Michael's Hotel's award-winning Flying Fish Restaurant bags a fabulous vista and has a genuine local flavour to its contemporary menus, with lots of Cornish seafood on offer such as whole dressed crab, oysters, Thai-style crabcakes and the Newlyn seafood grill. Inventive desserts too.

▶ PLACES NEARBY

Falmouth is close to the Lizard Peninsula (see page 129) and some of Cornwall's most beautiful sub-tropical gardens, including Glendurgan and Trebah. Watersports enthusiasts have two nearby lakes to choose from as well.

Glendurgan

nationaltrust.org.uk
Mawnan Smith, Falmouth,
TR11 5JZ | 01326 252020
Open mid-Feb–early Nov Tue–Sat
10.30–5.30 (also Mon in Aug and
BH Mon)

Glendurgan's sub-tropical gardens spread across three valleys and include 'giant rhubarb' (*Gunnera manicata*) plants, a huge laurel maze dating from 1833 and the Giant's Stride, a pole that the estate-owning family's children have been swinging round for a hundred years. Developed in 1820 by Alfred Fox, the brother of Charles Fox who created nearby Trebah, the National Trust estate includes trees and shrubs from all over the world, including the Japanese loquat and tree ferns from New Zealand. There are garden tours on the first Thursday of the month, and it is only the gardens that are open to the public – the house is not.

5 beach cafes

▶ Porthminster
  Beach Cafe
  page 240

▶ The Hidden Hut,
  Porthcurnick Beach
  page 223

▶ Gylly Beach Cafe,
  Gyllyngvase Beach,
  Falmouth
  page 99

▶ The Beach Hut,
  Watergate Bay
  page 183

▶ Kynance Beach Cafe,
  Kynance Cove
  page 143

Lizard lakes

Cornwall has few natural lakes of any size but there are reservoirs that make a pleasant change from the sea. The Argal and College Waterpark is only about 2 miles from Falmouth along the A394. The reservoir here is tree fringed and very peaceful, with much birdlife and pleasant paths skirting the shoreline. Coarse fishing is available all year and the fly-fishing season is Mar–end Oct. Stithians Lake is within easy reach of Falmouth and Helston along the A394. There is a car park on the east side of the lake near the dam and another at its north end, near the watersports centre.

Miss Peapod's

misspeapod.co.uk
Kitchen Cafe, Jubilee Wharf, Penryn, TR10 8FG | 01326 374424
An eco-eatery within Jubilee Wharf on Penryn's revitalised waterfront. The river views from the alfresco decking and the food are the stars, with excellent breakfasts, coffee and cakes and delicious lunches prepared from local produce, including organic meats from Rosuick Farm.

Penjerrick Garden

penjerrickgarden.co.uk
Budock, Falmouth, TR11 5ED
01872 870105 | Open Mar–end Sep
Sun, Wed, Fri 1.30–4.30
Far less commercial than some of the bigger Cornish gardens, you won't find a tea shop at Penjerrick but you will find a gardener's paradise with 15 acres of forest, jungle and huge tree ferns. The garden dates back 200 years when it was created by Robert Were Fox, another green-fingered brother of the Fox family behind the gardens at Trebah and Glendurgan. Look out for waterfalls, dense valleys, ponds and a tranquil garden, best in April and May.

Stithians Lake

www.swlakestrust.org.uk
near Redruth, TR16 6NW
01209 860301
The Outdoor + Active centre at Stithians Lake has options for watersports – sailing, windsurfing, kayaking and canoeing – as well as archery and climbing activities. Lessons and equipment hire are on offer and there are less strenuous activities such as a lakeside walk, a trim trail and a children's park. Birders will find bird hides and there's a cafe, a campsite and a fly-fishing area too.

Trebah

See highlight panel overleaf

▶ Trebah

trebahgarden.co.uk

Mawnan Smith, near Falmouth, TR11 5JZ | 01326 252200

Open all year daily 10–6.30

One of Cornwall's most exceptional gardens, Trebah is known for its hydrangea valley, excellent children's facilities including an adventure playground, and miles of trails that lead to a private beach on the Helford River. It also has an award-winning cafe and, seasonally, a beach cafe and ice cream hut. The gardens themselves cover 25 acres in a steep ravine running from a fine 18th-century house down to the river.

Charles Fox, Trebah's original creator, came to Cornwall in 1826 and planted a screen of maritime pines to protect the ravine from fierce coastal winds. Behind this shelter he was able to plant seeds collected from all over the world, and the garden has developed to become one of the finest in the county. More recent additions include a water garden in the upper part of Trebah, created in the 1980s, where small pools are edged with primulas and water irises, and bamboos and ferns provide a colourful background.

In the lower part of the ravine, the Brazilian 'rhubarb' is probably the largest you'll ever see. Follow a dense network of paths to find the koi pond and waterfall, or amble along the camellia walk to a viewpoint overlooking the beach. As much of the garden dates to Victorian times, you can expect to see a lot of rhododendrons. Many are spring and early-summer flowering – and the Trebah Gem, planted in 1900, now reaches 42ft in height. The garden has been created to have interest all year, with plants flowering through to Christmas.

Trebah is also famous for its tender trees and shrubs. A large Chilean laurel with bright green, aromatic leaves can be seen in the Chilean Combe, and the dogwood 'Bentham's Cornel', with its yellow bracts, does well. Magnolias, including *Magnolia x soulangiana*, and the pink tulip tree are also well represented, as are many varieties of eucalyptus, pieris and tree fern. Two extremely tall Chusan palm trees dominate the view down the ravine, and you can also see a pocket handkerchief tree and an exotic, though actually quite hardy, Chinese fir.

▶ Fowey

Fowey is one of the must-see maritime towns of south Cornwall. Pronounced 'Foy' (don't embarrass yourself by trying to call it 'Fow-ey'), this pretty town on the west side of the Fowey estuary attracts the boating fraternity with their yachts, foodies who love to eat the local seafood and Fowey River mussels in particular, and families and holidaymakers browsing interiors shops, supping tea in cafe gardens and playing on the beach at Readymoney Cove.

The town was a major port from medieval times – hence so many well preserved medieval houses – and supplied more boats to the Siege of Calais in 1346 than London. The town's sailors were well known for their arrogance and contempt for the law. Unsurprisingly, as time went on, this town became a haven for smugglers and you can still imagine them rolling barrels of rum up the narrow, cobbled streets in the moonlight. China clay exporting is one of the legal ways in which people have earned money around here for hundreds of years, and unlike the smuggling it's still going on today.

One of the first things you'll notice is that while Fowey is a waterfront town, it centres around a river rather than the sea, which gives it quite a different feel from other towns nearby. Pubs cluster down by the water with views of white-sailed yachts and the wide river beyond it from their terraces. The shopping is interesting too, with delis, craft shops, independent shops and plenty of nautical touches to bring home from the streets of the old town where medieval and Georgian buildings stand beside each other.

St Catherine's Castle, built by Henry VIII to protect the estuary from attack, stands at the edge of the harbour beside Readymoney Cove at the far end of the town and is its only bona fide sight. People don't visit Fowey to tick off attractions on their to-do list, though; it's a place to enjoy for its food and atmosphere. One great way to see it is from a river cruise departing from the Town Quay steps taking you out to sea. Cruising the other way, up the estuary in a canoe, gives you access to an array of river wildlife, and maybe a kingfisher if you're lucky.

Daphne du Maurier was the town's most famous resident. She lived and wrote nearby, inspired in part by this beautiful area.

▶ Washing rocks viewed from St Catherine's Castle

Access to Fowey

A word of warning: don't try to drive through Fowey. It's one of those towns where you might get stuck trying to turn a corner and will almost certainly not find anywhere to park. You'll certainly regret it. The main car park is at the entrance to the town. An alternative and relaxing way to visit is to take the ferry from Polruan. Park up and walk down to the slip; you can also take a bike. Ferries go about every 10–15 minutes and it saves a long drive round. In the summer, there's also a passenger ferry to Mevagissey, and if you have to bring the car, the Bodinnick to Fowey ferry is the one to look for. All are subject to weather conditions and have a reduced service in the winter months. Consult the website, ctomsandson.co.uk, to check timetables.

TAKE IN SOME HISTORY
St Catherine's Castle
english-heritage.org.uk
0870 333 1181
Open any reasonable time
All the way through Fowey
(park at Readymoney Cove),
this small 16th-century fort is
one of a pair built by Henry
VIII to defend Fowey Harbour.
Entry is free and there are no
facilities; climb to the top
storey for views of the town
and harbour.

VISIT THE MUSEUM
Fowey Museum
museumsincornwall.org.uk
Town Hall, Trafalgar Square,
PL23 1AY | 01726 833513
Open Easter–end Sep Mon–Fri
10.30–4.30
Housed in one of Fowey's
oldest buildings, this small
local museum shows
something of the history
and heritage of the little
harbour town. Some displays
are changed on a yearly basis;
regular items on show include
a cape worn by Garibaldi and
some archaeological finds
from the medieval period.

MEET THE SEALIFE
Fowey Aquarium
Town Quay, Fowey, PL23 1AT
01726 816188 | Open Easter–end
Sep 10–5
This small local aquarium
holds a collection of fish and
sea life from the waters around
Fowey. It looks a little scruffy
from the outside, but inside
you can get up close and
personal with eels, flatfish
and starfish and quiz the owner
on the lot. It's very different
from the big-budget aquarium
in Newquay.

HIT THE BEACH
A walk through the town and
up the hill takes you to a small,
sandy cove, Readymoney Cove,
just to the south. St Catherine's
Castle overlooks the beach,
which can be accessed by the
Southwest Coast Path. There
are no facilities; it's a safe place
to swim but can be very busy
in summer.

TAKE A BOAT TRIP
Fowey Quay
foweycruise.co.uk
07776 141241 | Open Apr–end Oct
Short harbour and longer river
cruises take place from the
town quay, running as far afield
as Polperro and Charlestown,
or closer to Lostwithiel, Lerryn
and around the town's historic
harbour. The crew aim to
provide an interesting
sightseeing tour and can
answer all questions.

EAT AND DRINK
Crumpets Tea Shop
1 Fore Street, Polruan-by-Fowey,
PL23 1PQ | 01726 870806
Just a 5-minute boat trip
across the estuary from
Fowey, Crumpets is a
traditional tea shop decked
out in yellow and blue, with
sea-related prints on the walls.
Just the ticket for light lunches,
home-cooked cakes or a
delicious cream tea, served
with homemade jam.

Fowey Hotel ⊛

richardsonhotels.co.uk
The Esplanade, PL23 1HX
01726 832551

This lovely Victorian hotel overlooking the River Fowey has a smart restaurant, Spinnakers, serving local produce, including seafood landed on the local quay in the form of pan-seared mackerel and scallops, as well as West Country lamb and local vegetables.

Lifebuoy Cafe

thelifebuoycafe.co.uk
8 Lostwithiel Street,
PL23 1BD | 07715 075869

This fun, friendly and bright tea shop specialises in homemade cakes and serves its tea in mismatched patterned china cups. Bread comes from the baker down the road, sausages from the local butcher and crabs are caught locally. Great for children too, the menu includes breakfast, sandwiches and afternoon tea.

Old Quay House

theoldquayhouse.com
28 Fore Street, PL23 1AQ
01726 83302

This chic boutique hotel has 11 rooms and the best river terrace in town. Non-residents can visit the Q restaurant for a relaxed waterfront lunch, enjoying the likes of Fowey River oysters, local scallops and West Country cheeses. You'll probably see a swan from the terrace – and if you're lucky maybe even a dolphin. Cream teas in the afternoon go down well too.

The Rashleigh Inn

therashleighinnpolkerris.co.uk
Polkerris, Par, PL24 2TL
01726 813991

Once a coastguard station, this 300-year-old pub between Par and Fowey at the end of a no-through road to Polkerris Beach faces west, so watching the sun set over St Austell Bay is a delight. In the bar you'll find a wide selection of real ales from Cornwall and good, locally sourced food includes pan-fried fillet of wild sea bass and roasted darnes of gurnard.

The Ship Inn

shipinnfowey.com
Trafalgar Square, PL23 1AZ
01726 832230

One of Fowey's oldest buildings, the Ship was built in 1570 by John Rashleigh, who sailed to the Americas with Walter Raleigh. It serves great pub grub with plenty of local fish on the menu (peppered smoked mackerel, breaded scampi and Ship Inn fish pie included). St Austell ales, real fires and a long tradition of genial hospitality add the final touches.

▶ PLACES NEARBY

The area around Fowey is fantastic for walkers – particularly Gribbin Head, with its striped tower. You'll also find the pretty village of Golant worth a visit.

Golant

This pretty village is 1.5 miles north of Fowey and is reached from the B3269. The small church of St Sampson in the middle of the village remembers one of Cornwall's great Celtic saints. The village holds a carnival in mid-August each year and has a friendly riverfront pub, the Fisherman's Arms.

Gribbin Head

nationaltrust.org.uk
Gribbin Head | 01726 870146
This headland, commonly known as the Gribbin, lies to the west of Fowey and has an unusual 84ft tower, the daymark, painted in barbershop red and white. It was put there to distinguish the Gribbin from St Anthony's Head at the entrance of Falmouth Bay – the two headlands look so similar from sea that sailors regularly mistook them, to catastrophic effect: St Austell Bay is in no way as deep as Falmouth's legendary natural harbour.

There's a circular walk from Fowey or Coombe around the headland. It's a rewarding path, with wildflowers and wild garlic in the woods in the spring and stunted elm trees running down to the shore, covered in lichen and blown into contorted shapes by the wind. Don't forget a camera – along with scenic views and wildlife, there are also Bronze Age barrows and some long-disused cliff gardens en route.

Inland from the Gribbin, Daphne du Maurier made Menabilly her home and found inspiration for a number of her novels there. In the eastern shelter of the Gribbin is Polridmouth Cove, with adjoining beaches and an ornamental lake.

The Gribbin can be reached on foot from a car park at Menabilly Barton, a mile inland. To the west, the small village of Polkerris faces into St Austell Bay; you can park halfway down the approach and walk to the beach.

▼ Fowey

Gunwalloe
see **The Lizard**, page 133

Gweek
see **The Lizard**, page 134

Gwithian

This coastal village 4 miles east of St Ives on the north coast is known for its sand dunes and has a church and a friendly pub. Gwithian Towans ('towans' means sand dunes) are the site of a Bronze Age farm, though nothing can be seen there today apart from glorious dunes and native wildlife. In summer, you might see butterflies and skylarks amid myriad mini-beasts. The local area was heavily mined for tin until the late 20th century, staining the river running through Gwithian red with iron ore. There are views across the nature reserve and beach to Godrevy Lighthouse and it's a great place to watch the sunset. Surfers love the beach, as do children, who can scramble across rocks and swim in natural pools. There is a local campaign ongoing to save the beaches here from sand extraction.

HIT THE BEACH

Gwithian's 3.5-mile-long sandy beach is popular with families and surfers and is backed with holiday chalets, a small tea room, a surf shop and the famous dunes. There is a lifeguard service here Easter–end Sep. Some of the rocks nearby and the beach bear witness to the iron-mining industry of the 20th century. At low tide there are caves and rock pools to explore; one of Cornwall's oldest churches is buried in the sand of the beach. You can park in the car park and walk through the dunes to the beach. Be aware that dogs are banned from the beach in the summer.

EAT AND DRINK

Godrevy Cafe

godrevycafe.co.uk

Godrevy Towans, Gwithian, TR27 5ED | 01736 757999

Godrevy Cafe, stands isolated within the dunes at Godrevy Beach near Gwithian. Beautifully designed, it has

5 local celebrities

▶ Dawn French

▶ Sir Ben Ainslie

▶ Rick Stein

▶ Tim Smit

▶ Richard and Judy
(ok, make that 6!)

spacious terraces that make the most of the view, and an unusual attic dining space. It's open all day, for breakfast, coffee and cakes, a light lunch, or a sunset dinner from the evening menu.

The Red River Inn

red-river-inn.com
1 Prosper Hill, TR27 5BW
01736 753223

The name of this 200-year-old pub reflects the colour of the village river when tin was mined locally. Among its attractions are up to five Cornish real ales on rotation, an Easter weekend beer and cider festival, and food that ranges from fresh crab sandwiches and haloumi salad to fresh sea bass, steaks and Middle Eastern, Mexican and Indonesian dishes. An in-house shop sells artisan bread, pastries and farm produce.

▶ Hayle

On an estuary surrounded by sand dunes up the coast from St Ives, Hayle is best known as a haven for wildlife with fantastic birding. The mudflats and sheltered estuary attract a vast number of rare overwintering migratory birds and wildfowl, along with water voles and wildflowers in the summer.

It has not always been this way: Hayle has an industrial past with tin and copper mining important in the Victorian era. Once you're away from the sea and the sand dunes, it's not a pretty place – the town's industrial heritage has yet to be brushed up and regenerated. Local names like Copperhouse and Foundry reflect that history.

The contrast between the dereliction of Hayle's harbour area and the spaciousness and brightness of its nearby beaches is quite startling. Take a brisk walk along the eastern side of the harbour and along the northern side of the large tidal pond, Copperhouse Pool, to see why. The beach is a big draw for most, with surfers, families and sunbathers flocking in the summer. The town has a choice of shops, galleries and craft shops, restaurants and several down-to-earth pubs.

MEET THE WILDLIFE

Paradise Park

paradisepark.org.uk
Trelissick Road,
TR27 4HB | 01736 751020
Open all year 10–6 (summer),
10–4 (winter)

Paradise Park is a mini-zoo with plenty of wildlife to meet, from red pandas to guinea pigs. The main event is the birds – they have more than 650 species to see, including parrots, flamingos, toucans

▲ Hayle Beach

and Cornish choughs. There's also a small petting zoo with donkeys and goats, and an indoor play barn for a rainy day.

HIT THE BEACH

Hayle Towans, along with Mexico and Upton Towans, provides plenty of sand for everyone. Backed by sand dunes, the beaches here are generally safe, good for surfing and have lifeguards in residence Easter–end Sep. There are mudflats by the River Hayle estuary, great for birding, and the sand dunes are full of wildlife, from wildflowers to rare butterflies and dragonflies. Hayle Canoe Club offers sea kayak and canoe lessons on the beach, and if you look out to see, you'll spot the 19th-century octagonal form of Godrevy Lighthouse which inspired Virginia Woolf's novel *To the Lighthouse*.

GO BIRDING

Hayle Estuary

Hayle's sheltered estuary is home to a vast number of birds and plays host to migratory species in the winter. Some very rare sightings are possible during autumn migrations when vagrant species from America may be pushed off their north-to-south migratory path and driven across the Atlantic to Cornwall.

The stretch between Copperhouse and Lelant Saltings is the best to begin with, accessed off the A30 on the Penzance and St Ives road by the Old Quay House Inn. There is a public hide at Ryan's Field, the Eric Grace Memorial Hide. Look out in particular for wintering wildfowl and migratory birds, golden and grey plover, widgeon, shelduck and curlew, and hovering kestrels and peregrine falcons. Water voles have burrows in the estuary bank and there is a select colony of European pond turtles here too. Grey seals sometimes make an appearance, as do basking sharks way offshore. There's plenty to look out for; bring binoculars if you can; spring, autumn and winter are the best seasons.

EXPLORE BY BIKE
Hayle Cycles
haylecycles.com
36 Penpol Terrace,
TR27 4BQ | 01736 753825
Open all year Mon–Tue, Thu–Fri 9–5.30, Sat 10–5
In the centre of Hayle, close to the Towans beaches, Hayle Cycles offers bike hire and servicing. There are some lovely routes along the coast and inland here, along quiet country lanes. You could tackle a route along the coast to St Ives (6 miles) and back, or over to Marazion and St Michael's Mount (5 miles).

GO SURFING
Shore Surf School
shoresurf.com
St Ives Bay Holiday Park,
TR27 5BH | 01736 755556
Various packages are on option for those wanting to find their feet on the waves, from a 2.5-hour taster to a 3- or 5-day course. The surf school has a centre of excellence at the St Ives Bay Holiday Park and a surf school at Godrevy National Trust car park. You can hire wetsuits and boards too.

EAT AND DRINK
Mr B's Ice Cream
mrbsicecream.co.uk
24 Penpol Terrace, TR27 4EQ
01736 758580
With a quite frankly ridiculous 260 flavours to choose from, Mr B's has been roundly declared one of Cornwall's top gourmet ice cream destinations. Strange to think, then, that former cockney Mr B himself spent 10 years making just vanilla ice cream before developing this extraordinary long list. Caramel and Homemade Fudge, Lemon Meringue Pie and Turkish Delight are among the top tastes to try.

Rosewarne Manor ⊛⊛
rosewarnemanor.co.uk
20 Gwinar Road,
TR27 5JQ | 01209 610414
This grand 1920s building has been remodelled and revamped and has a family-run restaurant serving seasonal Modern British food. You might set the ball rolling with Cornish blue cheese panacotta, then progress to an unusual assemblage of pork belly with dark chocolate, cauliflower and apple, or perhaps opt for line-caught sea bass and beef shin in a Cornish take on surf'n'turf.

▶ PLACES NEARBY
Close to Hayle is the attractive Godolphin House, while the small village of Gwinear has an interesting church with historical details.

Godolphin House

nationaltrust.org.uk

Helston, TR13 9RE | 01736 763194

Estate open all year; garden open most of year 10–4 (10–5 in summer); house selected weekends only – check website for details

This historic house with a medieval garden was one of Cornwall's most fashionable houses back in the 17th century and is a still a knockout today. The garden is one of the most important historic gardens in Europe and has barely changed since the 16th century. Its Tudor raised walkways and walls are of particular note; some parts of the side garden date from 1300. Godolphin Hill, on the southwesterly side of the estate, gives good views to St Ives Bay in the north and St Michael's Mount in the south.

St Winnear's Church

Gwinear, Churchtown, TR27 5JZ

This church's battlemented granite tower dates from 1441. Inside you can see much of historical interest including a carved roof screen, a Norman-based granite font and some interesting bench ends. Close by is part of a Celtic cross with a figure of Christ on it that may date back to the 9th century.

Helford

see **The Lizard**, page 135

Helston

see **The Lizard**, page 138

Kingsand & Cawsand

You don't have to drive miles into the depths of Cornwall to find a true Cornish experience – here, just 3 miles from Plymouth, the twin villages of Kingsand and Cawsand have narrow streets, pretty houses, gig boat races and cosy pubs. They are not the best known of Cornwall's villages, tucked away on the Rame Peninsula, and are all the better for it, with several pubs and cafes and only one or two shops selling paintings and photographs of traditional Cornish seaside scenes. Hidden from Plymouth by the high ground of Mount Edgecumbe, you'd never know the big city was so close.

Start in Cawsand, and do use the car park. The streets here are narrow, and watching a tourist in a large vehicle attempt to manoeuvre around them is considered a sport by the locals. Cawsand has a charming little square above its small, sandy beach, overlooked by a pub, and from here you can walk along

Garrett Street to Kingsand, and past a grand clock tower built to commemorate the coronation of George V (sadly damaged by storms in February 2014). Explore the narrow alleyways and flights of steps that sidle to and fro above the rocky shoreline.

Running south from Cawsand is a level walk that leads along part of a Victorian drive, built by the Earl of Edgcumbe. Wealthy landowners of the 18th and 19th centuries often built such driveways through their properties in order to show them off to their full advantage to arriving guests. The way leads through shady woods to Penlee Point, where there is a grotto built against the slope of the headland. From here you can enjoy views of the curve of Rame Head as it heads to the west. The villages have a strong smuggling and fishing past; sadly all the known smugglers' tunnels have been sealed up.

Kingsand has a wider and rockier beach, popular with children and dogs, as well as an ice cream cafe open in season, a beautiful art gallery and a pleasant pub. You can walk along the beach to Mount Edgcumbe, beside fishermen's boats.

Once upon a time, Kingsand and Cawsand were divided by the Devon–Cornwall border – and there's a sign to that effect on Garrett Street. For many generations those born in Kingsand were recorded as Devon-born, while those born in Cawsand were considered Cornish; today the merged villages are both considered Cornish.

▼ Cawsand

TAKE IN SOME HISTORY
Mount Edgcumbe Country Park and House
mountedgcumbe.gov.uk
Cremyll, Torpoint, PL10 1HZ
0844 6820380 | Park open all year;
House & Earl's Garden open Apr–
end Sep Sun–Thu 11–4.30
The original Tudor house at Mount Edgcumbe was destroyed by a bomb during World War II, a victim of the massive raids on Plymouth. It was rebuilt during the 1960s to replicate the original and has been handsomely restored. The landscaped park has many lovely features, including follies, mock temples and Gothic ruins, and exquisite formal gardens. The park's woodland has a network of paths and fallow deer roam among the trees. Nearby is the little river port of Cremyll from where there is a passenger ferry to Plymouth.

VISIT THE GALLERY
Westcroft Art Gallery
westcroftgallery.co.uk
Market Street, Kingsand,
PL10 1NE | 01752 822151
This fine, small art gallery attached to an exquisite B&B is worth looking out for its contemporary expressions of Cornwall by talented local artists, including watercolours, oils and pottery. It's a cut above the typical souvenir shop offering; the friendly owners can also arrange art tutorials and painting sessions around the coast with local artists.

HIT THE BEACH
Both Kingsand and Cawsand have safe beaches for families. Cawsand's sandy beach is overlooked by the Cawsand Bay Hotel and is the home of the local boat club. Kingsand's beach is longer and is sandy and shingly; it's better for rock pooling when the tide goes out. Both are dog friendly and there are several slopes and steps leading down to them.

EAT AND DRINK
Cawsand Bay Hotel
thecawsandbayhotel.co.uk
The Bound, Cawsand, PL10 1PG
01752 822425
If you want a drink, perhaps some local cider, plus a view of the sea, this is the place to go. The Cawsand Bay Hotel has a prime location on Cawsand's sandy beach and serves lunchtime soups, sandwiches and local fare. It's family friendly and there's also a coffee lounge bar to shelter in.

The Halfway House Inn
halfwayinn.biz
Fore Street, Kingsand, PL10 1NA
01752 822279
So named because the pub stands at the point that once marked the spot of the Devon–Cornwall border, this friendly inn is hidden among the narrow lanes and colourful houses of Kingsand. It's a relaxing place to enjoy a pint of Betty Stogs or locally caught mackerel, sea bass and crab.

The Rising Sun

The Green, Kingsand, PL10 1NH
01752 822840
One of the locals' favourites,
The Rising Sun is popular
because it serves great food,
has a fun and welcoming
atmosphere and is in the heart
of the village. With plenty of
local real ales on tap plus a
speciality fish soup, it's a real
Cornish experience. You can
also enjoy live music on a
Saturday night.

The View

theview-restaurant.co.uk
Treninnow Cliff Road, Torpoint,
PL10 1JY | 01752 822345
Just out of Cawsand on
the cliff road overlooking
Whitsand Bay, this modern
restaurant is sensational in
every aspect. Serving modern
European food with Cornish
specials and local ingredients,
it's high class in every regard
– but with reasonable prices.
Expect the likes of roast
scallop risotto, grilled dabs
and roast hake.

▸ PLACES NEARBY

Along the headland from
Kingsand and Cawsand,
Whitsand Bay is overlooked by
holiday chalets but remains a
beautiful, wild, unspoilt beach,
while the granite-faced
18th-century Antony House is
5 miles inland. The wonderful
Port Eliot country house can be
found at St Germans.

Antony House

nationaltrust.org.uk
Torpoint, PL11 2AQ
01752 812191 | Open weekdays
12–5, some seasonal variation; visit
the website for full opening hours
Antony House, home of the
Carew family for generations
and now cared for by the
National Trust, stands in more
than 100 acres of woodland
garden on the grassy banks
of the Lynher River near
Torpoint. The original Tudor
house was pulled down in the
early part of the 18th century
and replaced by the finest
Georgian house in Cornwall,
perfectly proportioned with fine
granite stonework facings of
Pentewan stone and elegant
colonnaded wings of red brick.

Port Eliot

porteliot.co.uk
St Germans, PL12 5ND
01503 230211 | Open 11 Mar–
6 Jun, 10 Jun–15 Jul, Sat–Thu 2–6
With vast lawns, woodland
gardens, a maze and a rip-
roaring summer festival, Port
Eliot is a particularly special
country house. As the historic
seat of the Earl and Countess
of St Germans, it's a grand
and impressive place, with
Rembrandts above the
fireplaces and a magnificent
collection of exquisite furniture
as well as some very odd
murals. The family still live
there and on a tour you may
meet their dogs. The
landscaped gardens were
laid out by Humphrey
Repton and the house was

remodelled by Sir John Soane in the 18th century. Its more recent claim to fame is as the setting for the Port Eliot Festival, a bohemian mix of writers, speakers, wild swimming and creativity, where the likes of Dominic West, Tracy Chevalier and Ali Smith have spoken. At other times of the year it's a great dog-walking and picnicking spot, regularly holds unique fairs and events, and has a buzzing, arty tea room called the Long Gallery.

Whitsand Bay

Whitsand Bay is a gorgeous curve of white sand – hence the name – and is popular with surfers. There's nothing here but sand and waves – no shops, no ice cream stalls, no surf hire – but that makes it all the more appealing.

Access is limited to the beach – the cliffs here are very steep so you have to tackle many steps – and there are some rip currents. A little further along the coast, Freathy Beach is a good place to swim, with a car park at the top and steep steps to the bottom of the cove.

Whitsand Bay Hotel and Golf Club
whitsandbayhotel.co.uk
Whitsand Bay, PL11 3BU
01503 230276 | Open all year
This testing seaside course is laid out on cliffs overlooking Whitsand Bay. It's pretty easy walking after first hole; the par 3 third hole is acknowledged as one of the most attractive holes in Cornwall. The hotel also has a spa, restaurant and bistro and is dog friendly.

Kynance Cove
see **The Lizard**, page 143

Lamorna
Lamorna, a small former fishing village turned artist colony 4 miles south of Penzance, is in the most sheltered of the narrow valleys that lead gently down to the south-facing shores of Mount's Bay. It's an arty community that drew the Newlyn School in the 19th and 20th centuries; these days it celebrates this heritage with an arts festival each autumn bringing together professional artists working in the area. Down at the cove, Colin Caffell's bronze sculpture 'Naiad' lends a little magic.

The road that leads down to Lamorna Valley is narrow and can become congested during Bank Holidays. It is quite a journey through shady woodland to reach an unexpected bay fringed by granite cliffs, but there is charm around every corner of Lamorna. On the way down to the cove is the Wink, a classic Cornish pub so named for the blind eye that locals turned to smugglers. The village has a granite quay and in Victorian times the granite from the hillside quarries was highly prized. Some went to build lighthouses while more went to construct the Thames Embankment.

Note that Lamorna's car park is pay-and-display; plenty of tourists have missed the notice and found themselves landed with big penalty fines.

HIT THE BEACH

Lamorna Cove does not have a lifeguard and is only a small curve of sand (read: busy in summer), but there is a car park right nearby, a cafe and, in season, motorboat and kayak hire. The small pebble cove is backed with boulders and is popular with swimmers and scuba divers.

EAT AND DRINK

Lamorna Cove Cafe

lamornacove.com

In a beautiful setting overlooking the cove, this cafe serves up breakfasts, and lunch dishes using local crabs and mackerel. Watch out if you park here – the pay-and-display car park is monitored stringently and many holidaymakers have been caught out with a fine.

The Lamorna Wink

TR19 6XH | 01736 731566

This characterful pub is popular with the locals and has a special place in local mythology; author Martha Grimes wrote a crime novel about it (called, indeed, *The Lamorna Wink*). It also acted as a station for rescue workers during the Penlee lifeboat disaster, and has hosted actors and crew during many filming sessions that have taken place in the cove. And that's without getting into the smuggling history of the pub...

▶ PLACES NEARBY

You might like to visit Penlee House (see page 201) if you're interested in the artists of the area; walkers can walk the coast path that runs through the cove, and just west of the valley there's a famous stone circle and a Bronze Age grave.

▼ Lamorna Cove

The Merry Maidens

A mile west of Lamorna Valley in a field alongside the B3315 is a stone circle dating from the early Bronze Age – the famous Rosemodress, or Boleigh, Circle of 19 upright stones. It is popularly known as the Merry Maidens, from the legend of young girls turned to stone for dancing on a Sunday. In nearby fields are two tall standing stones, the Pipers, who suffered the same fate. They are all more likely to have been ceremonial sites of the local Bronze Age peoples. A short distance west of the Merry Maidens, and close to the road, is the Tregiffian entrance grave. Also from the Bronze Age, it comprises a kerbed cairn with a chamber roofed with slabs.

▶ Land's End

And so to Cornwall's most southwesterly point, the start of many a walk to John O'Groats and the location of 'that' signpost. Land's End draws tourists like bees to honey so go with that expectation in mind. The 200ft granite cliffs are majestic when nobody else is around and the best way to get a clear shot is to walk there, along the cliff path. The Southwest Coast Path runs from Sennen (see page 256), one mile north, and Porthgwarra (see page 216) three miles southeast.

Otherwise, turning up by car introduces you to the delights of the Land's End entertainments complex: naked commercialism or a respite from wet weather for families, depending on how you look at it. Inside you'll find shops, exhibitions, cinemas and enough to keep you all busy for at least half a day. There is a good choice of cafes and restaurants within the complex and the Land's End Hotel is in a splendid position overlooking the Longships Lighthouse. There may, of course, be queues on the approach on popular public holidays and during peak holiday periods. The car park operates a flat fee for an all-day stay.

ENTERTAIN THE FAMILY

Land's End
See highlight panel overleaf

EAT AND DRINK

The First and Last Inn
firstandlastinn.co.uk
Sennen, TR19 7AD
01736 871680
This 700-year-old pub has a strong smuggling history, complete with smugglers' tunnels, and is haunted by the ghost of former landlady Annie George. Serving up sandwiches, pub grub and local ales, it's a popular spot for those on the longest walk, and visitors to the most southwesterly point too. The pub also has four modern and stylish rooms nearby for visitors.

▶ Land's End

landsend-landmark.co.uk

TR19 7AA | 0871 720 0044 | Open all year daily 10–4, later in peak season

This complex includes the West Country Shopping Village, for all your souvenir needs, along with Arthur's Quest, a 4D family cinema experience '20,000 Leagues Under The Sea', an Air Sea Rescue motion theatre attraction, the End-to-End exhibition and Greeb Farm, a family farm park with a small petting zoo. All the attractions are pay as you go, and there are restaurants and cafes in the complex too.

▲ St Mary Magdelene Church

▶Launceston

Launceston, on the A30 just over a mile west of the Tamar, is the largest town in the Cornwall/Devon borderlands and is dominated by its castle. Known as the gateway to Cornwall, it's a historic town with Georgian buildings, restaurants and museums that has suffered a little during the recession, with many shops closing down.

The key attractions are the town's 11th-century castle, which hosts the local Castle Rock music festival in July each year and is a good site for a picnic; the Lawrence House Museum, which showcases the town's history from the Bronze Age to World War II; and the dark granite and beautifully carved St Mary Magdalene Church.

To enjoy Launceston, park as soon as you can (there are car parks near the market and at Thomas Road and Tower Street) – Launceston's handsome South Gate forces traffic to pass through in single file while pedestrians pass comfortably three abreast beneath an adjacent arch.

At the centre of the town, the Square has some very fine Georgian buildings, including the White Hart Hotel, which has the added flourish of a Norman arch over its doorway. Launceston Castle is reached by going down Western Road from the Square. The Launceston Steam Railway is based at the bottom end of St Thomas Road and runs for 2 miles through the valley of the Kensey River.

TAKE IN SOME HISTORY
Launceston Castle
english-heritage.org.uk
Castle Lodge, PL15 7DR
01566 772365 | Open Apr–end
Jun and Sep daily 10–5, Jul–end
Aug 10–6, Oct 10–4; closed
Nov–Mar
Built by Henry III's brother
Richard in 1227, Launceston
Castle is a shell keep, a circular
wall with buildings inside it.
Richard later added to the
castle with another tower and a
fighting platform, making this
castle the dominant building for
miles around. It's still fairly
impressive today. Climb the
battlements for impressive
views, picnic on the grass
around it or read up on its
history in exhibitions inside.
The castle has an impressive
history not just as the fortress
of the Earl of Cornwall but also
as a prison in the 17th century
where George Fox, founder of
the Quakers, was imprisoned
for eight months. Today the
castle is the site of a summer
music festival, Castle Rock, and
the start of the Two Castles
walking trail, linking it to
Okehampton Castle.

▼ Launceston Castle

VISIT THE MUSEUM
Lawrence House Museum
nationaltrust.org.uk
9 Castle Street,
PL15 8BA | 01566 773277
This Georgian townhouse museum run by the National Trust preserves the town's history, focusing particularly on its links with Australia. There is also a display of costumes dating from the 18th century to the 1960s, and a toy room with historical exhibits and toys that visiting children may play with.

TAKE A TRAIN RIDE
Launceston Steam Railway
launcestonsr.co.uk
St Thomas Road,
PL15 8DA | 01566 775665
Open Jul–end Sep Sun–Fri; check the website for other times
The Launceston Steam Railway links the historic town of Launceston with the hamlet of New Mills in a five-mile round trip through the Kensey Valley. Tickets are valid for unlimited travel on the day of issue and you can break your journey. Launceston Station houses railway workshops, and a transport museum, gift shop and book shop.

GO WALKING
There are two long-distance walking trails starting in Launceston. The Tamar Discovery Trail is a 30-mile waymarked route from the town to Plymouth, through villages and woodlands. The Two Castles Trail is a 24-mile route from Launceston Castle to Okehampton Castle, waymarked through northwest Dartmoor. A visit to the Tourist Information Centre gives you access to leaflets on the routes and Ordnance Survey maps.

PLAY A ROUND
Launceston Golf Club
launcestongolfclub.co.uk
St Stephens, PL15 8HF
01566 773442 | Open all year
The highly rated Launceston Golf Club course has magnificent views over the historic town and moors and is noted for superb greens and lush fairways.

Trethorne Golf Club
trethornegolfclub.com
Kennards House,
PL15 8QE | 01566 86903
Open all year
A challenging and scenic par 71 parkland layout, with numerous water hazards and tree-lined fairways with greens built to USGA specification, making them playable all year.

▶ PLACES NEARBY
The villages around Launceston have several beautiful historic churches; families and nature-lovers will enjoy seeing otters in the wild at the Tamar Otter and Wildlife Centre, or enjoy some family fun at the Hidden Valley Discovery Park.

Hidden Valley Discovery Park

hiddenvalleydiscoverypark.co.uk
Tredidon, Launceston, PL15 8SJ
01566 86463 | Open daily last week
in May–end Sep 10–4.30, Mon–Fri
only in Sep; check the website for
other times

This mini family theme park is
great fun, with a miniature
railway, Forbidden Mansion
haunted house and the
'X'plorer's Path, an adventure-
themed detective treasure
hunt trail. There's also a
hedge maze, a Hobbit House
and a cafe.

St Paternus' Church

Hellescott Road, North
Petherwin, PL15 8LR

This is a very large and
splendid church for a small
rural community. The village
was originally in Devon, though
it lies west of the Tamar and
has always been part of the
archdeaconry of Cornwall.
The architectural features of
the church include round
columns with scalloped
capitals dating from around
1200, and a clerestory dating
from the 14th century.

St Petrock and St Keri's Church

Egloskerry, PL15 8RU

This church has Norman
details – a simple font and an
unusual pillar piscina
– alongside a section of early
17th-century stained glass and
the alabaster tomb probably of
Edward Hastings, Lord of
Penheale, dating from 1510. It
is interesting because he is
shown in civilian clothes,
not the military attire that
was the norm.

St Winwallo's Church

Tremaine, PL15 8SA

Set on its own among trees,
Tremaine's little church is
peaceful and rugged. It has
Norman details that include
a tympanum and window,
both on the north side of the
church, and, inside, a Norman
font with a round bowl and
cable moulding. The wagon
roof and its bosses date from
the early 16th century. The
unusual steps cut into the
thickness of the north wall
led to the rood loft.

Tamar Otter and Wildlife Centre

tamarotters.co.uk
North Petherwin, near Launceston,
PL15 8GW | 01566 785646
Open Apr–end Oct daily 10.30–6;
also opens Good Fri if earlier
than 1 Apr

Visitors to this wildlife centre
will see British and Asian
short-clawed otters in large
natural enclosures. They will
also be able to see fallow and
Muntjac deer, and wallabies
roaming around the grounds.
There are also owls, a pair of
Scottish wild cats, peacocks,
and a large selection of
waterfowl on two lakes. Otters
are fed at noon and 3pm,
accompanied by a talk.

▶ Lelant

The small, pretty village of Lelant is a mile west of Hayle and a little further than that up the coast from St Ives. With a sandy beach and sandy coves on the estuary, it's a pleasant spot – but beware fast-running tides on the estuary coves, which are not completely safe for swimming. Surrounded by countryside, dunes, and former tin mines and granite quarries, the village used to be a fishing port until the estuary silted up. Now it's best known as the start of St Michael's Way, a 13-mile pilgrimage route from Lelant church to St Michael's Mount, via the coast path to St Ives and an overland path. There's an information board on the route outside the church.

The village is a stop on the jaw-dropping St Ives Bay train line – if you get a chance to ditch the car and try it out, do. And Lelant Saltings is the place to leave your car for a park-and-ride service into St Ives in the summer months.

GO BACK IN TIME
Trencrom Hill

The rocky hill of Trencrom, the site of an Iron Age encampment and the highest hill in West Cornwall, stands above the Hayle Estuary and can be reached from Lelant or from the B3311 St Ives to Penzance road. Trencrom is in the care of the National Trust and there is a small car park on its southern side. The path to the summit is short and steep in places, but the views are outstanding. Just west of Trencrom is the little village of Nancledra, from where the green and peaceful Towednack Valley runs north to the sea through a gap in the coastal hills.

HIT THE BEACH

Carbis Bay beach is one of the finest in Cornwall, backed by sub-tropical plants. See St Ives, page 239.

SADDLE UP
Old Mill Stables
Riding School
Lelant Downs, Hayle, TR27 6LN
01736 753045

This riding school in nearby Hayle offers half-day rides and pony trekking on Lelant Downs. It's a wonderful scenic spot to ride along country lanes and farmland with views of the beach and sea.

PLAY A ROUND
West Cornwall Golf Club
westcornwallgolfclub.co.uk
TR26 3DZ | 01736 753401
Open all year

Established in 1889, this is a seaside links with sand hills and lovely turf adjacent to the Hayle Estuary and St Ives Bay. It's a real test of the player's skill, especially Calamity Corner starting at the 5th on the lower land by the River Hayle.

EAT AND DRINK

The Badger Inn
thebadgerinn.co.uk
Fore Street, TR26 3JT
01736 752181
This friendly St Austell Brewery pub is in the heart of the village by the Hayle Estuary and has rooms as well as a carvery restaurant. They have a large garden that hosts barbecues in the summer, and regular events and specials. Call in to enjoy steaks, roasts and locally caught fish.

The Watermill
Lelant Downs, Hayle, TR27 6LQ
01736 757912
Set in extensive gardens on the old St Ives coach road, the Watermill is a cosy, family-friendly pub and restaurant created in the 18th-century Lelant Mill. The old mill machinery is still in place. Downstairs is the old beamed bar and wood-burning stove, while upstairs in the open-beamed mill loft is the atmospheric restaurant where steaks and fish (sea bass, sardines and mackerel) are specialities.

▶ Liskeard

Liskeard is neither the prettiest town in Cornwall nor the most characterful but, placed between Bodmin Moor to the north and Looe to the south, it sees its fair share of tourist traffic in the summer months. This former market town has grand Victorian buildings and a number of high street shops. In recent times, in response to the Mary Portas High Street Review, it has made a lot of effort to develop its independent streak and embrace unusual ideas, holding regular festivals and events and introducing some more offbeat elements to the town, including yarn bombing. Under shadow of retail parks nearby, the town team have been keen to develop the personality of the town to attract shoppers into it.

As a coinage town in medieval times, Liskeard was always the seat of prosperity in this part of East Cornwall. When copper mining took off in the 19th century, the town grew ever wealthier. It's still important for its rail routes today, connecting with London and as the northern terminus of the branch railway connecting with Looe. There's a lovely train ride through the trees and along the estuary from Liskeard to Looe that's well worth the train fare, with sights of ancient woods, wading birds and sailing boats that you can't otherwise see unless you're on foot.

If Victorian market town architecture is your thing, the town has some key buildings to look out for: Webb's Hotel, which overlooks the Parade; the Guildhall and its Italianate tower on

Market Street; and the church of St Martin, which is the second largest church in Cornwall. There's also an ancient well, the Pipe Well, gated off on Well Lane, off Market Street.

Around Liskeard, reaching up to near Bodmin Moor (see page 62) and down to the area around Looe (see page 151), there are lots of attractions, walking routes and countryside sights.

VISIT THE MUSEUM
Liskeard Museum
liskeard.gov.uk/Museum.aspx
Foresters Hall, Pike Street,
PL14 3JE | 01579 346087
Open all year Mon–Fri 11–4,
Sat 11–1.30
This small town museum tells the tale of Liskeard, including its early days as a cattle-farming district right through to the copper boom of the 19th century. Much of the museum is about mining, of course. The museum is housed in the former East Cornwall Savings Bank, and is free.

TAKE A TRAIN RIDE
Looe Valley Line
Liskeard Station, PL14 4DX
08457 484950 | Trains run daily;
Sun in peak season only
A trip on the Looe Valley Line from Liskeard to Looe is a stress-free way of going to the seaside and back, recapturing some of the excitement of those days when such a journey as this was a rare treat. The trains descend through the lovely East Looe Valley from Liskeard Station, with station halts on the way giving access along narrow lanes to pleasant villages such as St Keyne.

EXPLORE BY BIKE
Liskeard Cycles
liskeardcycles.co.uk
Pigmeadow Lane, PL14 6AF
01579 347696
The narrow tree-lined lanes around Liskeard are the perfect place for a cycle ride. This bike shop offers cycles for all the family. From Liskeard, there are routes to Tavistock, Bodmin Moor and even Land's End, if you're game.

▶ PLACES NEARBY
The area surrounding Liskeard has a lot of activities, small museums, independent attractions and places to visit. Carnglaze Caverns in particular are a good spot on a rainy day, and host occasional concerts and events. See also Bodmin Moor (page 62).

Carnglaze Caverns
carnglaze.com
St Neot, Liskeard, PL14 6HQ
01579 320251 | Open Jan–end Jul daily 10–5, Aug daily 10–8, Sep–end Dec daily 10–5
Not just another Cornish mining heritage sight, the Carnglaze slate caverns and gardens are also a concert venue and have an intriguing history. Visitors can take a self-guided tour of the three

largest caves, one of which has a subterranean lake. Check the website for details on concerts and events in the Rum Store, the first of Carnglaze's caverns, which got the name because the Royal Navy used it to store its supply of rum during World War II. The acoustics are outstanding. There are also gentle walks to be had in the gardens around the caves, including an easy 25-minute loop around the woods with a view of St Neot's village. The woodland walk has a lot of bluebells in late spring and is open later on Tuesday evenings in season to view them.

King Doniert's Stone

english-heritage.org.uk
St Cleer | Open any reasonable time
For serious fans of ancient Cornish history and heritage, these two carved pieces of a 9th-century Celtic cross commemorate Dumgarth, the British King of Dumnonia, who drowned around AD 875. They are the only surviving examples of a 9th-century stone cross in Cornwall. The stones are in a walled enclosure by the road, a mile northwest of St Cleer. Visitors can park in the layby nearby.

Paul Corin's Magnificent Music Machines

paulcorinmusic.co.uk
St Keyne Station, between Liskeard and Looe, PL14 4SH
01579 343108 | Open May–end Oct daily 10.30–5

This quirky little museum down a narrow, tree-lined road celebrates music machines from the Edison phonograph to the pianola and the Wurlitzer organ. There's also a free car park, a picnic area by the river and dogs are welcome. About 15 minutes' walk up the road, you can also visit the Holy Well of Saint Keyne.

Trethevy Quoit

Tremar Coombe,
between St Cleer and Darite
Trevethy Quoit, or 'the Giant's House' as it's called locally, is an impressive 9ft tall megalithic tomb of five standing stones crowned by a large, flat, sloping slab. Originally covered by a mound, this type of grave dates from 3700–3500 BC. For those seeking Cornwall's ancient history, this site is one of the highlights.

TM International School of Horsemanship

tminternational.co.uk
Henwood, Upton Cross,
PL14 5BP | 01579 362895
This riding centre offers lessons, hacking on the moors and activities for children, as well as residential riding holidays for those aged 12 and up. Book in advance, at least up to a day before you wish to ride.

Adrenalin Quarry

adrenalinquarry.co.uk
PL14 3PJ | 01579 308204
Closed Nov-Feb
A 1,608-ft long,164-ft high zipwire above a flooded quarry.

▶ The Lizard

Along with rocks that make geography teachers' hearts beat double time, dolphins cruising in the sea, seabirds calling and wildflowers bending in sea breezes, the Lizard is visited by most people because its point is the most southerly piece of land on the UK mainland. But there's much more to the peninsula than that. None of this area is overdeveloped – although the number of pasty shops and ice cream parlours around Lizard Village can feel a little much – and if you can avoid the coach parties heading to the point, it feels a world away from touristy Cornwall.

Surrounded by the sea on three sides, with fishing villages seemingly untouched by time at the foot of dramatically steep roads, and with some of Cornwall's very best beaches to boot, it is a dazzling place to visit. Helston is held as the 'gateway' to the Lizard – meaning that it's the largest town hereabouts and you have to drive through it to reach the countryside and southernmost point beyond it. Back in the seafaring days, the rocky coast around here was considered highly treacherous and many sailors lost their lives on the Manacles and other protruding rocks nearby. The large lighthouse overlooking the point acknowledges this today, and churches remember the lost sailors in stained-glass windows.

Regardless of whether or not you're keen to check off the furthest points of land on the UK mainland, this peninsula

▼ Coverack

is worth a visit for Kynance Cove alone. This sensational beach has a long clifftop route down to it and a welcoming cafe on the cliffs when you make it, and features on many postcards and images of Cornwall. Other coves and beaches around the Lizard are family friendly, sandy and worth a visit for sure.

The Southwest Coast Path winds all the way around the peninsula and it's hard not to walk at least a mile of it while you're there, looking out to sea and perhaps spotting dolphins or basking sharks along with rare wildflowers and seabirds. The geology of the area is quite incredible: the rocks found here are not found anywhere else in the UK and are the result of the Earth's crust being pushed up many miles higher than it would normally sit. Just ask a geography teacher.

The Lizard Downs areas, including Goonhilly Downs and Predennack Nature Reserve, are rich in ancient artefacts dating from a time when early man found reasonable grazing on the poorly drained soil. The soil over serpentine rocks also supports a remarkable variety of rare plants. The Lizard's mild climate encourages these plants, but the main reason for the area's unique botanical nature is that the Lizard was joined to the European land mass thousands of years ago, when these plants spread and flourished on what are now the peninsula's coastal fringes. Look out for *Erica vagans*, a type of heather with dark green leaves and spikes of small pink or lilac flowers. It's only found in substantial quantities on the Lizard. Closer to the cliff tops, blue spring squill, pink thrift and creamy sea campion contribute to a mosaic of wild flowers in spring and summer.

▼ Beach from Halzephron cliffs, Gunwalloe

▲ Cadgwith

▷ Cadgwith

It feels a little as if time has stood still at Cadgwith, where a whitewashed pub stands beside thatched and slate-roofed cottages, waiting for the fishermen to come home with their catch. Aside from the odd blackboard advertising cream teas, it's as if the community here doesn't know that the rest of Cornwall has hi-tech aquariums, Wifi and a roaring surf-fashion industry. And in fact, fishing boats do still go out here to bring in the catch, with inkwell-shaped pots trapping lobster and crab, and nets for cod, pollock, monkfish and mackerel. Pilchards were the catch of the day here for decades, until the fishery declined in the early 20th century, and now the cellars where pilchards were once salted and pressed for oil have been converted for modern use.

The best way to visit is on foot. Park in the car park on the hill before you reach the village – the main street is very narrow and there's no parking. Cadgwith has a small, shingly beach called Cadgwith Cove, used mainly by fishing boats, with another beach, Little Cove, beyond it. There are some lovely cliff path walks from the village. A short walk south takes you to the spectacular Devil's Frying Pan, a huge gulf in the vegetated cliffs where a sea cave collapsed centuries ago leaving an arch of rock connecting both sides. On the cliff to the north of the cove there is a small building that was built over a hundred years ago and used as a coastguard watch house.

The Lizard area is especially noted for the variety and value of its plant life. Pink thrift, the powder-blue squill, cliff bluebells and kidney vetch grow in profusion here, but insignificant-looking plants may well be very rare and vulnerable. Visitors are asked not to pick even the most prolific wild flowers and to take care while walking.

HIT THE BEACH
Kennack Sands
Kennack Sands is everything that Cadgwith Cove isn't: a vast, wide, sandy beach with space to build sandcastles, fly kites, surf and grab a coffee or ice cream from one of the two beach cafes. The remains of boats that have run aground can be seen here at low tide. The beach is split in two, with a small hill, Carn Kennack, in the middle; the easterly beach is designated as a wildlife reserve.

▼ Devil's Frying Pan

GO FISHING
From Easter–mid-Sep, the Cadgwith Cove Inn (see below) runs daily fishing trips with breakfast from Cadgwith's beach. These 8am hour-long trips travel along the coast and finish up with a full English breakfast at the pub. From Easter to mid-October, longer fishing trips leave from Porthleven Harbour for some serious sea angling. Book via the Cadgwith Cove Inn again, and reserve in advance.

EAT AND DRINK
Cadgwith Cove Inn
cadgwithcoveinn.com
TR12 7JX | 01326 290513
Relics in this pub's atmospheric, simply furnished bars attest to a rich seafaring history; the cove itself is just across the old pilchard cellar from its sunny front patio. Meals include fish and chips, Cove crab salad, and roast belly of pork. Tuesdays are folk-music nights, and the Cadgwith Singers pitch up every Friday

▶ PLACES NEARBY
A couple of miles north of Cadgwith, beyond Ruan Minor, you'll find a wide, sandy, family-friendly beach that is popular with surfers.

Coverack

Towards the southeast tip of the Lizard Peninsula, Coverack is another of the area's characterful fishing villages, defined by steeply sloping roads down to the sea and encompassed by a dramatically undulating part of the Southwest Coast Path. Pilchard fishing was Coverack's main industry from the medieval period until the early 20th century and it still feels like a busy fishing town today. Despite modern developments around the area, the village retains its authentic atmosphere.

The sand and pebble beach is fun to visit; offshore you can see the Manacles, a group of dangerous rocks that have sunk many a ship. Today it's a popular dive site. And if you should wonder why a Cornish fishing village has a Paris Hotel, it is named after a ship that was stranded off the coast of Coverack in 1899, rather than the glamorous French city.

GO WINDSURFING

Coverack Windsurfing Centre
coverack.co.uk
Cliff Cottage, Sunny Corner,
TR12 6SY | 01326 280939
Open Apr–end Oct
This local RYA-recognised windsurfing centre makes use of Coverack's protected sandy bay and offers windsurfing lessons at all levels plus surf kayak hire. Residential courses are on offer for a weekend or longer, and all courses are small with groups having a maximum size of 12.

Gunwalloe

South of Helston and bordering The Loe (see page 139), Gunwalloe is a small fishing cove with a church, pub and sandy beach, with lifeguards in season and a beach cafe. Following the road to the sea brings you to Church Cove, where an intriguing little 15th-century church nestles close to the edge of eroded cliffs. North of the church is the noisily named Jangye-ryn, or Dollar, Cove and inland are extensive sand dunes.

If the beaches could talk, they'd tell lively tales of seafaring, fishing, smuggling and shipwrecks: the price of not giving the Lizard a wide enough berth was grief on Gunwalloe's shoreline. Dollar Cove saw the wreck of a Spanish treasure ship in the 1780s – if you have a metal detector, bring it here as much of the treasure was lost and is said to be in the bay. Halzephron and Gunwalloe Fishing Coves are just north of Church Cove and can be reached along the coast path. The waves are still heavy and threatening today, especially in the winter; to combat coastal erosion large blocks of granite have been tipped on to the beach. Parking is in the National Trust car park on the approach to Church Cove.

EAT AND DRINK

The Halzephron Inn

halzephron-inn.co.uk

TR12 7QB | 01326 240406

Perched high above Gunwalloe Fishing Cove, this 500-year-old stone inn has stunning views. All the food is homemade, with plenty of fish on the menu. Main courses include cottage pie and baked fillet of hake. Bag a front bench and savour a pint of Skinner's Betty Stogs while admiring the view of St Michael's Mount.

Gweek

The little village of Gweek, 3 miles east of Helston, is known to visitors mainly for its seal rescue centre, the saviour of many a rainy day in the area. The name, by the way, doesn't come from the noise an injured seal makes but is derived from the Cornish word 'gwig' meaning 'forest village'.

At the head of navigation of the Helford River, Gweek was an important port in Tudor times and has been active since Roman times. You will certainly see yachts and fishing boats pulled up on the bank at low tide today – try to imagine the scene in the late 19th century when Gweek had at least 200 boats working in the pilchard-fishing industry, as well as scores of boats importing timber, coal and limestone and exporting ore, corn and oysters. It must have been like Piccadilly Circus at rush hour – so very unlike this tranquil little spot today.

There's an annual summer fair and a fun band week each July, where the local Gweek silver band plays with two other local groups, and events include a pig roast, clay pigeon shooting, a tug of war and sheaf pitching.

MEET THE SEALIFE

Cornish Seal Sanctuary

sealsanctuary.com

TR12 6UG | 01326 221361

Open all year daily 10–5, winter 10–4

This small sea life centre exists to rehabilitate injured seals and home those that wouldn't be able to make it out in the sea today. Alongside a range of seals swimming in and around a large swimming pool, there are playful otters, comical penguins and happy ponies, goats and sheep. The rock pool experience allows children to touch starfish and other marine life safely, and there is a small cafe and kiosks as well as a lovely walk in the woods to be had.

EAT AND DRINK

The Black Swan

blackswangweek.co.uk

TR12 6TU | 01326 221502

Next to the Cornish Seal Sanctuary, this delightful inn has been restored to its former glory, serving pub classics and a selection of Cornish ales including the landlord's own, named after his dog Hamish. Look out for details of their beer and mussel festival in autumn. The pub also has four en suite bedrooms.

The Grange Fruit Farm
thegrangecornwall.com
TR12 6BE | 01326 221718
This fruit farm has a farm shop and a country kitchen restaurant. It's a great spot for Sunday lunch or a cream tea with fresh strawberries, and also has plenty to entertain the children, including pitch and putt, giant skittles and a sandpit.

▶ **PLACES NEARBY**
The tiny village of Mawgan is close to Gweek and has an interesting and ancient church.

St Mawgan in Meneage Church
Gear Hill, Mawgan, TR12 6BU
St Mawgan, who may have founded the church here in about AD 700, appears as a statue on the church tower, which also has carved shields of arms on it. The church dates from the 16th century and has a variety of Gothic window types. It also still has much of its original wagon roof, complete with bosses and angels.

▶ Helford

This pretty village on the Helford Estuary, east of Helston at the top of the Lizard Peninsula, gives you the chance to plunge into a romantic world of woodland and riverside paths. Nearby you'll find Frenchman's Creek, a winding inlet that inspired Daphne du Maurier's tale of the same name. Like many of the routes round here, it's best discovered on foot; parking is difficult. It's one of the many fine walks you can start in Helford; another path leads east to the coast at Dennis Head and to St Anthony and Gillan.

A passenger ferry sails to Helford Passage on the north bank from Helford Easter–end Oct, giving you access to some of the area's most lush sub-tropical gardens. Glendurgan (see page 100) , Trebah (see page 102) and Penjerrick gardens (see page 101) are the best known, where hydrangeas, camellias and rhododendrons flourish amidst lovely woodland on the banks of the estuary and beyond.

EAT AND DRINK
The Shipwrights Arms
TR12 6JX
01326 231235
Stunningly located on the banks of the Helford Estuary, the narrow approach road is restricted to pedestrians only. The pretty, thatched 300-year-old pub was saved from closure in 2012 by a determined consortium of local people.

▶ Aerial view of Helford river estuary (overleaf)

It has a terraced garden and picnic benches on the water's edge plus two dining rooms and a conservatory, added in 2013. The bar is traditional, with rustic furnishings and plenty of nautical bits and pieces.

▶ PLACES NEARBY

Helford is surrounded by beautiful countryside and is close to Helston. There is a golf course on the outskirts of the village.

Budock Vean Hotel Golf Course

budockvean.co.uk
Helford Passage, Mawnan Smith, near Falmouth, TR11 5LG
01326 252102 (course information)
Open all year
Set in 65 acres of mature grounds with a private foreshore to the Helford River, this 18-tee undulating parkland course has a tough par 4 fifth hole (456yds) which dog-legs at halfway around an oak tree. The 16th hole measures 572yds, par 5.

Manaccan

Just south of Helford, Manaccan is a pretty little village with a 12th-century church famed for the 200-year-old fig tree growing from its steeple wall. If you needed further proof of Cornwall's sub-tropical climate, there it is. As well as a church, the village has a pub, a cafe and a deli. Wooded lanes lead to Gillan Creek and Helford River. You can walk from here around Gillan harbour and to Gillan Cove, a sand/shingle beach.

▶ Helston

Helston is the true gateway to the Lizard – if you're on the way to the southernmost point of land in the UK, you'll certainly drive past it. It's the most southerly town in the UK and the second oldest town in Cornwall. The streets are lined with miners' cottages, Georgian houses, pasty bakeries and old pubs, and there are large supermarkets on the outskirts.

Helston's history was connected to its position as a port on the River Cober, until it silted up, and from the medieval period it was a thriving market town and the area's trading centre. The name of Coinagehall Street bears witness to the town's history and it's still a good shopping centre today, as Cornish towns go. There is a great view down Coinagehall Street to the Gothic-style gateway of the bowling green and to the fields beyond. The Guildhall dominates the top of the street and the nearby Victorian Market House is quite stylish for its time.

The town's annual Flora Dance, or Furry Dance, is held on 8 May and possibly dates from a pre-Christian time; it certainly has medieval links. This is when Helston-born people dance through the streets and in and out of buildings and shops from 7am to welcome the summer.

In terms of sightseeing, there is a folk museum in the Market House and Loe Pool, the largest freshwater lake in the county, is nearby. There's also a boating lake and a skate park. Goonhilly Satellite Station nearby was once the largest satellite station in the world and is presently not in use and awaiting a government grant so it can be reopened as a space science centre. Off the B3293 St Keverne road, located about 3.5 miles from Helston, is Trelowarren House. It has been the home of the Vyvyan family since the early 15th century and has a craft centre and restaurant.

VISIT THE MUSEUM
Helston Folk Museum
museumsincornwall.org.uk
Old Butter Market, Church Street, TR13 8TH | 01326 564027
Open Mon–Sat 10–1; check the website for extended opening times
Behave yourself – this folk museum in the old butter and meat markets of Helston has a Victorian schoolroom, complete with a strict teacher, Mrs Crawford. The collection here focuses on Victorian life and covers the whole Lizard Peninsula. In the loft there's a display on Bob Fitzsimmons, a boxer who in the 1890s won three world championships, in three weight divisions.

ENTERTAIN THE FAMILY
Flambards Theme Park
flambards.co.uk
Culdrose Manor, TR13 0QA
01326 573404 | Open 26 Mar–1 Nov from 10.30am, with more limited hours in winter
This family theme park delivers what it promises: something to do when it's raining on the Lizard. Undercover attractions include a life-size and authentic re-creation of a Victorian village, complete with cobbled streets, a Britain in the Blitz exhibition with a bomb shelter, and an indoor play park. Outside, rollercoasters, drop towers and merry-go-rounds cater for children of all ages. Dads, you know who you are...

GET OUTDOORS
Loe Pool
The Loe, the largest natural freshwater lake in Cornwall, is part of the Penrose Estate. Originally the estuary of the River Cober, over time it was cut off from the sea by a broad shingle bar created by rough Atlantic seas in the 13th century. It's a unique habitat with rare moths and woodlice living there, alongside a number of rare plants, algae and other insects. It also attracts more than 80 species of bird and many more wildfowl in winter.

Local people would have you believe that the Loe is the place where Sir Bedivere cast Excalibur, King Arthur's sword, on his request. It's one of a number of lakes to have that story attached to it. There's a superstition that the Loe claims a victim every seven years and Cornish legend tells of the demon Jan Tregeagle (see also Bodmin Moor, page 62), who was doomed by his bad deeds to remove the sand from Gunwalloe to Porthleven. While doing so, he dropped a bag of sand at the end of Helston Harbour, forming the bar.

Penrose Estate
nationaltrust.org.uk
Penrose, TR13 0RD
01326 561407 | Accessible all year
Penrose Estate, beyond Loe Pool, has beautiful woodland and farmland paths to explore. One way to see it is by bike; you could also strap on hiking boots and walk from here to the Southwest Coast Path. There is an outdoor gym trail and in summer, the Stables cafe is open serving cream teas. Also within the estate is St Winwalloe Church, tucked into the rocky headland at Church Cove overlooking sandy beaches and clear aquamarine water. The Gunwalloe Valley is a good spot for birding. Penrose can be reached from the Coronation Gardens and Boating Lake at the bottom end of the town.

Trelowarren Estate
trelowarren.com
Mawgan, TR12 6AF
01326 221224 | Open to non-residents Apr–end Sep 11–5
This working estate, plus tourist accommodation, has spent 600 years in the hands of the Vyvyan family. With 1,000 acres of pasture and woodland down to the Helford River, rococo gardens, a restaurant using only local food, a Cornish art gallery and a mysterious Neolithic cave system, there's plenty to explore. Guests staying on the estate have access to everything, including tennis courts and a swimming pool. The four-mile woodland walk takes in a Victorian folly, an Iron Age Hill fort, an 18th-century garden and the highest point on the Lizard; a leaflet is available from the reception office detailing the route. Dogs are not permitted.

The pleasure gardens are open for Estate guests only, and comprise 12 acres of 18th-century landscaping by Dionysus Willams. Funds are being raised to develop and extend them in the future.

GO BACK IN TIME
Halliggye Fogou
english-heritage.org.uk
Trelowarren Estate, 5 miles
southeast of Helston off the B3293
This mysterious place dates from the Cornish Iron Age and is a complex of well preserved underground tunnels roofed and walled in stone. 'Fogou' in Cornish means 'cave' and nobody really know what these were used for, though it has been suggested that they could have been refuges, storage chambers or shrines. The fogou is part of the Trelowarren Estate but it is free to enter and is under the care of English

Heritage. You may have to pay their car park fee unless you're a member. Dogs on leads are welcome. Bring a torch.

EXPLORE BY BIKE
Family Cycles
7 Church Street,
TR13 8TA | 01326 573719

Porthleven Cycle Hire
porthlevencyclehire.co.uk
Commercial Road, Porthleven,
TR13 9JE | 01326 561101
Open end Mar–end Oct
Hire bikes here to tour the local quiet roads down to the beach and estuary, or around the Penrose Estate and Loe Pool where there are cycle paths and woodland routes. Porthleven Cycle Hire offers free bike delivery to those staying in the local area and has road bikes, mountain bikes and trailer bikes for children.

PLAY A ROUND
Helston Golf and Leisure
on the B3297 just outside Helston,
TR13 0LX | 01326 565103
Open all year
Set in delightful countryside a mile north of Helston, this 18-hole, par 3 short golf course is always in good condition and has panoramic views of the downs and coast. An ideal approach course for beginners, novices and golfers alike. Suitable for players of all levels. Pay as you play.

EAT AND DRINK
The Blue Anchor
spingoales.com

10 top beaches

▶ Kynance Cove, Lizard Peninsula
page 143

▶ Constantine Bay beach, near Padstow
page 194

▶ Gyllyngvase Beach, Falmouth
page 97

▶ Polzeath Beach
page 211

▶ Porthmeor Beach, St Ives
page 238

▶ Harlyn Bay beach, Padstow
page 194

▶ Porthcurno Beach
page 214

▶ Perran Sands, Perranporth
page 208

▶ Watergate Bay, Newquay
page 183

▶ Bedruthan Steps beach
page 56

50 Coinagehall Street,
TR13 8EL | 01326 562821
This 600-year-old building was built as a rest house for monks, and today has a skittle alley, a large garden and welcoming bars. Traditional recipe Spingo ales have been brewed here for 150 years and are a speciality today. There's a restaurant next door and the pub serves soup, light bites, and Spingo ale and beef pie.

The Queens Arms

queensarmsbreage.co.uk
Breage, near Helston, TR13 9PD
01326 573485

It's not so apparent from outside, but this is a 15th-century pub where the workmen building St Breaca's Church lived. Its age is more obvious indoors, particularly in the beamed, open-fired bar, where real ales include Penzance Brewing's Potion No. 9. Sample the simple, home-cooked food which makes good use of local produce, including allotment-grown vegetables. There's also a children's play area.

▶ **PLACES NEARBY**

As well as all the attractions of the Lizard Peninsula, the mining district of Wendron is close to Helston, complete with its independent mining attraction, Poldark Mine. In Constantine, you'll also find the Potager, a delightful garden and cafe.

Poldark Mine

poldark-mine.co.uk
Trenear, Wendron, near Helston,
TR13 0ER | 01326 573173
Open daily 10–5.30; closed Sat
mid-Apr–mid-Jul and Sep–Oct

Poldark has been the site of tin production above and below ground for thousands of years. As another of Cornwall's mining heritage sites, Poldark Mine offers exhibitions, a mining museum and Cornwall's only complete underground tin mine tour, complete with hard hats and an underground Post Office post box. It's an interesting introduction to mining history in the county, and is great for children, with multiple attractions including gold panning and a ghost tour.

▼ Kynance Cove

The Potager
potagergarden.org
High Cross, Constantine, TR11 5RF
01326 341258 | Open all year
Fri–Sun 10–5
Once an abandoned plant nursery, the Potager is now a beautiful garden with hammocks to laze in, boules, ping pong and badminton to play and the Glasshouse Cafe where you can enjoy homemade cakes, lunches, teas and ice cream. It's a unique, relaxing spot – and quite different from the other garden delights in the county.

Kynance Cove

The stunning beach at Kynance Cove is the cover star of many a Cornwall calendar. This is one of the best beaches not just in Cornwall but in the world, enhanced by a long, steep walk down and a pretty beach cafe serving delicious Cornish ice cream on arrival. Dramatic and historic, it's easy to imagine mermaids swimming in Mermaid's Pool, the part of the beach surrounded by boulders on three sides and only accessible at half tide. The legend goes that a local man living in Cury near Mullion found a sobbing mermaid here, cut off by the tide from the sea and her family. He helped her back to the sea, and she in return granted his wishes to break evil spells, become a healer and find stolen property.

It's not just an appealing place for mermaids and dreamers; Kynance was visited and much loved in the Victorian times by Prince Albert and Lord Tennyson, as it perfectly satisfied the Romantic ideal of the Picturesque in nature. Countless artists still paint scenes of the beach, completely under water at high tide with gnarled monoliths of serpentine rock islanded in the deep sea. The largest of these is called Asparagus Island, with Steeple Rock and the Sugar Loaf lying between it and the mainland.

The cove and the cliff land to the east are in the care of the National Trust, which has a car park above Kynance and a viewpoint for visitors with disabilities. Descent to the cove is steep, and the return is quite strenuous. Care should be taken if swimming off the cove – the tide comes in rapidly and the currents close to shore are dangerous. There are great rock pools to play in and caves to explore at low tide.

The Kynance area is of great biological importance. Rare species grow in the area, including sedges and tiny liverworts. Spiders, moths and even a rare European woodlouse are also found here. The mild climate and a maritime environment partly explain the richness of local wildlife.

▶ Lizard Point

Starting at Lizard Village, where you can park the car, the walk down to Lizard Point is an easy one, next to the road and along a small coast path. You can also park at the Point, near an old lifeboat station. Breathe deeply and look out to sea: birds hang in the air, the water churns and you might see a dolphin or two. The air is mild here even in midwinter, and it's a key breeding ground for choughs, which have been breeding on the point since 2001, after an absence of 50 years. The RSPB runs a Chough Watchpoint in spring.

The coast path leads west above high cliffs. To the east it passes through a green, sheltered landscape above cliffs draped with the invasive Hottentot fig. The Lizard's position, jutting out into the Channel approaches, has made it dangerous to vessels. For a mile seaward off Lizard Point the sea tumbles in frightening overfalls during stormy weather. To the northeast lies the blunt promontory of Black Head and beyond here the deadly Manacles Reef.

The fortress-like Lizard Lighthouse dominates the coast to the east. A warning light was first established here in 1612. Today's powerful light flashes every three seconds and can be seen in clear weather from up to 29 miles away. The fog signal is delivered by siren every 60 seconds on gloomy days. About 1.5 miles east of Lizard Point is Church Cove and its attractive little church of Landewednack. The cove is reached on foot from the car park past thatched cottages. A short walk south along the coast path leads to the remarkable cliffside site of the Lizard-Cadgwith lifeboat house.

EAT AND DRINK

Housel Bay Hotel ⊛
houselbay.com
Housel Cove, TR12 7PG
01326 290417
Britain's most southerly hotel on the mainland was built in the 1890s and has dramatic views and fantastic food. The kitchen's requirements are met by small Cornish producers, and just about everything is made on the premises. From grilled sea bass with clam and coconut velouté, to panacotta with lemon tart, the menu is a slate of interesting ideas.

Polpeor Cafe
Lizard Point, The Lizard, TR12 7NU
01326 290939
At Britain's most southerly cafe, perched high on the cliffs on Lizard Point, you can watch waves crashing onto the rocks and choughs wheeling around the cliffs while you tuck into a local crab salad and sandwiches or a traditional cream tea. On fine summer days, the suntrap terrace right on the cliff edge is the place to eat.

▶ The Manacle rocks

▶ Mullion

On the west coast of the Lizard, between Gunwalloe and Lizard Point, Mullion is a bustling community full of shops, restaurants and tea rooms. The Church of St Melanus in the village has a remarkable collection of bench ends depicting characters, including a jester and a monk. The biggest attraction here is Mullion Cove, the 19th-century harbour a little way from the village, reached by road. Pass through Mullion Meadows, an area of craft galleries, workshops and tea rooms, on the way there.

GET OUTDOORS
Mullion Cove

The dramatic sight of Mullion Cove tells you plainly why there are so many artists in the area. Built in 1893 to help the ailing pilchard fishing industry, it's still in use today and is maintained by the National Trust. Big cliffs and sea stacks, gold-leafed with yellow lichen, enclose the narrow inlet and its substantial piers while offshore the bulky mass of Mullion Island lies flickering with seabirds.

The coast to the south is pleasantly remote, especially around Predannack Head, where you'll find rare wildflowers, and Vellan Head, with delightful coast walks to either side of the cove. Just to the north of Mullion is Polurrian Cove where there is a large sandy beach, and further north again is the popular Poldhu Cove with its sandy dunes.

HIT THE BEACH

The large sandy beach at Poldhu Cove is a big draw for local holidaymakers. With lifeguards in the summer, a beach cafe and a shop, it's one of the largest beaches on the peninsula with some of the best facilities. In the summer, the cafe serves pizza in the evening too. It's a safe beach for swimming.

PLAY A ROUND
Mullion Golf Club

mulliongolfclub.co.uk
Cury, Helston, TR12 7BP
01326 240685 (secretary)
Open all year

Founded in 1895, Mullion Golf Club's clifftop and links course with panoramic views over Mount's Bay is the most southerly course in England. A steep downhill slope on the 6th and the 10th descends to the beach with a deep ravine alongside the green.

GO HORSE-RIDING
Newton Equestrian Centre

www.newton-equestrian.co.uk
Newton Farm, Polhorman Lane,
TR12 7JF | 01326 240388

For beach rides, countryside hacks, horse-riding holidays and yoga, this equestrian centre on the Lizard caters for all levels of experience and also has accommodation on site. Deals and offers can be found on their website; their spa, gym and yoga facilities are not just for horse-riders. Contact direct for beauty treatment details.

EAT AND DRINK
Mullion Cove Hotel ⊛
mullion-cove.co.uk
Mullion Cove, Lizard Peninsula, TR12 7EP | 01326 240328

The hotel's location could hardly be bettered: it's perched on the top of cliffs overlooking Mullion's harbour, with spectacular coastal views. There's a timeless elegance to the Atlantic Restaurant, where window tables are inevitably at a premium, with menus changing daily and plenty of seafood thanks to the local fishing boats.

▶ Porthallow

The small fishing cove of Porthallow, between St Keverne and Roskorwell on the east coast, was known for its pilchards, hence the name of the local pub. These days it's known for being the midway point on the Southwest Coast Path – there's a waymarker on the beach acknowledging it – and to geologists as the geological boundary fault line separating the Lizard from the rest of Cornwall. The village has a small, shingly beach where you can park and watch the waves in winter. The village beach committee organises events through the year, including Easter egg hunts, duck racing and summer beach parties. There are lovely coastal walks from the village to Nare Head and beyond to Gillan Creek.

EAT AND DRINK
Fat Apples Cafe
The Old Vineyard,
TR12 6QH | 01326 281559
This friendly, community-run cafe welcomes walkers, dogs and holidaymakers as well as locals catching up on the village gossip. Serving homemade cakes, pies, coffee, lunches and snacks, it's just a short walk from the beach and also has a wild camping spot in the orchards.

The Five Pilchards
thefivepilchards.co.uk
TR12 6PP | 01326 280256
This beachside pub is chock-full of nautical memorabilia and dates from the time when pilchards were fished in the cove and counted out in groups of five. The pub has a menu of classic pub staples – fish and chips, pasties, burgers and steaks – and also has rooms above it.

▲ Loe Bar

▶ Porthleven

Great Britain's most southerly point, the village of Porthleven
centres around the harbour, as it has for centuries. It was a
notable fishing and shipbuilding village in days gone by and
those industries still survive today, with concessions to the
tourist trade including an interesting mix of galleries, shops,
pubs and restaurants around the inner harbour and quays.
At low tide you can see Giant's Rock, a huge boulder on the
north side of the outer harbour. It is believed to be a glacial
'erratic' carried here probably embedded in an ice floe during
the last Ice Age.

It's a pleasant place to visit, with grand Victorian villas on
the south quay and a bustling quayside. To the southeast, a
road lined with cottages leads along the cliff edge and Loe Bar
Road leads to a car park, for the short walk to Loe Bar and the
Penrose Estate (see Helston, page 138).

Be warned that Porthleven Harbour is very vulnerable to
high tides and you should never walk along the outer piers.
Swimming in this area is dangerous. Porthleven Beach is very
popular with surfers, but Praa Sands, a beautiful, long, sandy
beach just 4 miles away, is a much better bet for families.

EAT AND DRINK

Kota Restaurant ◉

kotarestaurant.co.uk
Harbour Head,
TR13 9JA | 01326 562407
Chef-proprietor Jude Kereama
has Maori, Chinese and
Malaysian blood in his veins,
so you can expect vibrant
Pacific Rim fusion cooking in
his relaxed bistro in an
18th-century corn mill on
Porthleven Harbour. In such
a setting, local fish naturally
plays a starring role – Kota
is Maori for 'shellfish',
by the way.

The Ship Inn

theshipinncornwall.co.uk
TR13 9JS | 01326 564204
Dating from the 17th century,
this smugglers' inn is actually
built into the cliffs. It's
welcoming, with good food:
expect a good selection of
locally caught fish and seafood.
The pub has declared itself a
'chip-free zone' and has good
provision for children with a
family room in the old Smithy
building, attached.

▶ PLACES NEARBY

A short drive along the coast
takes you to one of Cornwall's
finest sandy beaches; Helston
and the other delights of the
west coast of the Lizard are
also close by.

Praa Sands

TR20 9TF
Four miles from Porthleven,
Praa Sands is a wide swathe
of golden sand beloved by
families, swimmers and
surfers alike – and there's
room for all of them in a mile
and a half of beach, dunes
and natural habitats. It's in a
sheltered position on Mount's
Bay and has cafes and
lifeguards in season. Dogs
are banned Easter–end Sep
and there's parking just by
the beach.

The village nearby is the site
of Pengersick Castle, said to be
one of the most haunted
buildings in the UK. It's due to
reopen to the public in 2014;
interestingly, the Cornish name
for Praa Sands, *Poll an wragh*,
means 'witches' cove'.

▶ St Keverne

Just north of Coverack on the southeast coast of the Lizard
Peninsula, St Keverne is a village full of character with a small,
square and impressive church. St Keverne's church was
important for more than spiritual reasons: as the tallest
landmark roundabout, highly visible from the sea, its spire was
a key sight for local fishermen and aided navigation. The
Manacles, a series of vividly named treacherous rocks, lie
offshore; their Cornish name, *Maen Eglos*, meaning 'the Church
Stones', seems even more menacing.

St Keverne Church is one of Cornwall's largest and
architecturally most intriguing churches and dates mostly from

the 15th century, with some pillars from the 13th century. Parts of the church were rebuilt after the spire was struck by lightning in 1770. As well as an interesting interior, the church's graveyard is worth a look, full of memorials to drowned sailors.

As well as the church, there are a number of welcoming pubs in the square, and for children, families and ice cream lovers, a visit to Roskilly's farm can't be beaten.

SEE A LOCAL CHURCH
St Keverne Church
North end of High Street,
TR12 6NE
As mentioned, St Keverne Church was important spiritually to the local area, and also as a navigational tool when sailing off the south coast, and the church's stained-glass windows remember shipwrecks and lives lost at sea over the past centuries. Remarkably, the 13th-century pillars are not made from local stone and it is thought that they might have originated in Brittany. The 15th-century font is another interesting feature, with angels at each corner and AM, for Ave Maria, and IHS, for Jesus, carved into it.

▼ St Keverne Church

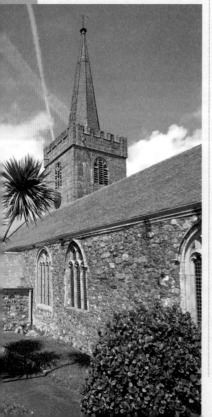

EAT AND DRINK
Roskilly's
roskillys.co.uk
Tregellast Barton Farm, St Keverne, Helston, TR12 6NX | 01326 280479
Please check the website or call for opening times
Roskilly's is a family-run, working organic farm where they make one of Cornwall's much-loved ice creams, as well as clotted cream, fudge, preserves, jams and juices. A great family day out on the farm can culminate with a homemade lunch, tea and cake, or a delicious cream tea with warm scones and their famous clotted cream and fruity jams, all washed down with apple juice or cider made on the farm. There's a viewing gallery so you can watch the cows being milked (at 5am or 4.30pm).

▲ The harbour at Looe

▶ Looe

Looe is a brash, tourist-focused town in high season, with arcades blaring tinny music at sunburned families, barely a space to sit on the harbour for all the children crabbing, and a beach with attractions such as bouncy castles and funfairs around the edges. This is not traditional Cornwall – you won't find thatched cottages or peaceful walks here – but it's full of kiss-me-quick fun and, when you look a little closer, there are some interesting places to visit, including ancient woodlands and a beautiful estuary.

You can blame the railway for the development of Looe as a holiday destination. Popular with tourists since the early 19th century, when war with France sent the leisured classes to Southwest England in search of a home-grown alternative to the French resorts, the bathing machine arrived at Looe beach in 1800, and when trains came to the area there was no stopping them. Incidentally, the train line running from Liskeard to Looe is a real delight, running on a track beside the estuary overhung with trees.

Looe divides into East Looe and West Looe; West Looe is the more upmarket side, with a few knick-knack shops leading through to a shingle beach with a view of Looe Island (and free parking beside the road), while East Looe is where you'll find the town centre, shops, restaurants, sandy beach and harbour.

A walk round to the far end of East Looe's beach takes you to a cave used by smugglers. The old pilchard-curing cellars by the quay here are built from unadorned stone and many of the cottages have an outside stone staircase, showing that the ground floors were used as pilchard-processing cellars and net stores. Looe is Cornwall's second largest fishing port and you can sit and watch the boats go by, with a crab line or ice cream in hand on the quay. Looe's viewpoint, Banjo Pier, can be reached from the quay.

Access to Looe

The main car park for East Looe is at Millpool and there's another car park in the town. Both are pay-and-display; the Millpool car park has a children's playground and a small pleasure boating lake beside it.

The delightful Kilminorth Woods are reached easily from the Millpool car park. Waymarked walks lead through a splendid oak wood and alongside the West Looe River. The woods and river are rich in plant, insect and bird life, including herons, which nest in the trees on the opposite bank. Further information can be obtained at the Discovery Centre.

VISIT THE MUSEUMS AND GALLERIES

Old Guildhall Museum

eastlooetowntrust.co.uk/looe-museum.php

Higher Market Street, East Looe, PL13 1AA | 01503 263709

Open late Mar–mid-Oct 11–4

This small, local museum gives a flavour of the history of Looe and its smuggling, fishing and boatbuilding past. The building itself was East Looe's Town Hall and Magistrates Court and has ancient cells and items from homes dating to the 18th century, plus a genuine cat o' nine tails.

South-East Cornwall Discovery Centre

Millpool, West Looe, PL13 2AF

01503 262777 | Open daily 10–5 (summer), 11–3 (winter)

This small visitor centre promotes green tourism in southeast Cornwall and has a shop and a booking service.

MEET THE MONKEYS

The Monkey Sanctuary

monkeysanctuary.org

Murrayton House, St Martins, PL13 1NZ | 08442 721271

Open daily Mar–3 Nov

Wild Futures' Monkey Sanctuary cares for unwanted and former pet monkeys. Visitors can meet some of these characters – Capuchin monkeys, woolly monkeys and Barbary macaques – dependent on the stage of their rehabilitation, and keepers are on hand to talk about the Sanctuary's rescue work, as well as the charity's wider work.

GET OUTDOORS
Kilminorth Woods
Millpool car park | 01503 262777
This glorious nature reserve
and woodland area is within
easy reach of Looe. The valley
traces the West Looe River and
is a pretty backdrop for it, with
blossom in spring. It also
includes a huge, ancient
earthwork, the Giant's Hedge,
which runs from Lerryn to
Looe. Locals say the woods
are haunted.

Looe Island
Also known as St George's
Island, Looe Island is just
offshore and is open to day
visitors in the summer. It has a
lovely history – in the 1960s, a
pair of sisters were determined
to own their own island and
bought this beautiful place,
living on it until they died. Now
under the care of the Cornwall
Wildlife Trust, it's a natural
sanctuary for seabirds and
seals and was a known
smuggler's haunt. It also has
the ruins of a 12th-century
Benedictine chapel on it. The
ferry service for visitors runs in
the summer, tides permitting,
taking 20 minutes and allowing
visitors 2 hours on the island.
Look for The Islander board on
the quay near the lifeboat
station in East Looe.

For the Looe Valley Line
see **Liskeard**, page 127

HIT THE BEACH
Plaidy Beach in East Looe is the
most obvious choice, backed
with ice cream parlours and
beach shops, but it's not exactly
beautiful, with concrete steps
and a far from natural appeal. It
gets very busy in summer.
Hannafore Beach, in West Looe,
is shingly with some sand and
is good for rock pooling at low
tide. There's a walk along the
promenade on West Looe from
here too, with views of Looe
Island. East up the coast from
Plaidy Beach, Millendreath
Beach is in a sheltered cove
with rock pools at high tide and
some sand, just under a mile up
the coast towards Whitsand Bay
on the Southwest Coast Path.

TAKE A BOAT TRIP
Looe's seafaring and fishing
history means that there
are plenty of sea cruises and
fishing trips available from the
harbour. The Islander Ferry
takes visitors to Looe Island
in season (see left) and
charter boats even take visitors
out shark fishing. A good
evening trip is up the West
Looe River to the Watergate,
where you can see herons and
other riverbank wildlife. Check
the boards in East and West
Looe for both sea and river
trips, which all depend on
weather and tides.

HIRE A BIKE
Cornish Cycle Hire
cornishcyclehire.co.uk
Pensilva, PL14 5PJ | 07526 317737
Cornish Cycle Hire delivers
mountain bikes in the Looe area
direct to your accommodation
so you can spend a day cycling

along the shore, exploring the country lanes and woodlands around the town. Adult and child bikes plus trailers and HD cameras are available.

GO FISHING
Looe Pet Supplies
Buller Street, PL13 1AS
01503 263535

Looe Chandlery
looechandlery.co.uk
Millpool Boatyard, West Looe,
PL13 2AF | 01503 264355
East and West Looe Rivers both have a trout and salmon fishing season from 1 April to 15 December. You need a permit to fish, available from Looe Pet Supplies on Buller Street. There are also plenty of sea-fishing trips on offer from Looe Quay. Check the boards for details – mackerel is the catch of the day typically, but some operators promise shark fishing too. Looe Chandlery sells fishing supplies and can offer advice on spear fishing, and river and sea fishing.

PLAY A ROUND
Looe Golf Club
looegolfclub.co.uk
Bindown, PL13 1PX
01503 240239 | Open all year
Designed by Harry Vardon in 1935, Looe Golf Club's downland and parkland course commands panoramic views over southeast Cornwall and the coast. It's an easy-walking course with views across to Dartmoor to the east,

countryside and moors to the west and north, and Looe Island to the south.

EAT AND DRINK
Barclay House ⊛⊛
barclayhouse.co.uk
St Martin's Road, PL13 1LP
01503 262929
One of Looe's most distinguished eateries, Barclay House is a snow-white country villa overlooking the harbour. Fish and seafood comes straight from the quayside and Cornish produce is the theme. On the seafood front, dishes range from Looe Bay scallops to Fowey River mussels steamed in Cornish Orchards cider, while West Country meat includes local duck breast.

The Ship Inn
staustellbrewery.co.uk
Fore Street, PL13 1AD
01503 263124
This lively pub stands on a corner a minute's walk from the working harbour. The menu includes burgers and hot baguettes, steak and ale pie and hunter's chicken. Tribute is on tap. A quiz is held on Mondays throughout the year and live bands play regularly.

Squid Ink
squid-ink.biz
Lower Chapel Street, PL13 1AT
01503 262674
This bijou seafood-focused restaurant in the East Looe lanes is one of the town's best, a friendly spot serving the likes

of tempura tiger prawns, lemon sole, Cornish seafood risotto and local Cornish cheeses. The style is Modern British with Mediterranean and Asian accents; the welcome is warm and genuine.

Trelaske Hotel and Restaurant ⓐⓐ
www.trelaske.co.uk
Polperro Road, PL13 2JS
01503 262159
This lovely, small-scale hideaway sits in 4 acres of woodland and attractive, well-tended gardens between Looe and Polperro. Modern Cornish food menu specials include cod fillets, Cornish black pork loin, Cornish cheeses and spotted dick.

Ye Olde Jolly Sailor Inn
jollysailorlooe.co.uk
Princes Square, PL13 2EP
01503 263387
One of the UK's oldest pubs, dating to 1516, The Jolly Sailor is a whitewashed pub in West Looe with rooms above it and a colourful history. The Jolly's main beam comes from a French ship captured at the Battle of Trafalgar, and the pub is reputedly haunted. It was a known smugglers' den too, with a quick-thinking landlady who hid barrels of spirits under her skirts during an unexpected customs visit, so the story goes. It serves local ales and cider today and has regular live music.

▶ PLACES NEARBY
Near to Looe, the small village of Duloe has an award-winning pub. Seaton Beach and nature reserve are easily reached. Port Eliot (see page 116) and Paul Corin's Magnificent Music Machines (see page 128) are also worth a visit.

The Plough
ploughduloe.co.uk
Duloe, near Looe, PL14 4PN
01503 262556
Linked to Barclay House, Looe's flagship restaurant, the Plough has been quietly carving out a reputation as one of the best gastro pubs in Cornwall. From the St Austell ales and Cornish Orchards cider to the nettle soup, everything is local. Lunch, dinner and Sunday roast are served, and bar snacks include Cornish-style scotch duck eggs. Great mulled cider in winter.

Seaton Beach
Four miles east of Looe on the Southwest Coast Path, the village of Seaton has a sand and pebble beach and a divers' centre and beach cafe. It's popular with families, with a car park adjacent to the beach. There are no lifeguards and dogs are welcome year round. Take care in the sea as the current can be unpredictable. Nearby, Seaton Valley Countryside Park is a former caravan park turned nature reserve with otters and kingfishers, and has a sensory garden, cycle paths, play area and woodland walks.

▶ Lostwithiel

John Betjeman reputedly said that there is history in every stone of Lostwithiel – he wasn't wrong, but he didn't mention that you'd find it in every shop too. Located between St Austell and Liskeard in east Cornwall, Lostwithiel is the county's antiques capital. Crammed with antiques shops and with an antiques market running on alternate Fridays in the community centre, it's the place to come to find vintage items, furniture, militaria, silver and more.

In medieval times, the town was a busy port, but the silting up of the river put a stop to that. It has a beautiful 13th-century bridge with five pointed arches spanning the river and the ruined Restormel Castle nearby, also 13th-century, is considered the best-preserved military building in Cornwall.

Further history can be seen today alongside independent shops, antiques shops and delis, in the arches and buttresses of the Duchy Palace on Quay Street and the 13th-century tower and 14th-century spire of the Church of St Bartholomew. Guided historic walks of the town take place on Thursdays in the summer from outside the Tourist Information Centre. There is a town museum in Fore Street. Coulson Park is by the River Fowey and there are pleasant riverside walks.

TAKE IN SOME HISTORY
Restormel Castle
english-heritage.org.uk
Near Restormel Road,
PL22 0EE | 01208 872687
Open daily Jul–Aug 10–6, Apr–Jun and Sep 10–5, Oct 10–4
A mile upriver from Lostwithiel, Restormel Castle was built during the Norman period on the site of a wooden fortification and was twice visited by Edward the Black Prince. Today the impressive ruins of the circular keep have fabulous views and make a good picnic spot. You can climb the castle steps for views and look down on the remains of the rooms. In the woodlands around it, you might see black pheasants and beautiful wildflowers. In the summer, theatre performances take place here; in the spring the bluebells and daffodils are worth a visit.

VISIT THE MUSEUM
Lostwithiel Museum
Fore Street, PL22 0BW
01208 873005
Open Easter–end Sep
Mon–Sat 10.30–4.30
This small town museum celebrates the history of Lostwithiel with artefacts and photographs spanning the past 200 years. It's very small – in 2007 it became the smallest museum in the country to have Museums and Galleries Commission accreditation – and is much used by those wanting to find out more about their family history.

▲ Restormel Castle

PLAY A ROUND
Lostwithiel Hotel, Golf and Country Club
golf-hotel.co.uk
Lower Polscoe, PL22 0HQ
01208 873550 | Open all year
The 18-hole course at the Lostwithiel Hotel is one of the most varied in the county, designed to take full advantage of the natural features of the landscape, combining two distinct areas of hillside and valley. The challenging front nine has magnificent views of the surrounding countryside, while the picturesque back nine runs through parkland flanked by the River Fowey.

EAT AND DRINK
Asquiths Restaurant ⊕⊕
asquithsrestaurant.co.uk
19 North Street,
PL22 0EF | 01208 871714
Located opposite the medieval church in Lostwithiel, there's a serenity about Asquiths that is wholly inviting. It took silver in the Cornish Tourism Awards for Restaurant of the Year in 2012, and is a serious restaurant with Cornish credentials, creating skilfully cooked modern dishes from well-sourced local ingredients. Good beers and wines, too.

▶ PLACES NEARBY
Cornwall's biggest exotic animal sanctuary, Porfell Animal Land, is just outside Lostwithiel.

Porfell Animal Land and Wildlife Park
porfell.co.uk
Lanreath, near Lostwithiel,
PL14 4RE | 01503 220211
Open all year daily 10–6
This wildlife sanctuary looks after more than 250 animals from around the world that otherwise would be neglected or no longer wanted. Including lemurs, meerkats, emus and coatis, they are an unusual and exotic bunch. It takes about half a day to explore the woodlands, African area and children's farm. There's also a cafe.

Marazion

It's impossible to mention Marazion without first mentioning St Michael's Mount. This distinctive and beautiful part-time island lies just off the coast, connected to the town twice a day when the tide is low. The romantic twin to Mont St Michel in Normandy, this former monastery, prison and castle-under-siege has been reached by pilgrims via its cobbled causeway for centuries, and we're still visiting today. But more of that later – there's a little more to Marazion than the Mount.

Marazion Marsh is an important breeding ground for birds and is looked after by the RSPB; whatever time of year you visit, there's something to watch here. The wide sandy beach is safe for bathers and attracts watersports fans, with private suntraps in the dunes behind it. And the town has a few pubs, restaurants, cafes and shops to browse too. Formerly the main trading port of Mount's Bay, Marazion was upstaged when Penzance developed its own market and port in the 16th century and it's never really got over it. What it does have in spades is art galleries – if you're looking to bring home a scenic painting of a Cornish harbour or romantic windswept headland, look no further.

Nearby, the quiet village of Perranuthnoe, a short distance southeast, has a south-facing beach which provides reasonable surfing for the south coast. A few miles further east lies Prussia Cove, a secluded rocky inlet of great charm reached most rewardingly by a pleasant 2-mile walk along the coast path. The whole Mount's Bay area was a prime smuggling district and walks around the coast uncover secret coves and inland paths with a dark history.

▼ Marazion Causeway

▶ St Michael's Mount

stmichaelsmount.co.uk
TR17 0HS | 01736 710265 | Island accessible daily, year round on foot at low tide; also by boat in the summer at high tide

You don't have to be visiting on a misty day to see the magic, myths and legends swirl around St Michael's Mount. According to Cornish legend, in the fifth century AD a group of fishermen saw the Archangel St Michael perched on a ledge of rock on the western side of the Mount, and it has been called St Michael's Mount ever since. Whether that was a seal, a hardy swimmer or a trick of the light, it really doesn't matter – this is a magical place.

It was also said that the giant Cormoran lived on St Michael's Mount and waded ashore to feast on local cows and sheep; felled by a local lad named Jack, the story has become the Cornish folk tale of Jack the Giant Killer.

Atop the island, reached by a granite causeway strewn with bladderwrack at low tide, there's a 12th-century castle surrounded by sub-tropical gardens; although these have distinct opening and closing times, the island can be visited year round, and has pubs, a shop and a harbour with charming whitewashed cottages.

History

Bronze Age finds on the island, including an axe head and a dagger, show that the mount was an important place long before the religious vision gave it its name. The castle was built in 1135 by the Abbot of Mont St Michel in Normandy, but the original building was destroyed by an earthquake in 1275. Rebuilt, it has been used as a church, priory, fortress and private home over the past 700 years and it was seen as a strategically important place during the Wars of the Roses, the Prayer Book Rebellion, the attack of the Spanish Armada and the English Civil War, when in 1646 it was a Royalist stronghold forced to surrender to Parliament.

In the 18th century, the St Aubyn family made it a permanent family residence, constructing a new wing and Victorian apartments with armour, oil paintings and Chippendale furniture.

The castle

Open 18–22 Feb daily 10–4,
18 Mar–3 Nov Tue and
Fri 10.30–5 (Jul–end Aug
10.30–5.30)

With everything from suits
of armour to a Samurai
warrior and a mummified cat
to see, the castle is a great
place to start. Used as a family
home since the 18th century,
there's plenty of family history
to view, including oil portraits
of the former owners, a
beautiful library and a historic
tidalclock made in the 1780s,
enabling the family to plan
their crossings to the mainland.
The Priory Church includes
500-year-old alabaster
panels depicting religious
scenes, and in the map
room there's a model of St
Michael's Mount made by the
butler from Champagne corks
in 1832. Best of all, on a sunny
day, are the views from the
terraces of the gardens,
the Lizard Peninsula and
Mount's Bay.

The gardens

Gardens open 15 Apr–27 Sep,
Tue and Fri 10.30–5 (May–Jun
daily, Jul–Aug 10.30–5.30)

The tiered gardens clinging
to the steep granite slopes of
the mount are exotic in the
extreme – the granite holds
heat well so plants from
Mexico, South Africa and the
Canary Islands have flourished
in the sea breeze. There's
a children's trail and a free
map too; access is restricted
to the gardens because of
their fragile nature, but they
look just as good viewed from
the castle.

Visiting

You should allow around
3–4 hours to experience the
whole island on a day when
all the attractions are open.
On Tuesdays and Fridays
there are free guided walks
around the village and harbour
side of the island, which
are led by an local resident
and focusing on island
daily life.

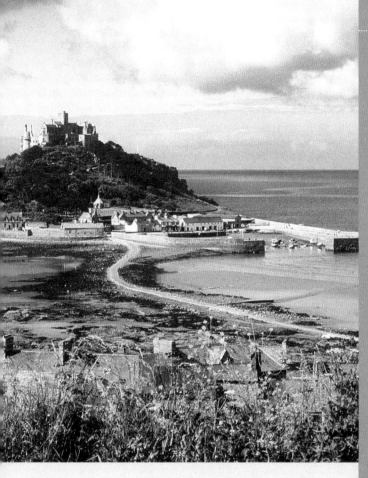

▲ St Michael's Mount viewed from Marazion

EAT AND DRINK

The Godolphin Arms

godolphinarms.co.uk
St Michael's Mount,
TR17 0EN | 01736 710202
Standing atop the sea wall at
the end of the causeway to St
Michael's Mount, the sea is so
close that it splashes at the
windows of this pub/restaurant
in winter. Seafood from the
Newlyn fish market is on the
daily specials board; crab is a
speciality. You could also opt for
bangers and mash, cream teas,
and Cornish ales and ciders.

Island Cafe and Sail Loft Restaurant

nationaltrust.org.uk
The Harbour, St Michael's Mount,
TR17 0HS | 01736 710748
This excellent tea room in a
converted laundry is welcoming
and cheerful, with a
mouthwatering array of treats
and six varieties of tea. As well
as traditional teas there are
light lunches and snacks, with
local Cornish pasties as a
speciality. The Sail Loft serves
Newlyn crab, Cornish cheeses
and local fresh fish.

VISIT THE MUSEUM
Marazion Town Museum
marazion.info

Town Hall, The Square, TR17 0AP
01736 711061 | Open weekdays
through the summer

Marazion's museum is in
the town hall, with plenty of
quirky touches including a
re-creation of a gaol cell and a
unique exhibition devoted to
HMS *Warspite*, a ship that
served in both world wars. It
also includes a host of
memorabilia about the town
and its history.

HIT THE BEACH
For the best views of St
Michael's Mount, Marazion
Beach is spectacular. It's wide,
sandy and exposed, and attracts
windsurfers, kite surfers, jet
skiers and sailors. There's a
lifeguard here in season and a
windsurfing school at the end of
the beach. Dogs are banned
Easter–end Sep.

Nearby Perranuthnoe
Beach is a sand and shingle
beach, safe for swimming,
with St Michael's Mount views
and a sandbank forming at
the centre of the beach. It's
very popular with surfers
and has a cafe, toilets and
a pub. Dogs are banned
Easter–end Sep.

Praa Sands, see page 149,
is another much-loved beach
just down the coast at the start
of the Lizard Peninsula.

▼ St Michael's Mount viewed from Marazion

GO BIRDING
Marazion Marsh
rspb.org.uk/reserves/guide/m/
marazionmarsh

Marazion Marsh is a key birding area, described by the RSPB as one of the best wildlife areas in the UK. It's open year round and is free; dogs must be kept on leads. More than 250 bird species and 18 mammal species have been recorded here in Cornwall's largest reed bed, with star species including heron and egret. Check the RSPB website for further information on seasonal spotting and their work here.

EAT AND DRINK
Ben's Cornish Kitchen ✿
benscornishkitchen.com
West End, Marazion, TR17 0EL
01736 719200

Ben Prior's friendly and award-winning neighbourhood restaurant ticks all of the right boxes, serving the sort of straightforward, contemporary food made from lovingly sourced seasonal ingredients that we all want to eat these days. The first-floor dining room not only lets more lucky punters in, but also gives sweeping sea views to St Michael's Mount.

Mount Haven Hotel and Restaurant ✿✿
mounthaven.co.uk
Turnpike Road, Marazion,
TR17 0DQ | 01736 710249

This former 19th-century coach house is now a chic hotel with a restaurant that is a cut above the competition. Expect to find the likes of pea and ham hock soup, local John Dory and local venison on the menu, followed by apple fritters with cinnamon ice cream and vanilla syrup.

▶ PLACES NEARBY
St Hilary, a couple of miles east of Marazion, has a church with an intriguing history.

St Hilary's Church
St Hilary, reached off the
B3280 beyond St Hilary School,
TR20 9DQ

Dedicated to a 4th-century French bishop, the shape of the churchyard suggests that it may have originally been a Roman fort guarding the tin mines that attracted traders to Cornwall for more than 2,000 years. Two stones here mark its remarkable history: one is a Roman milestone, from AD 306; the other is a stone inscribed 'Noti Noti', possibly a memorial to 'Not son of Not', dating from the 6th or 7th century.

The church was almost entirely destroyed by fire on Good Friday 1853, with only its ancient spire, a shipping landmark for Mount's Bay and St Ives Bay, surviving, and was rebuilt in 1854 by architect William White of Truro, who retained as much as he could from the old church. A later vicar commissioned decorations by local artists, but many were sadly vandalised in 1932 by 'extreme Protestants'.

▶ Mawgan Porth

This lovely, sandy cove between Padstow and Newquay is linked to both via the Southwest Coast Path and is good for swimming, sandcastle-building, cave exploring and coasteering.

Overlooked by Cornwall's top eco-friendly hotel the Scarlet, and its sister hotel, the award-winning family-friendly Bedruthan Steps Hotel, it has a pub and cafe and both the restaurants plus Scarlet's spa open to non-residents. Just up the coast towards Padstow is Bedruthan Steps itself, a National Trust beach and clifftop area (see page 56).

HIT THE BEACH

Mawgan Porth's award-winning beach has a lifeguard Apr–end Sep and is dog friendly. Rock pools and caves are exposed at high tide. There's a beach shop nearby and a cafe serving ice creams. Surf hire can be found at Bedruthan Steps Hotel – follow the path up from the beach to the back of the hotel to find its surf shack.

BOOK BEAUTY TREATMENTS

The Scarlet

scarlethotel.co.uk

The Scarlet, Tredragon Road, TR8 4DQ | 01637 861800

Scarlet's luxury spa focuses on tailor-made Ayurvedic treatments and has relaxation pods in tented rooms, swimming pools and a scarlet-coloured outdoor hot tub for seaweed treatments. There's also a rhassoul mud treatment therapy. Everything is designed with the environment in mind.

PLAY A ROUND

Merlin Golf Course

merlingolfcourse.co.uk

St Eval Road, TR8 4DN | 01841 540222

Open all year

The Merlin Golf Course is a heathland course with fine views of the coast and countryside. It's fairly easy walking. The most challenging hole is the par 4 18th with out of bounds on the left and ponds on either side of the green.

EAT AND DRINK

Bedruthan Steps Hotel

bedruthan.com

Trenance, TR8 4BU

01637 860860

This hotel has two restaurants, one resolutely child friendly and the other with a more adult focus. The Wild Cafe has floor-to-ceiling windows with views of the beach, a good selection of children's meals and friendly staff on hand to offer you bibs, high chairs and plastic cutlery, as required. The Herring is a more select affair, open in the evenings and serving an Ottolenghi-inspired fish-based menu.

The Park Cafe

mawganporth.co.uk

TR8 4BD

01637 860594

This family-friendly cafe has won multiple awards and

serves wholesome food with an emphasis on the slow food movement. Expect the likes of dippy eggs, homemade fish fingers, and delicious and inventive home baked cakes. It's part of The Park, a holiday complex, but non-residents are welcome.

The Scarlet ⊛⊛
scarlethotel.co.uk
Tredragon Road, TR8 4DQ
01637 861800
Huge windows opening on to the terrace, with wonderful views of the beach, sea and headland, dominate the restaurant at this modern hotel, which was built along eco-friendly lines. The kitchen's larder has been 'grown, reared, caught or foraged to taste as it should', according to the hotel, and the dishes are praiseworthy for the freshness of the ingredients. Vegetarians are properly catered for, and desserts have the wow factor, among them ginger pannacotta with sea buckthorn sorbet and micro shoots.

▸ Mevagissey

This lovely, traditional fishing village is one of south Cornwall's most charming, with narrow streets lined with cafes, pubs and gift shops leading to a harbour bobbing with colourful boats. Fishing was always a major part of the village's history: today boats bring in skate, mackerel and lobster. You can walk past the boats unloading their catch and round the quay to the point, where there's a small shingle beach to the left and a coast path.

The village dates from at least 1313, and was a major pilchard-fishing port in Tudor times. Like many Cornish fishing villages, Mevagissey has great character, especially in the old part of the village between the Fountain Inn and the Battery on the eastern side of the harbour. Many of the houses are colour-washed, and despite the fact that the harbour area has seen some rather brutal modern development, the village has retained its Cornish charm. A Feast Week is held in the village in June every year, with dances and music during the week and a grand carnival with fireworks to close it.

The aquarium at the old lifeboat house on the South Quay gives an insight into life in deeper waters (profits go to the upkeep and improvement of Mevagissey Harbour) and there is a little museum of local history on the East Quay. The biggest draw, apart from dinner in a Mevagissey restaurant followed by a moonlit stroll around the quay, is the Lost Gardens of Heligan, which are found on the cliff above the village and reached by the B3273 St Austell road.

VISIT THE MUSEUM
World of Model Railways
model-railway.co.uk
Meadow Street,
PL26 6UL | 01726 842457
Open mid-Mar–2 Nov daily 10–5
(10–6 in summer); check website
for other opening times
This model railway museum
is a bit out of step with the rest
of the seafaring town, but if
you're into trains rather than
boats, if it's raining or if you're
with a transport-mad toddler,
it's a neat place to spend half
an hour or so, watching the
large model train collection
go round and round in circles.
Highlights include a set
reflecting the local scenery,
clay pits and all, and steam
and diesel trains.

MEET THE SEALIFE
Mevagissey Aquarium
South Quay, PL26 6QU
01726 843305 | Open Apr–end
Sep daily 10–5
Housed in the old RNLI lifeboat
house on the quay, this small
aquarium holds plenty of local
Cornish sea life, including crabs
and lobster, and has a small
film on the pilchard-fishing
industry. It's a bolthole in the
rain, and all proceeds go to
support the harbour.

TAKE A BOAT TRIP
Mevagissey Ferries
mevagissey-ferries.co.uk
07977 293394 | Open end Apr–
1 Oct
There are plenty of boat trips to
take from this little harbour in
the summer. Boards and

booking offices at the harbour
provide full information. You
could also take a ferry that runs
from Mevagissey to Fowey and
back again, lasting 35 minutes
and offering views of the
contrasting harbours, and
hopefully the sighting of a seal
or dolphin along the way. All
sailings are weather and tide
permitting. See also Mevagissey
Shark Angling Centre, below,
for boat charters.

GO SEA FISHING
Mevagissey Shark
Angling Centre
mevafishingshop.co.uk
West Quay, PL26 6UJ
01726 843430
Whether you're looking for an
hour's mackerel fishing or a full
day's charter with spear fishing,
there are plenty of options in
Mevagissey. The Shark Angling
Centre on the quay sells fishing
tackle and bait, and offers a
booking service and advice.
They have 2-, 4- and 8-hour
fishing trips on offer Apr–end
Sep for 8 to 12 people with
various different skippers; call
for more information.

EAT AND DRINK
The Ship Inn
theshipinnmeva.co.uk
Fore Street, PL26 6UQ
01726 843324
This 400-year-old inn stands
just a few yards from
Mevagissey's picturesque
fishing harbour, so the choice
of fish and seafood dishes
comes as no surprise: moules
marinière, beer-battered cod

and oven-baked fillet of haddock topped with prawns and Cornish Tiskey cheese. The popular bar has low-beamed ceilings, flagstone floors and a strong nautical feel.

▷ PLACES NEARBY

On the hill above Mevagissey is one of Cornwall's best-known gardens, the Lost Gardens of Heligan. And nearby you'll also find a small local vineyard that makes the best of the area's sunshine.

The Lost Gardens of Heligan
See highlight panel overleaf

The Dodman
Dodman Point, south of Gorran Haven, is the highest headland on the southern coast of Cornwall and has historical significance. The headland, known locally as the Dodman, is enclosed by a massive Iron Age earthwork nearly 730 yards long and 20ft high, which it is thought could have housed a cliff castle or a promontory fort. There is a circular path around it leading to the Southwest Coast Path. The point also has an 18th-century watch tower with a large granite cross on it, visible from several miles away and created to help navigate the coastline from the sea.

Gorran Haven
This unspoilt coastal village centres around a secluded cove with fishermen's cottages arranged around it. At the

▲ Fishing port at Mevagissey

easternmost point of the peninsula, it's a sheltered spot with two safe, sandy beaches good for swimming. Walkers of the Southwest Coast Path stop by this way. Steep lanes and passageways climb from the harbour and there's an intriguing little chapel dating from the 15th century built on solid rock. The village has a bakery, a fish and chip shop, a Post Office and several beach shops.

Polmassick Vineyard
polmassickvineyard.co.uk
St Ewe, near Mevagissey, PL26 6HA
01726 842239 | Open last weekend of May–end Sep Wed–Sun 12–5 or on request
Cornwall's oldest vineyard will be running guided tours from 2014 and offers 'cellar door' tasting sessions. They also sell their wines here and have a pretty and peaceful wine garden where they invite you to bring a picnic and enjoy wine by the glass. There's a free car park, no admission fee and dogs on a lead are welcome.

▶ The Lost Gardens of Heligan

heligan.com
Pentewen, St Austell, PL26 6EN | 01726 845100 | Open Apr–end Sep daily 10–6, Oct–end Mar daily 10–5

With one of the most romantic back-stories of all of Cornwall's lush gardens – and that's going some – the Lost Gardens of Heligan are *the* garden to see. Even the least green-fingered will enjoy this one – it's not just about tropical plants that make you feel as if you're in an exotic rainforest, there's also a sculpture trail and a neatly planted Victorian garden complete with a pineapple pit.

The story goes like this: Heligan was the seat of the Tremayne family from the mid-18th century. At the end of the 19th century, its thousand acres were at their zenith, with 22 gardeners tending the trees, rhododendrons and melons. When World War I struck, everything changed. Sixteen of the gardeners went to war and never returned. Jack Tremayne, the family heir, left England for Italy and settled there, leasing out the estate. Only a few years later, bramble and ivy started to climb and the once well-tended estate fell into a deep sleep.

Upon Jack's childless death, the estate passed to a trust. A member of the extended Tremayne family introduced then-record producer Tim Smit to the gardens and he was, forgive me, smitten. Along with a group of other enthusiasts, Smit brought the gardens back to life in a process filmed by Channel 4. He remains involved here and after bringing the gardens back to life, he went on to create the Eden Project; if you visit both attractions you get a discount as a thank-you.

Today, they are an exciting place to visit, with 200 acres including the Lost Valley, the Jungle, where visitors are overshadowed by enormous ferns, and more delicate and precise Italianate gardens. There are also productive gardens, pleasure grounds, sustainably managed farmland, wetlands, ancient woodlands and a pioneering wildlife project.

Check the website for regular events, walks and talks, which all enrich a visit. Well-behaved dogs on leads are welcome all year. Allow a good half day or longer for a visit. There's a tea room, a shop and a plant centre, and you can bring a picnic.

▶ Morwenstow

The parish of Morwenstow lies at the northern extreme of Cornwall near Bude (see page 70) on the Devon border. Its coastline is awesome, yet unexpected: dramatic ravaged and twisted slabs of rock and 300ft cliffs bordered by flat green fields. This is the land of the famous Culm Measures, great pieces of layered shale that rise from boulder-strewn beaches striped with dark rock. At times, with a boiling sea, it looks otherworldly.

Its natural beauty apart, Morwenstow owes much of its fame to the reputation of the Victorian parson, eccentric and unsuccessful poet, Robert Hawker, who was vicar at the Church of St Morwenna for many years – see below.

Southwards from Morwenstow is the hamlet of Coombe, set in a shady, wooded valley. The river reaches the sea at Duckpool where the pebble beach has built up to dam a small pool of fresh water. Just north of Coombe, the coast path passes above Lower Sharpnose Point, where spectacular natural piers of rock jut out into the sea like the massive walls of ruined temples. Inland, the smooth satellite dishes of the Cleave Camp Satellite Station strike an incongruous note amidst such raw natural beauty, and dominate the view for miles around.

Cliff-path walks and beach visits are a must-do in the area.

▼ Hawker's Hut

GO BACK IN TIME

Hawker's Hut

www.robertstephenhawker.co.uk

A 3-mile circular walk from Morwenstow Church takes you to this tiny wooden cabin built overlooking the cliffs from timbers of wrecked ships. It's a National Trust-owned place, and is much frequented by passing walkers, who over the years have carved their initials in the driftwood planks.

Morwenstow's Victorian vicar, Robert Stephen Hawker, was a rather eccentric figure who was dedicated to recovering the bodies of drowned sailors – in no short supply along this treacherous coast. He's said to have smoked opium and dressed up as a mermaid, and lives on as one of Cornwall's most colourful characters. Sitting here, overlooking the waves, it's impossible not to think of him watching ships wrecked on the rocks, and saving those whom he could. Some less fortunate were buried in the graveyard of his church.

SEE A LOCAL CHURCH
St Morwenna Church
EX23 9SR

It's hard to miss this large Norman church, beautifully situated among trees in a shallow combe that leads towards the sea. Inside, it's pleasantly melancholic, especially at dusk, when there is a wonderful feeling of isolation. From 1835–37, Robert Hawker was the vicar of the parish here. In the graveyard is a preserved figurehead from a ship wrecked on the rock nearby. Rev. Hawker is credited with reintroducing Harvest Festival celebrations into the church, and wrote the 'Song of the Western Men', now Cornwall's anthem, especially at rugby matches. Hawker built a new vicarage – three of its chimneys were modelled on the towers of favourite churches, another on the tower of an Oxford college. The kitchen chimney was a replica of his mother's tomb.

The land around the church and the stretch of cliffs to the west are owned and conserved by the National Trust.

EAT AND DRINK
The Bush Inn
bushinn-morwenstow.co.uk
EX23 9SR
01288 331242

This 13th-century pub with rooms is set in an isolated clifftop hamlet. Flagstones, beams, inglenooks and old settles preserve the character of the bar. There's a contemporary feel to the dining room, which offers dishes such as Thai scallop salad and whole roast John Dory, while traditional ploughman's lunches and cream teas are served in the bar.

Rectory Tea Rooms
rectory-tearooms.co.uk
Rectory Farm,
EX23 9SR | 01288 331251

This 13th-century farmhouse just 10 minutes from spectacular Cornish cliffs is full of atmosphere. Heavy oak beams salvaged from wrecked ships, ancient flagstone floors worn by countless feet, and large, open fireplaces all help to make a memorable visit. Freshly prepared food includes ploughman's platters, soups and pasties, as well as light, home-baked scones served warm with jam and copious amounts of clotted cream.

▶ Mousehole

Named for its small harbour and tight harbour mouth, Mousehole (pronounced 'Mouz'l') is a picturesque fishing village with evocatively narrow streets, tempting alleyways and passages, and brightly painted boats in the harbour. The far end of Mousehole's tiny harbour has a splendid inner wall of irregular granite blocks, a perfect subject for imaginative photography or sketching, and 440 yards off the harbour there's a little island, St Clement's Isle, named after a hermit who lived there and lit the hazard for ships. When the tide is low, there's a sandy beach in the harbour; just east of the harbour wall, visitors can access a shingle beach too.

While any time of year is good for exploring the town's harbour, craft shops, galleries, cafes and pubs, it is particularly special in November and December. On 23 December, the town celebrates Tom Bawcock's Eve, a night commemorating a local hero from the 16th century who ventured out into stormy weather to bring back fish for a starving town. Stargazey pie, a pastry-topped pie with fish heads poking out, is the traditional dish of the day. And around the festive period, the town goes into Christmas lights in a big way, with floating lights in the harbour and beautiful displays around the town.

Dylan Thomas visited the town, as he had a friend living here, and it supposedly inspired *Under Milk Wood*. A more recent inspiration was the terrific bravery of the *Solomon Browne* lifeboat crew, which folk singer Seth Lakeman used as an inspiration for his RNLI benefit song. In 1981, eight volunteer lifeboat men died while repeatedly attempting to save eight people on the wrecked cargo ship *Union Star* on a stormy night with hurricane force 12 winds. There is a memorial to the crew in the Church of St Pol-de-Leon, on the steep hill leading inland to the village of Paul.

▼ Mousehole

The road out of Mousehole to the west leads up the dauntingly steep Raginnis Hill. Part way up is the famous Mousehole Bird Hospital, a refuge for countless injured birds, many of which are the victims of oil pollution.

A word of warning: Mousehole's narrow streets are not built for cars. Park outside the village on the road from Newlyn as the harbour car park is often full.

MEET THE BIRDLIFE

Mousehole Bird Hospital

mouseholebirdhospital.org.uk
Raginnis Hill, TR19 6SR
01736 731386 | Open all year

This small independent bird hospital is set up to help birds in distress, receiving and rehabilitating wild birds where possible, and with a number of permanent and unusual residents in their aviaries. They are open daily and ask for a donation rather than admission fee; every year on average 1,500 birds pass through their doors.

GET ON THE WATER

In the summer months, charter boats are available from the harbour, offering pleasure trips and short fishing trips for mackerel, dab and other local fish. Dolphins, seals and basking sharks are occasional visitors nearby and the town looks even prettier from the sea. All trips are weather and tide dependent.

EAT AND DRINK

The Cornish Range ⊚

cornishrange.co.uk
6 Chapel Street, TR19 6SB
01736 731488

Squirrelled away down one of Mousehole's skinny back lanes (leave your car at the outskirts of the village), this delightful stone-built restaurant with rooms is rooted deep in local fishing heritage, and was once a factory for salting and packing the local pilchard catch. Prime fish and seafood still drives the activity here, albeit in a more sophisticated manner.

10 top fishing villages

The Old Coastguard Inn

www.oldcoastguardhotel.co.uk
The Parade, TR19 6PR
01736 731222

This one-time coastguard station is perched high above the village. Although more of a hotel than a pub, there is a light and airy bar with real ale on tap. Contemporary menus take in delicious lunchtime soups, sandwiches and salads, and fresh fish.

The Ship Inn

shipinnmousehole.co.uk
South Cliff, TR19 6QX
01736 731234

This characterful old Cornish inn on the edge of the harbour has eight seaside-chic bedrooms and a welcoming bar serving local ales and cider as well as classic pub lunches and dinners. Speciality dishes include mussels, the catch of the day and local fishcakes. Great views of the harbor too.

▶ Mylor

Dense with trees and bordered by tidal creeks, the parish of Mylor is between Truro and Falmouth. A network of country lanes north of Falmouth links Mylor Bridge, Restronguet Passage, Mylor Creek and Mylor Churchtown, where there was once a royal dockyard. The Church of St Mylor has some unique features – a turret rises from its west gable and it has Norman doorways and a fine interior. Look out for the headstone of Joseph Crapp with its lyric epitaph, near the east window, and that of Thomas James, a smuggler, near a fork in the churchyard path. South of Mylor Bridge, the village of Flushing faces Falmouth across the river and a passenger ferry links the two.

Restronguet Creek was an important port for the export of tin and copper until the 20th century, and it has a character-packed 13th-century pub, the Pandora Inn. Named after the ship sent to Tahiti in 1790 to bring back the mutinous crew of Captain Bligh's HMS *Bounty*, a ship that sank on the Great Barrier Reef with great loss of life, the inn was owned by the captain of the *Pandora* who returned to Cornwall after being court martialled. It was badly damaged by fire in 2011, but has been restored using traditional materials and methods.

TRY SAILING

Mylor Sailing School

mylorsailingschool.co.uk
Mylor Yacht Harbour,
TR11 5UF | 01326 377633
Open all year
As well as sailing courses, this school runs open days, half-term activity days and pirate adventures aboard pirate ships. Family holidays are on offer for those aged seven and up; individual tuition and Sunday-morning sessions for

those who can already sail are also an option.

EAT AND DRINK
The Pandora Inn
pandorainn.com
Restronguet Creek, TR11 5ST
01326 372678
This 13th-century inn has Cornish Rattler ciders and St Austell Brewery ales on tap and has a colourful history (see opposite). Today, despite a scorching in a fire in 2011, the low-beamed ceilings and flagstone floors, along with the wood-pegged green oak beams of the dining room, display plenty of character. The kitchen serves good local fish, and home smoked chicken breast and mackerel.

▶ Nare Head

This stretch of south-coast Cornwall between the Roseland Peninsula and Dodman Point includes small villages, the parishes of Gerrans, Veryan and St Michael Caerhays, rocky and sandy beaches, and the 19th-century estate of Caerhays, known particularly for its magnolias. There aren't many sights, as such, but it is wonderful walking territory, particularly around the coast path, and feels like a hidden part of Cornwall. The best way to get there is to use the A3078, then follow signs to Veryan, a village with remarkable round thatched cottages and a large, dark church.

The best beaches are at Pendower and Carne, where there is parking and easy access to Nare Head. There are beaches all the way along the shores of Gerrans Bay and Veryan Bay, and there's also a beach at Porthluney Cove below Caerhays Castle.

Walks around Nare Head itself are highly recommended. On a good day you can see miles out to sea, and the headland includes a Bronze Age barrow, Carne Beacon, a World War II decoy bunker, an Iron Age earthwork, wooded valleys and views over to St Agnes Beacon.

For other attractions in the nearby area, see Roseland Peninsula, page 222.

TAKE IN SOME HISTORY
Caerhays Castle
www.caerhays.co.uk
Gorran, St Austell, PL26 6LY
01872 501310 | Gardens open mid-Feb–mid-Jun; castle open mid-Mar–mid-Jun Mon–Fri
This 19th-century Gothic castle and estate is famed for its magnolias and a visit in springtime when they are in bloom is highly recommended. Caerhays holds the largest collection in England and is one of four gardens in the National Magnolia Collection.

John Charles Williams created the gardens here in the

19th century and financially supported plant hunters to amass this beautiful collection. As well as creating this unrivalled collection of magnolias and shrubs, he specialised in the cultivation of daffodils, another good reason for a springtime visit.

There are four marked routes through the 120-acre estate, red, yellow, blue and green, and guided tours with the gardeners, lasting 1–2 hours, can also be booked. The red route takes in magnolias, rhododendrons and azaleas just to the west of the castle; the yellow route traces round the hill at the back of the castle, behind Mr Roger's Quarry, where you can admire the best variety of *Magnolia campbellii* at Caerhays, *mollicomata* 'Lanarth', which produces cyclamen-purple flowers; the blue route is a long circuit around the back of the castle and hills and the estate's two quarries; and the green route skirts around the outside of the estate from the main drive to the Japanese hydrangea planting, the fernery and the old cart road. There's a lot to see, including *Rhododendron arboreum* hybrids that are more than a century old, and an oak that was probably sent to Caerhays from Louisiana by the great plant collector Professor Charles Sprague Sargent.

The beautiful castle is open for guided tours on weekdays only mid-Mar–mid-Jun and is still inhabited by the family.

Expect to see gilded frames holding oil paintings, a Georgian hall, and lavish furnishings and fixtures. Book in advance for tours and check the website's events listings if you're interested in gardening, as they run popular lectures in association with the Royal Horticultural Society in the spring, and various events and fairs.

EAT AND DRINK
The Nare ⊛
narehotel.co.uk
Carne Beach, Veryan-in-Roseland, TR2 5PF | 01872 501111
The setting is one to savour, as the hotel perches above a secluded sandy beach, with full-length windows on three sides. It has two restaurants: the Dining Room for a formal table d'hote dinner (jackets required), and the Quarterdeck, a more relaxed eatery. There's a great wine list too.

The New Inn
newinn-veryan.co.uk
Veryan, TR2 5QA
01872 501362
This unspoiled, part-thatched pub in Veryan has open fires, a beamed ceiling, a single bar serving St Austell ales and a warm, welcoming atmosphere. Sunday lunch is a speciality. On other days expect superior pub grub and traditional puddings such as apple crumble and sticky toffee pudding.

▼ Nare Headland

▸ Newquay

Chances are you've heard of Newquay. It's Cornwall's best-known tourist town, a place alive in the summer with parties, clubs, and teens and twentysomethings. It's also the UK's surf capital, where international surfers battle it out on Fistral Beach every year in the country's only top-rated surf championships. Run to the

▲ Surfers at Watergate Bay

Sun takes place here every May, a festival of music, mods and VWs. Teenagers camp and celebrate or commiserate after their exam results come in; packs of stag nighters stalk the streets, hen nighters drink cocktails and shots in beach bars, and families build sandcastles on the beach and play ankle-deep in the sea. There's a lot to this town – you couldn't ever write it off as boring.

The beach is the big draw no matter who you are – mod or tot, surfer or drinker. Fistral is the best-known beach, a surf beach where in the summer months the water is packed with the yellow and blue foam boards of learners and the waves are nearly always lacklustre. A word of warning: if you want to

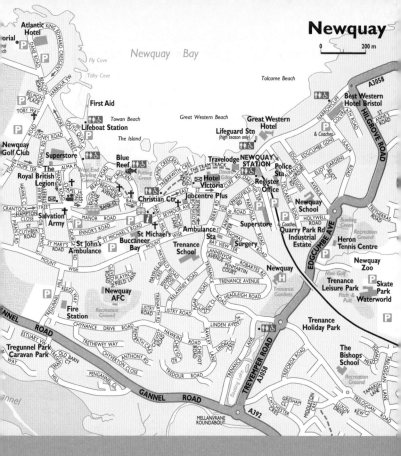

learn to surf, there are less crowded spots, and the local residential surf schools will probably take you there, rather than Fistral Beach, so you have a fair shot at riding a wave rather than running over other learners. As well as Fistral Beach, there are four other beaches walkable from the town centre, and the watersports centre at Watergate Bay just up the coast is a good bet for activities.

Despite Newquay's reputation as a party town, it's also a good place for a family holiday, with the aforementioned beaches plus attractions such as a zoo, an aquarium and a swimming pool. Check that you're not staying in a party hotspot before you book your accommodation, though: some campsites have banned large single-sex groups for this reason, because they want family visitors.

Near to the town you'll find the Elizabethan manor house Trerice, a National Trust property, while up the coast there's Rick Stein's empire at Padstow.

◄ Towan beach Island bridge

ENTERTAIN THE FAMILY
Buccaneer Bay
buccaneerbay.co.uk
22 St Michael's Road, Newquay,
TR7 1RA | 01637 873379
Open 28 Mar–end Oct daily 10.30–3
It's not a swashbuckling
holiday in Cornwall without a
glimpse of some real live
pirates, me hearties, so get ye
down to Buccaneer Bay to meet
'em. Young'uns can follow a
treasure trail and unlock the
Cap'n's treasure chest, and
brave souls can detour into the
Sunken Village of the Damned.
Cornish myths and legends are
alive and well here in
Buccaneer Bay. Aaarr.

Newquay Zoo,
Trenance Gardens
newquayzoo.org.uk
Newquay, TR7 2LZ
0844 474 2244 | Open all year
Apr–end Sep daily 9.30–6, Oct–end
Mar daily 10–5 (last entry 1 hour
before closing)
Set within exotic lakeside
gardens and with more than
130 species, Newquay Zoo is
one of Cornwall's most popular
attractions. The Madagascar
Walkthrough features crowned
lemurs, vasa parrots, striped
mongoose and more. Animal
feeds and informative talks run
throughout the day. Children
can also enjoy the Tarzan Trail
and Dragon Maze. Other
highlights include the Tropical
House, Oriental Garden,
Penguin Pool, Village Farm and
lots more.

MEET THE SEALIFE
Blue Reef Aquarium
bluereefaquarium.co.uk
Towan Promenade, Newquay,
TR7 1DU | 01637 878134
Open all year daily from 10am
Discover Cornish marine life
from native sharks and rays to
the frighteningly intelligent and
playful octopus in this large
aquarium. From here, journey
through warmer waters to
watch the magical seahorses,
unusual shape-shifting,
jet-propelled cuttlefish and the
vibrant, swaying tentacles of
living sponges and anemones.
The safari continues through
the underwater tunnel below a
tropical sea. Daily talks and
regular feeding demonstrations
bring the experience to life.
Events all year; check the
website for details. The
aquarium is right next to
Towan Beach.

HIT THE BEACH
There are plenty of beaches to
choose from in the Newquay
and Watergate Bay area – good
to know when it's busy in high
season. Dogs are banned
Easter–end Sep and lifeguards
patrol in peak season. See also
St Agnes for other nearby sandy
spots (page 224).

Fistral Beach
For more information on events,
visit fistralbeach.co.uk
This large sandy beach is
Newquay's best-known beach,
the site of the annual

▶ Beach from cliff, Whipsiddery

Boardmasters international surf contest and festival and the host space for a number of big family events in the summer months. It's a world-class surf beach and there are surf hire companies and a BSA-registered surf school just off the beach, next to beach bars and shops. Lifeguards patrol in peak season. Little Fistral, a cove at the north end of the beach, is only accessible at low tide and has no lifeguard cover.

Great Western Beach

One of the four beaches accessible on foot from the town centre, Great Western is a sandy beach with rock pools and caves to explore at low tide, when it combines with Lusty Glaze, Towan and Tolcarne Beaches to become a mile-long stretch of sand. Access is via a steep cliff path at high tide, or via the other beaches at low tide. It's a popular family and surf beach, with cafes, surf hire and surf tuition, and a lifeguard May–end Sep. The nearest car park is in town.

Lusty Glaze

For full event details, see lustyglaze.co.uk

This horseshoe-shaped beach, backed by cliffs, has a restaurant and bar, regular events and Sundowner Sessions in summer, a programme of free evening gigs on the beach. The name derives from the Cornish for 'a place to view blue boats' – but there's not much

fishing going on these days. There's a surf school and the Adventure Centre, which offers children's activities, abseiling, a 750ft-long zip wire and jet-ski adventures. There are lifeguards on the beach in peak season and the beach is home to the National Lifeguard Training Centre. It's a decent family and surf beach.

Porth Beach

This large, sandy beach is safe for swimming and is sheltered at its mouth by Porth Island, which can be walked round at low tide. At mid-tide on a windy day there's a blowhole just at the end of the island for added drama. It's narrow, family friendly and easily accessed, with a pub on the beach and cafes across the road. Surfing is banned here in the summer season.

Tolcarne Beach

Tolcarne is the largest of Newquay's beaches, a stretch of sand between Great Western and Lusty Glaze surrounded on three sides by cliffs. Access is via the steep steps in the cliffs or at low tide from Newquay's other beaches. There is no car park nearby. The beach has all the usual facilities, including a surf school and surf hire, and it's safe for swimmers. There are rock pools at low tide, caves in the cliffs, and the Tolcarne Wedge, a punchy high-tide wave that attracts the UK's top bodyboarders.

Towan Beach

The westernmost of Newquay's beaches, Towan is the closest to the town centre. It's notable mostly for its private island, connected by a bridge to the mainland, which has a luxurious holiday home available to rent on it. The beach is sandy and safe for swimmers. Parking is in the town and there are plenty of cafes and beach shops nearby. The Blue Reef Aquarium is right by the beach.

Watergate Bay

extremeacademy.co.uk
Extreme Academy, Watergate Bay,
TR8 4AA | 01637 860840
Open all year daily 9–5
This large, west-facing beach is home to the Extreme Academy and is a great place to go if you want to learn to surf or kite surf, wave ski or stand-up paddleboard (depending on the weather). Last-minute lessons are usually available. It can be breezy. There's a lifeguard here in season and a great beach cafe, the Beach Hut. Jamie Oliver's restaurant (see page 186) and the Watergate Bay Hotel are just beyond the beach.

GO ON A BOAT TRIP

Newquay Harbour Boatmen's Association
newquay-harbour.com
South Quay, The Harbour,
TR7 1HR | 01637 876352

Lusty Glaze beach, Newquay (overleaf)

Open May–end Sep daily 10–6, weather and tides permitting
A variety of boat trips are on offer from Newquay Harbour, including speedboat hire, pleasure cruises and deep-sea angling trips. Mackerel fishing trips involve trawling a few lines and taking the catch home for tea. In the harbour, the seals are usually there to greet you; on the water you'll see the beautiful craggy cliffs and headlands, Newquay from the sea and perhaps a dolphin or two. Call in advance for fishing trips in particular.

EXPLORE BY BIKE

Cycle Revolution
7 Beach Road, TR7 1ES
01637 872634
There are some lovely routes along the golf course and the cliffs and around Newquay,

which is on National Cycle Route 32 running from Land's End to Bodmin (see sustrans. org.uk for full details). The Camel Trail is also within reach of the town. Cycle Revolution hires out bikes from a base near Crantock, just outside the town centre.

GO FISHING
Porth Reservoir
swlakestrust.org.uk
near Newquay
01566 771930
For coarse fishing, Porth Reservoir near Newquay is a good bet. As well as being a coarse fishery, it's also a bird reserve with specialist hides. The reservoir is stocked with carp and has some large fish, with 32lb carp, 24lb pike and 10lb bream being caught. Call for details on permits.

GO SWIMMING
Waterworld
tempusleisure.org.uk
Trenance Leisure Park,
TR7 2LZ | 01637 853828
Open all year Mon–Fri 9am–9.45pm, Sat–Sun 10–5
Good to know about for a rainy day with children, Waterworld is a large swimming pool with a six-lane 80ft pool and a tropical fun pool with two waterslides, a waterplay hut, an erupting volcano and a snake fountain. There's also a gym and exercise classes.

PLAY A ROUND
Newquay Golf Club
newquaygolfclub.co.uk

Tower Road, TR7 1LT
01637 874354 | Open all year
One of Cornwall's finest seaside links with magnificent views over Fistral Beach and the Atlantic Ocean. Open to the unpredictable nature of the elements and possessing some very demanding greenside bunkers, the prerequisite for good scoring at Newquay is accuracy.

EAT AND DRINK
Fifteen Cornwall ⓐ
fifteencornwall.co.uk
On The Beach, Watergate Bay,
TR8 4AA | 01637 861000
Jamie Oliver's flagship Cornish restaurant has an antipasti bar and kitchen open to view, along with a fantastic beach view and a decent children's menu. Straightforward, unfussy Italian cooking is the order of the day, with dishes of upfront rustic flavours. Start with pasta – gnocchi with oxtail and sage, or taglierini with squid and mussels – and proceed to a steak with marrowbone and horseradish, monkfish with cime di rapa and rosemary, or duck with polenta and salsa verde. Had enough of tiramisù? Then go for lemon tart with rhubarb and clotted cream.

Lewinnick Lodge
hospitalitycornwall.com
Pentire Headland,
TR7 1QD | 01637 878117
For panoramic Atlantic views on a terrace overhanging the ocean, and modern British food,

the upmarket Lewinnick Lodge is the place. A typical menu could include roasted wood pigeon breast to start, followed by tiger prawn linguine – one of its signature dishes – and clotted-cream rice pudding as an indulgent dessert.

Trenance Cottage Tea Rooms and Gardens

trenancecottagesnewquay.co.uk
Trenance Lane,
TR7 2HX | 01637 872034
Escape the bustling beach in this award-winning Georgian tea room. You can lunch on fresh local crab, home-baked pasties and local cheese ploughman's lunches, or peruse the extensive tea list, which offers a brew that matches your meal or one of the homemade cakes.

▸ **PLACES NEARBY**

Newquay is surrounded by tourist attractions for those of all ages, as well as beautiful beaches, a steam railway and the Elizabethan estate of Trerice.

DairyLand Farm World

dairylandfarmworld.com
Summercourt, near Newquay,
TR8 5AA | 01872 510246
Open 25 Mar–3 Nov daily 10–5
Visitors can watch while the cows are milked to music on a spectacular merry-go-round milking machine. The life of a Victorian farmer and his neighbours is explored in the Heritage Centre, and a Farm Nature Trail features

informative displays along pleasant walks. Children will have fun getting to know the farm animals in the Farm Park. They will also enjoy the playground, assault course and indoor play areas.

Holywell Bay

Six miles west of Newquay, this mile of sandy beach with dunes is popular with families and surfers, and is usually a lot less packed and more friendly in the height of summer than those in the town itself. There are streams and rock pools at low tide to paddle in; dogs are welcome and it's safe for swimmers. The twin rocks offshore are called Gull Rocks, or Carter's Rocks. There's said to be a holy well in one of the caves at the northern end of the beach, only accessible at low tide; it certainly has an unusual rock formation inside it. There are facilities nearby and a car park.

Holywell Bay Fun Park

holywellbayfunpark.co.uk
Holywell, TR8 5PW
01637 830095 | Open May–end Sep, plus public holidays and some weekends, from 10.30am
A family fun park with rides, water attractions, pitch and putt, trampolines and plenty more rides, all paid for individually. Free car parking and free entry. Check the website for full opening hours – it's open late in July and August and at various times depending on the season.

Holywell Bay Golf Park

holywellgolf.co.uk
TR8 5PW | 01637 832916
Open all year

Situated beside a family fun park with many amenities, the course is an 18-hole short course with great sea views. Fresh Atlantic winds make the course hard to play and there are several tricky holes, particularly the 18th over the trout pond. The site also has an excellent 18-hole pitch and putt course for the whole family.

Lappa Valley Steam Railway

lappavalley.co.uk
St Newlyn East, near Newquay
01872 510317 | Open 27 Mar–1 Nov Sun–Fri 10–5.15

This little Lappa Valley attraction has three miniature railways running in its grounds plus a steam railway running on a track dating from 1849. More for families than for serious rail enthusiasts, there's also a boating lake, crazy golf, pedal cars and play areas. The average visit takes around 4 hours. There are two stations, Benny Halt is where the ticket office and car parking are found. All other activities are at East Wheal Rose. There are special events all year, including Santa Specials.

The Smugglers' Den Inn

thesmugglersden.co.uk
Trebellan, Cubert, near Newquay,
TR8 5PY | 01637 830209

Truly a pub that lives up to its name, the Smugglers' Den is a 16th-century thatched inn just 15 minutes' drive from Newquay, serving local food, real ales and a decent Sunday lunch. They are enthusiastic about local food and drink, and hold a regular real ale and pie event in the spring. Ask the bar staff about the resident ghost and the pub's smuggling past. It's certainly worth the trip here from Newquay – it's a world away from arcades and themed pubs.

Trerice

nationaltrust.org.uk
Kestle Mill, near Newquay,
TR8 4PG | 01637 875404
Open Mar–4 Nov daily
10.30–5, 9 Nov–22 Dec,
weekends only 11–4

This glorious Elizabethan manor surrounded by Tudor gardens is a lovely place to visit. The architecture dates from the 1570s, and the plaster ceilings of the Great Hall and Great Chamber are a particular delight. Outside, you can try your hand at the Cornish form of bowls, with games known as kayling or slapcock, and wander through an orchard of Cornish apple trees. There are regular events and family adventures to be had – see the website for full details – and the National Trust has put in a lot of work to make this place come alive, with Tudor music drifting out into the gardens, and old-fashioned purple carrots and salad leaves planted in the cottage garden.

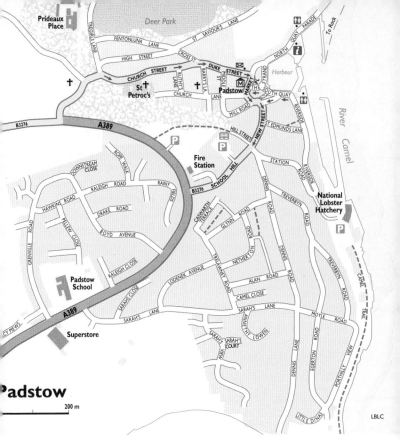

Padstow

Padstow

On the Camel Estuary north of Newquay, Padstow has acquired the nickname 'Padstein' for its celebrity chef connection. Mr Stein has not one but three restaurants in the small town, plus a fish and chip shop, and he's been the driving force that has made this working harbour an attractive prospect for holiday visitors. It's a delightful place to visit, with art shops, boutiques and cafes in the maze of narrow streets around the harbour, and an easy place to spend a morning or afternoon and a lot of money, if you're keen to shop.

Shoppers and foodies should note, though, that Padstow has a lot more to it than sublime fish and seaside knick-knacks – it's been a significant town in Cornwall for a long, long time. Padstow was a busy trading port from the earliest times, and Welsh and Irish saints of the Dark Ages landed here. St Petroc arrived from Wales in the 6th century AD and stayed for 30 years, founding a monastery which thrived until 981 when it was destroyed by marauding Vikings.

The town has a couple of interesting local traditions, including Obby Oss, a festival on May Day, and Mummers' Day, a celebration on Boxing Day that can be traced back to an ancient midwinter party.

Along with boat trips and the National Lobster Hatchery, the town has three significant walking trails. The Saints Way, *Forth an Syns* in Cornish, is a 28-mile route from Padstow to Fowey. It can be walked in 2 days and is best started at the Church of St Petroc, Padstow. The first part of the walk to Little Petherick, 2 miles south of Padstow, is worth doing for its own sake. The Camel Trail runs along a disused train line from Padstow to Wadebridge (see page 268) and can be cycled or walked, and the Southwest Coast Path winds along the cliffs here with lovely views of the estuary and its mussel and oyster farms.

TAKE IN SOME HISTORY
Prideaux Place
prideauxplace.co.uk
PL28 8RP | 01841 532411
House open Easter Sun–early Oct Sun–Thu 1.30–4; grounds and tea room 12.30–5. Also open through the year by appointment.
Closed 30 Apr–1 May
This Elizabethan estate overlooks Padstow, a house surrounded by 40 acres of landscaped gardens that dates from 1592. It's still occupied by the Prideaux family, which can trace its ancestry back to William the Conqueror. Overlooking a deer park, this splendid house contains a wealth of family and royal portraits, a fine porcelain collection, a growing teddy bear collection and a magnificent 16th-century plaster ceiling in the Great Chamber, which has some marvellous views across countryside to Bodmin Moor. There's plenty of opportunity for walking in both formal gardens and woodland, and there is also a peaceful tea room. The house

has been featured in many film and TV productions. Of the house's 81 rooms, 46 are bedrooms and only six of those are habitable; the remaining rooms are as the US army left the house after World War II.

MEET THE LOBSTERS
National Lobster Hatchery
nationallobsterhatchery.co.uk
Padstow, PL28 8BL | 01841 533877
Open spring 10–5, summer 10–7.30, autumn 10–5, winter 10–4
This pioneering marine research facility is on the quay by the car park and provides an interesting insight into the country's vulnerable lobster populations and the situation facing them in the sea. Its main aim is to preserve the species and conserve vulnerable populations, and it focuses a lot of attention on the issue of biodiversity and sustainable fishing. The visitor centre is an interesting way to learn more about the issue, get up close and personal with lobsters and local sea life in the mini aquarium, and find out why you

should be picky about where you buy your fish and chips.

HIT THE BEACH
Padstow's beaches are at the north of the town and accessed by the Southwest Coast Path. The walk takes about 10 minutes to St George's Cove, and on to Harbour Cove and Hawker's Cove. You can also walk to the headland and Stepper Point ('the sleeping dragon') with views across to Rock. There is a ferry running to Rock (see page 221) at high tide and a lovely beach there too. The beaches are all sandy with rock pools at high tide and some strong currents. Dogs are banned Easter–end Sep.

EXPLORE BY BIKE
Padstow Cycle Hire
padstowcyclehire.com
South Quay, PL28 8BL
01841 533533 | Open all year daily 9–5
Cycle along the coast, around the town or along the Camel Trail, which runs from Padstow to Wadebridge. Padstow Cycle Hire rents men's, women's and children's bikes, trailers, tandems, baby bike seats and tagalong bikes, and runs evening cycle rides in the summer months too. Part-day hires, after 3pm, are also possible.

TAKE A BOAT TRIP
Padstow Sealife Safaris
padstowsealifesafaris.co.uk
North Quay, PL28 8AF
07754 822404

Padstow Sealife Safaris runs nature-focused boat trips from the harbour, taking visitors out to see seals, dolphins, basking sharks, puffins and much more. Various trips include a 1-hour voyage to Seal Cave, a 1-hour powerboat tour of the coast and 2-hour sea safaris exploring the coastline, history and wildlife of the local area.

LEARN TO COOK
Padstow Seafood School
rickstein.com
Riverside, PL28 8BP
01841 532700 | Check website for course calendar; book in advance
Where better than Padstow to get a handle on how to cook fish, with a view of the working harbour out of the window? Half-, 1- and 2-day courses are available on a variety of topics, including classic seafood dishes, cooking from India, Italian seafood cookery, and Spanish tapas. Advance booking is essential.

GO SEA FISHING
Emma Kate II
emmakate2.com
North Quay,
PL28 8AF | 07970 595244
Padstow is a working harbour and in the summer months sea fishing trips can be booked to catch mackerel and more. *Emma Kate II* is one of the regular boats offering fishing trips all year, including wreck, reef and all day trips, 2-hour mackerel and 4-hour bass fishing trips. Enquire along the quay for other trips.

EAT AND DRINK

Margot's ◉
margotsbistro.co.uk
11 Duke Street,
PL28 8AB | 01841 533441
This modest little bistro with a marine-blue frontage tucked away in the narrow streets of the town centre serves straightforward, direct and high-impact bistro cookery from chef-patron Adrian Oliver. Padstow runs on fresh fish, and just as well when you contemplate a starter of grilled mackerel dressed in cucumber, capers and lemon, or a main such as whole lemon sole in citrus oil. Meats are good too.

The Metropole ◉
the-metropole.co.uk
Station Road,
PL28 8DB | 01841 532486
'The Met', to its friends, is just about Padstow's most imposing building, a Victorian grande dame that is a local landmark. It's a great place holding its own among the town's great eateries. Expect the likes of surf and turf-style combos of scallops with hog's pudding, confit duck leg with braised Puy lentils, and lemon posset with blackcurrant ice cream and homemade shortbread.

Paul Ainsworth at No. 6 ◉◉◉
number6inpadstow.co.uk
6 Middle Street,
PL28 8AP | 01841 532093
There's more than one celebrity chef in this town:

▲ Padstow

Paul Ainsworth has wowed telly audiences on *Great British Menu* and continues to draw crowds to his Georgian townhouse restaurant. Think Cornish classics brought bang up to date – lobster tail and claw with perfectly made ravioli, served with sea purslane and cheddar – served in a contemporary dining room.

Rick Stein's Cafe

rickstein.com

10 Middle Street, PL28 8AP

01841 532700

The most relaxed of Rick Stein's restaurants is a casual cafe with rooms decked out with a nautical theme. It's open all day, so call in for breakfast or an excellent cappuccino and peruse the papers, or arrive early for deliciously simple lunches and dinners – salt and pepper prawns, whole grilled mackerel with tomato and onion salad, or chickpea, parsley and salt cod stew.

St Petroc's Hotel and Bistro ✿

rickstein.com

4 New Street, PL28 8EA

01841 532700

Rick Stein's bistro has bare wooden tables, white walls hung with bold artwork, and a courtyard and garden for alfresco dining. The focus, as expected, is on seafood in various guises, although there are a few token meat dishes in the shape of pan-fried chicken breast with black pudding, and steaks. For dessert, expect something such as panacotta with vanilla-poached rhubarb.

The Seafood Restaurant
🅰🅰🅰
rickstein.com
Riverside, PL28 8BY
01841 532700
This is where the Stein empire began, a humble, large, ever-packed restaurant set around a central seafood bar. Fish is the thing, of course – deep-fried river prawns, palourde clams à la plancha, roast slab of turbot or a luxuriant Newlyn fish pie. Oysters and mussels are farmed just steps away in the estuary.

▸ **PLACES NEARBY**
There are some lovely beaches near Padstow, along with a golf course by Constantine Bay and a pub run by Rick Stein in St Merryn. Rock (see page 221) is just across the water.

Constantine Bay
This long sandy beach just north of Padstow is popular with surfers and families alike, with a food wagon on the sands on its approach, lifeguards in peak season and dogs allowed all year. At low tide rock pools are exposed and a little pool forms in the middle of the beach, thanks to a sandbank. Parking is difficult close to the beach – parking at Treyarnon Bay and walking 10 minutes along the coast path is an option. There are toilets by the small car park and there's a small shop in Constantine village a short walk away.

Harlyn Bay
This sheltered, sandy beach with dunes is considered one of Cornwall's best beaches for families. It's a safe beach for learner surfers and swimmers alike, and popular with sea kayakers too. Lifeguards patrol in the summer. There are surf schools on the beach and it's a short walk to Harlyn village. Dogs are allowed all year and there's a car park just by the beach.

Trevone Bay
Two miles from Padstow, Trevone Bay is another sandy beach popular with families and surfers. Dogs aren't permitted Easter–end Sep. There are lifeguards through the summer season and the sea is safe for swimmers. Scramble over the rocks and you'll find another rocky beach here, great for rock

pooling and with a natural swimming pool that appears at low tide. There's also a blowhole in the cliffs, and during the summer months the beach and the village beside it often hold events. There's a car park by the beach and it's just a short walk from the beach to the village tea shops and pub.

Treyarnon Bay
Another great sandy family beach with rock pools, Treyarnon is 11 miles north of Newquay and has a car park, a beach shop and lifeguards in summer. There can be strong undercurrents and large waves. It's a popular surfing spot for intermediate surfers. At low tide, a large rock pool great for paddling in is exposed. Parking is in a car park beside the beach.

Trevose Golf Club
trevose-gc.co.uk
Constantine Bay, near Padstow,
PL28 8JB | 01841 520208
Open all year

The well-known links course at Trevose Golf Club has its early holes close to the sea on excellent springy turf. A championship course with varying degrees of difficulty appealing to professionals and higher handicap players, it's a good test with well-positioned bunkers and a meandering stream. It can be windy.

The Cornish Arms
rickstein.com
Churchtown, St Merryn,
near Padstow, PL28 8ND
01841 520288
Rick Stein runs this whitewashed, traditional Cornish pub in St Merryn so you can expect good seafood; there are cask ales and St Austell Brewery real ales on tap plus Stein's own home-bottled brews Chalky's Bark and Chalky's Bite. The menu is a Stein variation on simple pub food, with roasts, real beef burgers and mussels.

▸ Pendeen
This straggling line of small communities on the north coast of the Land's End peninsula all link to the former tin and copper mines of the area. The smaller villages of Carnyorth, Trewellard, Boscaswell and Bojewyan make up the roll call of this, the last of Cornwall's coastal mining communities. It's a startlingly dramatic place to visit, where the fractured mining landscape meets the raw beauty of the Atlantic coast.

Pendeen's Geevor Mine closed in 1991 in the face of international market pressure, but was previously the mainstay of the larger area. It can be visited today, transformed into an informative heritage centre with mine workings, a museum and a fascinating underground tour.

Just south of Geevor at Levant, the power of steam is harnessed to a restored working beam engine at Levant Mine, looked after by the National Trust.

GET INDUSTRIAL
Geevor Tin Mine
See highlight panel opposite

▷ **PLACES NEARBY**

As befits the former tin mining area, there's more to see in nearby Trewellard and open moorland at Penwith is lovely walking territory.

Levant Mine and Beam Engine

nationaltrust.org.uk
Levant Road, Trewellard,
TR19 7SX | 01736 786156
Open all year daily 11–5

This unique steam-powered Cornish beam engine is the only one in the world still in steam on its original site. Perched in a stone-built engine house overlooking the cliffs, it's an evocative spot. A local team, known as 'the Greasy Gang',

restored it after 60 years lying idle; for 110 years, Levant Mine was worked and stretched a mile out to sea at a depth of nearly 2,000ft.

Penwith Moors

Penwith Moors run parallel to the north coast of the Land's End Peninsula through an undulating series of hills crowned with granite tors. They are noted for their ecological value and their unique concentration of Neolithic, Bronze Age and Iron Age remains, which include burial chambers, settlements, stone circles and standing stones. Most of the northern moors are at the heart of the Environmentally Sensitive Area within which farmers are compensated for working in sympathy with the traditional structure of the ancient landscape.

The high ground begins at Rosewall Hill just west of St Ives and is continuous throughout the beautiful parishes of Zennor and Morvah. Smaller areas of moorland continue the westward-leading sequence to Chapel Carn Brea above the wide, flat coastal plateau of Land's End itself. The moorland is a splendid counterpoint to the peninsula's outstanding coastline and is easily accessible from a number of points.

▼ Pendeen Lighthouse

Geevor Tin Mine

geevor.com

TR19 7EW | 01736 788662

Open Apr–end Oct Sun–Fri 9–5, Nov–end Mar Sun–Fri 9–4

This preserved tin mine and museum provides an insight into the methods and equipment used in the industry that was once so important in the area. The Geevor Tin Mine only actually stopped operation in 1990 and was closed completely a year later. Guided tours let visitors see the tin treatment plant, and a video illustrates the techniques employed. There is also a museum of hard rock mining, and the underground tour is well worth the trip.

▶ Penzance

This grand seaside town, the capital of West Cornwall, is all palm tree-lined streets, sunshine and stunning sunrises over Mount's Bay and St Michael's Mount. The old town has beautiful Georgian and Regency buildings, there's a 19th-century seaside promenade and the jewel in its crown, a 1930s lido. The water is a bit on the chilly side, mind, but you can warm up afterwards in one of the town's characterful pubs, which are welcoming and have Cornish ales and ciders on tap. Penzance is a lively spot that saw its heyday in the 19th century as a popular holiday spot. Gilbert and Sullivan's opera *The Pirates of Penzance* was a little dig at the holiday scene here, rather than a reference to a historical smuggling past.

Today it's a great place to visit, particularly if you're into art, as the town has long had associations with artists and the arts. Three top quality art galleries to visit are the Exchange, Penlee House and Newlyn Art Gallery; there are also countless art shops selling seaside and Cornish-themed prints. If you are more interested in modern and contemporary art than that of the Newlyn School, be sure to visit Tremenheere nearby. As the newest garden in Cornwall, it has a distinctly different feel to the county's historic garden estates, and it is peppered with experiential art and sculptures.

Penzance is not the most gorgeous town in Cornwall – the modern additions to the town's architecture are bland and characterless to say the least – but it is a living town, rather than a tourist attraction, and has a distinct character and spirit. It has a summer festival called Golowan that lasts for eight days in late June and involves numerous cultural events and entertainment, culminating in Mazey Day when the streets of Penzance are closed to traffic and the main street, Market Jew Street, hosts a street fair. Other unique-to-Penzance experiences include Allantide, a Cornish celebration of Hallowe'en where children are given a large red apple, and the Montol Festival in December, where traditional Cornish customs including ceidlidhs and a lantern procession take place. Both are believed to date from pre-Christian times.

Talking of history, Penzance gets its name from the Cornish for 'holy headland', referencing a chapel called St Anthony's that is said to have stood for more than 1,000 years on the headland where Penzance harbour is now.

Penzance's main street, Market Jew Street, holds all kinds of shops, including Pellow's Bakery, where you can find the largest pasties in town. Towards the sea are Morrab Gardens and Penlee Park; the former is a lovely ornamental garden, the latter houses Penlee House Gallery and Museum.

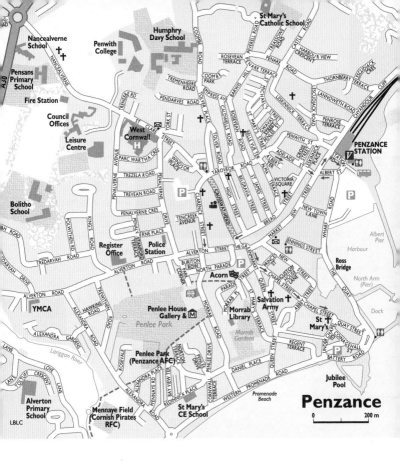

To the west, Penzance merges with Newlyn, the major fishing port in the southwest of the county. Newlyn harbour is full of life and colour. Scores of fishing boats of all types and sizes work from here in spite of the increasing difficulties of the modern international industry. The large fish market bustles with activity in the early morning as boats land a remarkable variety of fish. Parking at Newlyn is difficult, and most visitors find that a walk along Penzance's spacious promenade and on along the seafront to Newlyn is a pleasant alternative, which can be combined with a visit to the Newlyn Art Gallery along the way.

Just outside Penzance is the National Trust's Trengwainton Garden, a complex of five walled gardens set amid mature woodland, at its best during the spring and early summer months. Trengwainton Garden can be reached via Heamoor, or from Tremethick Cross on the St Just road.

Another sight to visit on the outskirts of the town is Chysauster Ancient Village, the remains of an Iron Age settlement from almost 2,000 years ago with a mysterious tunnel or 'fougou'.

A ferry goes to the Isles of Scilly from Penzance Harbour, offering day trips and longer; there's also a helipad at Eastern Green. The harbour is also the place for sea safaris, where you might spot sunfish, basking sharks and dolphin, and sea fishing trips, which could result in a mackerel or two for tea; they taste great on a barbecue with a little lemon squeezed over them. For walkers and cyclists, there are some lovely routes nearby, including the Southwest Coast Path and the First and Last Trail, linking Penzance with Land's End.

If you're looking for a beach, Long Rock Beach is a broad sandy beach safe for swimming and good for families, leading around Mount's Bay to Marazion, and Sennen, 9 miles down the coast, is your best bet for surfing; see page 256.

TAKE IN SOME HISTORY

Trereife

trereifepark.co.uk
Trereife, TR20 8TJ
01736 362750 | House and gardens open to visitors summer only; Stableyard Café open summer Sun–Thu 11–5

This Queen Anne manor house, some of which dates from the Elizabethan age, is in a stunning location near Penzance. It's open year round for bed and breakfast – unusual for an estate of this style – and is open to day visitors during the summer months only. The garden has modern parterre gardens, laid in 1999 and planned to suit the Queen Anne front of the house; there's also a ha-ha and parkland beyond it. In the house, plasterwork ceilings were created by Italian workers in the early 1700s and are a key feature.

As well as an estate to explore, the Stableyard Cafe has a menu including Cornish crab and pilchards. Check the website for events and fairs which take place at Trereife all year, including an Easter fair, a food, craft and beer festival at the end of May, the Cornwall Design Fair in August and a Christmas gift fair in November.

VISIT THE MUSEUMS AND GALLERIES

Newlyn Art Gallery and the Exchange

newlynartgallery.co.uk
New Road, Newlyn, TR18 5PZ
01736 363715 | Open summer Mon–Sat 10–5, public holidays 11–4, winter Tue–Sat 10–5

This contemporary art gallery, housed in two rather wonderful modern buildings (the Exchange, a former telephone exchange, is on Princes Street), shows some of the finest modern art in Cornwall. The focus is on paintings and drawing, with some events, performances and film screenings at the Exchange. Newlyn Art Gallery's Studio Cafe has a fantastic view of the sea and both venues have great shops showcasing books, art, and the best local crafts and ceramics.

Penlee House Gallery and Museum

penleehouse.org.uk
Morrab Road,
TR18 4HE | 01736 363625
Open Easter–end Sep
Mon–Sat 10–5, Oct–Easter
Mon–Sat 10.30–4.30

This museum and gallery in a grand Victorian house specialises in the works of the Newlyn School artists, painting from around 1880–1940, along with West Cornwall's archaeology and social history. The park includes sub-tropical gardens, a sensory garden, an open-air theatre and a children's play area. Follow an enlightening gallery tour with lunch or afternoon tea in the Orangery Cafe. Cakes and pastries are freshly baked, while lunches include crab sandwiches, quiche and fish pie.

GO ROUND THE GARDENS

Tremenheere Sculpture Garden

tremenheere.co.uk
Gulval, near Penzance,
TR20 8YL | 01736 448089
Open Easter–3 Nov Mon–Sat 10–5, Sun 10–4, winter Fri–Sun; check website for hours

So much more than a sub-tropical garden – though that's interesting and exciting enough – Tremenheere opened in 2012 as a sculpture garden with woodlands, streams and views of the coast offsetting contemporary art, experiential art and installations. With a monthly market, a singing group, a cafe and views of St Michael's Mount through the trees, it's a very special place. Installations are atmospheric and magical, and fit in beautifully with the surrounding countryside. There's an adventure map for children and well-behaved dogs are welcome.

Trewidden Garden

trewiddengarden.co.uk
Buryas Bridge,
TR20 8TT | 01736 363021
Open 3 Mar–21 Sep daily 10.30–5.30

Trewidden Garden, one of the Great Gardens of Cornwall, is a 15-acre, 19th-century garden with one of the largest tree fern dells in Europe and an impressive camellia and magnolia collection. The owners have designed a trail for children and have a cafe and plant shop on site. Head gardener Richard Morton takes free guided tours on Thursdays Feb–end Apr – ring to book a place in advance. At other times, garden tours can be booked but cost extra. Dogs are welcome.

GO BACK IN TIME

Chysauster Ancient Village

english-heritage.org.uk
Newmill, TR20 8XA
07831 757934 | Open Apr–end Jun and Sep daily 10–5, Jul–end Aug daily 10–6, Oct daily 10–4

Chysauster Ancient Village is what remains of an Iron Age settlement occupied almost 2,000 years ago. The village

▲ Chysauster Ancient Village

consisted of stone-walled homes known as 'courtyard houses', found only on the Land's End Peninsula and the Isles of Scilly. The houses line a 'village street', and each has an open central courtyard surrounded by a number of thatched rooms. The site also has the remains of a 'fogou', an underground passage of uncertain purpose.

MEET THE WILDLIFE
Marine Discovery
marinediscovery.co.uk
Shed 5, Albert Pier,
TR18 2LL | 01736 874907
Sailings Mar–end Oct,
weather permitting
Penzance is a great place to take safari trips to watch seals, seabirds, sharks and dolphins out on the open sea. Marine Discovery runs catamaran sailing trips along the southwest coast, ranging from 1.5 to 4 hours long. Some voyages are for children aged 3 and up; others only take over-6s, or those over 12. The best time to see whales – minke whales are the most common ones seen – is at the end of the summer and start of autumn; basking sharks are most commonly seen late May–end June.

HIT THE BEACH
Long Rock Beach is a large swathe of golden sand and shingle stretching as far as Marazion at low tide. It's an easy beach to reach from the town centre and is very safe for

swimmers, particularly children, as it takes a lot of walking through the shallow, gently deepening water to get waist deep for a swim. There are lifeguards in season.

EXPLORE BY BIKE
Pedals Bike Hire
Kiosk 17, Wharfside Shopping Centre, TR18 2GB
01736 360600

Cycle Centre
cornwallcyclecentre.co.uk
1 New Street, TR18 2LZ
01736 351671
There are plenty of great scenic bike rides around Penzance, including to Marazion along Mount's Bay, with a view of St Michael's Mount all the way. It's part of the First and Last Trail that runs from Land's End and links Penzance with Mousehole in the opposite direction.

SADDLE UP
The Old Vicarage
oldvicaragepenzance.co.uk
Churchtown, St Hilary,
TR20 9DQ | 01736 711508
The Old Vicarage runs a slightly unusual programme of horse-riding and pony trekking activities. Along with classic beach canters and coastal and inland treks, they model themselves on the classic American ranch with Western riding, natural horsemanship, carriage driving and family bonding holidays all on offer too. Book in advance; consult the website about riding holidays.

VISIT THE SCILLYS
Isles of Scilly Steamship Company
ios-travel.co.uk
Quay Street,
TR18 4BZ | 0845 710 5555
The boat sails every day in summer and Mon, Wed, Fri, Sat the rest of the year. Some sailings are affected by tides, so you should check the website before booking
The Isles of Scilly Steamship Company runs day trips to St Mary's from Penzance on *Scillonian III*, taking 2 hours 45 minutes. Sailings leave Penzance at 9.15 and leave St Mary's at 4.30. Wildlife cruises are also on offer from the same company, with a chance to see seals, puffins and dolphin. The company offers a fly one way, sail the other option for day trips too. For more about the Isles of Scilly, see page 246.

GO SEA FISHING
Bite Adventures
biteadventures.com
Penzance
01736 711764
Penzance has fleets of ships out fishing every day and you can join them, on a private or group sea angling trip seeking shark, wrecks, mackerel or pollock. The best wreck fishing is in the spring. Bite Adventures is a Cornish record-breaker for its shark fishing, having brought in the biggest blue shark found in Southwest waters in over a decade in 2013.

10 top pubs

GO SWIMMING
Jubilee Swimming Pool
jubileepool.co.uk
Battery Road, Promenade,
TR18 4UU | 01736 369224
Open end May–1 Sep 10.30–6
Penzance's art deco lido is the largest seawater lido in the UK and is a lovely spot for swimming and sunbathing away from the beach. It dates from 1935 and is a wonderful place to spend a day, all white and blue with a hint of the glamorous Mediterranean to it, and with views of Newlyn and Mount's Bay. There is a large triangular pool plus a children's pool, and it's beautifully sheltered from the wind. Bring a picnic or buy lunch from the cafe.

EAT AND DRINK
The Admiral Benbow
46 Chapel Street,
TR18 4AF | 01736 363448
One of the most famous names in piratical pubs, the Admiral Benbow was apparently Robert Louis Stevenson's inspiration for his dark and moody pub in *Treasure Island*. It's a characterful place today, a whitewashed pub complete with a smuggler on the roof and 200-year-old smugglers' tunnels underneath it used by the infamous Benbow Brandy Men in the 19th century. Today there are Skinner's ales on tap, and classic pub grub and sandwiches served amid the maritime knick-knacks and antiques.

The Bay @ Hotel Penzance ◉◉
thebaypenzance.co.uk
The Bay, Britons Hill,
TR18 3AE | 01736 366890
A light, relaxed restaurant with all-day dining and particularly lavish Sunday roasts. The Hotel Penzance and its Bay restaurant both have permanent exhibitions by local outstanding artists on their walls. The kitchen has strong

links with local suppliers and caters well for vegans, those who love shellfish, foodies looking for a tasting menu and fans of Modern Cornish.

The Coldstreamer Inn ◉

coldstreamer-penzance.co.uk
Gulval, TR18 3BB
01736 362072

This local village pub has a reassuringly rustic ambience, with candles lit in the evening. Modern Cornish cooking is on the menu and Penzance Polgoon apple juice, rare Irish whiskey and Cornish alcoholic ginger beer are served as thirst-quenchers. The pub also has rooms and holds occasional art shows.

The Dolphin Tavern

dolphintavern.com
Quay Street, TR18 4BD
01736 364106

Sir Walter Raleigh is said to have smoked the first pipe of tobacco in England at this lovely 16th-century pub. These days, it serves great homemade food accompanied by a full range of St Austell beers, and has rooms. A typical menu might feature steak and ale pie or Newlyn crab salad.

Harris's Restaurant ◉

harrissrestaurant.co.uk
46 New Street,
TR18 2LZ | 01736 364408

This unshowy, traditional family restaurant an engaging atmosphere. The emphasis is on seafood, with Newlyn nearby providing most of it, but meat features on the menu too along with divine desserts.

The Navy Inn ◉

navyinn.co.uk
Lower Queen Street,
TR18 4DE | 01736 333232

This small, whitewashed pub just off the seafront is an atmospheric place with a nautical theme. It looks like a traditional place, with its bare board floors, but its food is a notch up from expectations: seafood comes from nearby Newlyn Fish Market and meat from Cornish farms or the local butcher, and it all gets turned into some bright, contemporary dishes.

The Turks Head

turksheadpenzance.co.uk
Chapel Street,
TR18 4AF | 01736 363093

This popular terraced side-street local is the oldest pub in Penzance, dating from

▼ Penzance Harbour

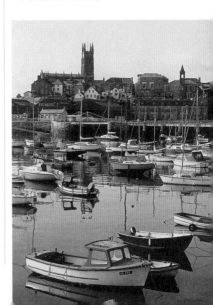

around 1233, and was the first in the country to be given the Turks Head name. Sadly, a Spanish raiding party destroyed much of the original building in the 16th century, but an old smugglers' tunnel leading directly to the harbour still exists. Wash down hearty pub food with a cracking pint of Sharp's Doom Bar, and don't miss the annual beer festival.

▶ PLACES NEARBY

Around Penzance you'll find one of Cornwall's most highly regarded ice cream parlours, a handful of classic Cornish pubs, and banana plants and rhododendrons in Trengwainton Garden.

Jelberts

New Road, Newlyn, Penzance,
TR18 5PZ | Open Easter–end Sep
This far from glamorous-looking ice cream parlour is regularly hailed as one of the best in the county, and serves up just one simple, divine flavour: vanilla. Worth the drive, especially if you like to load your cone up with clotted cream on the top too. Expect queues.

The Star Inn

Crowlas, near Penzance,
TR20 8DX | 01736 740375
A couple of miles east of Penzance, the Star Inn in Crowlas is known for having a beer list as long as some restaurants' wine lists, with real ales and brews

from its microbrewery on a regular rotation with other Cornish ales and ciders. The locals are friendly and it's most certainly not a gastropub – people really are only here for the beer. Locals take a stoppered 4-pint jug home with them from the microbrewery – why not do the same if you're headed back to a holiday home or campsite?

Trengwainton Garden

nationaltrust.org.uk
Madron, near Penzance,
TR20 8RZ | 01736 363148
Open mid-Feb–early Nov,
Sun–Thu and Good Fri
10.30–5
With plants from around the globe scattered throughout this 25-acre garden, there is something to inspire around every corner at Trengwainton Garden. Champion magnolias and vibrant rhododendrons make way for lush banana plants and soaring echiums. Unusually, the restored walled kitchen garden was built to the dimensions of Noah's Ark and showcases contemporary varieties of fruit and vegetables. A colourfully bordered stream leads up to a shady pond and a sunny terrace, with stunning views across Mount's Bay. Special events take place throughout the year; check the website for details.

▲ Perran Beach

▶ Perranporth

A little way south of Newquay on the north coast, Perranporth is known for its wonderful beach, backed with a mile of sand dunes. What you find in the sand dunes, known as Penhale Sands, depends on where you walk and what time of year you visit: there's a golf course, butterflies, lizards and plenty of rare plants and other insects, orienteering routes, and the odd naturist here and there. Probably not in the winter, though.

The beach itself is well worth the trip – a huge slice of sand with natural arches and rock stacks at the south end and Ligger Point exposed at low tide, 2 miles out. There's enough space for everyone and it's walking distance from the village, making it a great family holiday spot. It's also one of Cornwall's key surf beaches.

One of the loveliest stories about Perranporth surrounds its churches. Because of drifting sands, Perranporth has had three St Piran's churches. They keep getting lost under sand: one, dating from the 7th century and apparently founded by St Piran himself, has been dug up twice in the last 100 years, but was reburied in the 1970s for its own preservation. The second church was abandoned in the 15th century and the latest was built in a village nearby when local architects had learned their lesson.

Ask your parents about Winston Graham and the *Poldark* series: these novels, which were televised in the 1970s, were set here, and the author lived here for a while.

Other notable things about Perranporth include its surf lifesaving club, one of the oldest in the UK, which puts on an extreme triathlon in the autumn; the beach is popular with kite surfers as well as surfers, thanks to its exposed position. In the early morning, you might see dog walkers and horse-riders in the surf; in peak season the beach is closed to dogs 9–5.

HIT THE BEACH

Perranporth Beach, as mentioned, is a glorious family beach with lifeguard cover in season. Watch out, though, for rip tides around Chapel Rock. Combined with Perran and Penhale Sands to the north, it's a popular surf destination, and lessons and surf hire are available. There's also a cafe, the Watering Hole (see right) right on the beach, and at low tide there's a nice walk to Ligger Point along the sands, then back through the dunes as the tide comes in.

PLAY A ROUND

Perranporth Golf Club
perranporthgolfclub.com
Budnic Hill, TR6 0AB
01872 572454 | Open all year
There are three testing par 5 holes on the links course at Perranporth Golf Club (2nd, 5th, 11th). This seaside links course has magnificent views of the north Cornwall coastline, and excellent greens. The drainage of the course, being sand-based, is also exceptional.

EAT AND DRINK

The Watering Hole
the-wateringhole.co.uk
Perranporth Beach,
TR6 0JL | 01872 572888
This pub serves food and drink right in the middle of the beach and has been set in this location for 35 years. It's a popular spot, with lovely views of the sandy beach and plenty of events, gigs and sporting tournaments keeping it busy. It serves breakfast, lunch, evening meals, hog roasts and barbecues, and has the likes of nachos, burgers, salads and pasta on the menu.

▶ Polperro

West of Looe on the south coast, Polperro is another of Cornwall's picturesque fishing villages, with tightly packed fishermen's houses leading to a small harbour. It's an ancient place that has seen action as a fishing village for centuries, and has hosted many a smuggler since the 12th century. The pattern of narrow lanes and alleyways and steep flanking streets is enclosed by a wooded valley and the Rafiel, a boisterous stream, runs alongside it, beneath a Saxon bridge and beside the House on the Props, a historic house with rough wooden supports and a secret staircase to the sea. Polperro is thronging with tourists in the summer, so you need a little imagination to see the village as it was in days gone by, when supplies were brought in by boat from Plymouth just once a week. Today only a dozen or so fishing boats are in operation from the harbour, as tourism has taken over as the main economic activity. There are lots of pretty cafes, pubs and tea gardens where you can have a freshly baked scone and homemade jam while enjoying Polperro's unique atmosphere.

Taking a walk around the harbour is recommended; there's also a great walk from here to Looe, via the shingly Talland Bay, which has a beach hut cafe and a boutique hotel serving slap-up cream teas. A bus can take you back. It's all along the Southwest Coast Path, which in the 18th century was the haunt of the King's men, looking for smugglers.

The village heritage centre can tell you more about this particular time in history, and especially about local man Zephaniah Job, a merchant known as the 'Smuggler's Banker' who helped Polperro men sent to prison and hired London lawyers for them when they were taken to court.

A word of warning: Polperro is a car-free village, because the streets are very narrow. Park in the Crumplehorn car park and walk down the hill to the village. For those who find walking difficult, there's a shuttle service into the village from the car park.

VISIT THE MUSEUM
Polperro Heritage Museum of Smuggling and Fishing
Harbour Studio, The Warren, PL13 2RB | 01503 272423
Open Mar–end Sep daily 10–6
This small and characterful museum in the town's former pilchard factory brings the fishing and smuggling past of Polperro back to life with memorabilia dating to the 18th century on display alongside 19th-century photographs and model ships.

ENTERTAIN THE FAMILY
Polperro Model Village
polperromodelvillage.com
Mill Hill, PL13 2RP
01503 272378 | Open Easter–end Sep daily 10.30–6
Polperro's Model Village and Land of Legend has been going for more than 60 years, with a quaint reproduction of the village in miniature plus a show taking in seven stories of ancient Cornwall, myths, legends and smugglers' tales included. Two children are free with two paying adults.

TAKE A BOAT TRIP
The Polperro Boat Men
contact Jackie Ruscoe 01503 272476
Easter–end Oct daily from 10am,
weather permitting

Various boat trips operate out of the harbour on a daily basis with fishing trips, half-hour coastal trips and trips to Looe or Fowey on offer. It's a great way to see the coastline and the native wildlife, and is useful if you're keen to walk the delightful coast path route to/from Looe one way.

EAT AND DRINK
The Blue Peter
thebluepeter.co.uk
Quay Road, PL13 2QZ
01503 272743

A tiny, unspoiled fishing pub built into the cliffside facing Polperro's harbour, this cosy wood-floored bar oozes character, with flickering candles and walls chock-full of fishing paraphernalia. Simple, hearty bar food, tip-top Cornish ales and ciders, and sea views complete the picture.

The Old Mill House Inn
www.oldmillhouseinn.co.uk
Mill Hill, PL13 2RP
01503 272362

In the heart of historic Polperro, this old inn was once the house and storage area of a 17th-century grain mill. Sample well-kept local ales and cider beside a log fire in the bar, or sit out over lunch in the riverside garden during fine weather. A beer festival is held on the first weekend in October.

The Plantation
The Coombes, PL13 2RG
01503 272223

On the banks of the River Pol, this is a traditional Victorian tea room with wooden beams, a fireplace and a cosy atmosphere. Friendly service delivers homemade cakes, excellent Cornish cream teas and hearty lunchtime meals. There's also a leafy terrace outside.

▶ Polzeath

World renowned as a surfing destination, Polzeath is 6 miles north of Wadebridge and has a sandy beach exposed at low tide only. There is wetsuit and board hire on the beach, but beware if you're a beginner; this may not be the place for you, as it has a few rips and can have heavy waves.

The main street of Polzeath runs along the shore and includes beach shops, ice cream parlours and cafes, largely catering for holidaymakers. There are also a lot of caravan parks and campsites nearby.

There are some lovely walks to take from Polzeath and around the beach. Start by taking the coast path west to Greenaway Beach, a family spot with rock pools, and on to

Daymer Bay, a calm beach good for swimming. The route leads on to the 12th-century St Enodoc Church, which was almost buried by sand for centuries. Another lovely walk to take is from Polzeath around Brea Hill to Rock, where you can catch a ferry across the Camel Estuary to Padstow. Puffins nest in the cliffs nearby in the summer months.

Sir John Betjeman loved Polzeath and wrote many verses about it. He's buried nearby at St Enodoc Church.

SEE A LOCAL CHURCH
St Enodoc Church
Trebetherick, nr Polzeath,
PL27 6LD
This church is in the sand dunes east of Daymer Bay and in the 16th century was nicknamed 'Sinking Neddy' or 'Sinkiniddy' because it looked as if it was sinking in the sand. As the wind blows on shore, sand banks up around it. At one time, it was buried almost completely in sand and the vicar and parishioners had to enter via a hole in the roof; today it's accessible as normal through a door, but is surrounded by sand banks. Elements of the church date from the 12th century; former Poet Laureate John Betjeman wrote about the church in his poems and you'll find him buried in the churchyard.

HIT THE BEACH
Polzeath is a busy family beach and a legend in the surfing community. Lifeguards are on hand in the summer season and there are beach facilities nearby. Note that at high tide, there's not much sand to speak of. Dolphins have been seen offshore.

GO SURFING
Surf's Up
surfsupsurfschool.com
21 Trenant Close,
PL27 6SW | 01208 862003
This renowned surf school has turned out a few local champs in its time, and runs courses for beginners, intermediates and experienced surfers in the area, with taster lessons for those as young as 7. Weekend intensive courses involve three 2.5-hour sessions over 2 days and are great value.

▶ Port Isaac
Lovely Port Isaac on the north coast between Padstow and Tintagel is a popular fishing village and former pilchard-fishing port with a great fish market, characterful restaurants and pubs, and short coast path walks. Park on the outskirts of town and walk in around the headland for beautiful views and perhaps the odd dolphin.

Best known in recent times for being the location of Port Wenn in the popular *Doc Martin* television series, visitors tend to walk through the town and stop for a photo at the white house that is used as the doctor's house in the show, before wandering back down to the narrow streets to cafes serving cream teas, restaurants with fresh, fish and souvenir shops.

Whitewashed cottages crowd the narrow streets and lanes, one of which is so cramped that it is graphically called Squeezebelly Alley. Rose Hill, a crooked lane festooned with rambling roses, steepens and dwindles to little more than a path as it nears the harbour. Fishing boats, nets and calling gulls lend atmosphere to a port from which Delabole slate, which has been quarried nearby since the early 17th century, was once shipped. Port Isaac was also a thriving fishing port up to the 19th century, when the vast shoals of pilchards made their regular appearances along the Cornish coast. Today, the pilchards are replaced by tourists, both in numbers and in economic value.

The handsome 15th-century parish church to the south at St Endellion is built in the Perpendicular style; it has a beautiful timber roof with modern bosses depicting bishops, and bench ends are carved with heraldic motifs.

A couple of miles to the east you'll find the double ramparts of Tregeare Rounds. This Celtic hill fort was excavated in 1904,

▼ Port Isaac

and pottery from shortly before the Roman period was discovered. The fort has been identified with the Castle Terrible of Thomas Malory's 15th-century epic *Le Morte D'Arthur* – the spot where Uther Pendragon besieged the Duke of Cornwall. With Tintagel Castle just up the coast, it's a legend that seems to make sense.

EAT AND DRINK

The Slipway

portisaachotel.com
Harbour Front, Port Isaac,
PL29 3RH | 01208 880264

With a reputation for seriously good fresh fish and seafood, this 16th-century, one-time ship's chandlery could hardly be closer to Port Isaac's tiny harbour. Cornish Orchards cider, and real ales from Tintagel and Sharp's breweries are on hand pump in the bar. On summer evenings the covered terrace overlooking the harbour is a good place to dine and enjoy music from the local bands.

▶ PLACES NEARBY

Not far from Port Isaac in the pretty village of St Endellion there's a Victorian garden and a tea room to visit.

Long Cross Victorian Gardens

longcrosshotel.co.uk
Trelights, near Port Isaac,
PL29 3TF | 01208 880243

In the grounds of the Long Cross Hotel and Restaurant, these Victorian gardens are the only public gardens on the north coast and include windblown, lichen-clad sculptures of cherubs, a round tower, mazes and a lake. There's a plant shop too. The grounds here are deeply affected by the salty sea air and apparently receive a hundredweight – 8 stone – of salt per acre every year.

Port Quin

Between Port Isaac and Polzeath, Port Quin is a small hamlet and peaceful cove where you can see sensational sunsets. The National Trust owns a couple of fishermen's cottages now turned into holiday homes in the village, which never really prospered, some say because a fishing disaster took the local men, others because the mines and pilchard harvest failed.

Trevathan Farm Tea Room

St Endellion, near Port Isaac,
PL29 3TT | 01208 880164

This charming tea room has stunning views, serves superb teas and is also a quality farm shop, all on the edge of St Endellion village. Part of a working farm that has been farmed by the same family since 1850, it serves a famous Cornish cream tea and has a shop stocked with the farm's own fresh meat, jams and chutneys. There is also a children's play area and pets' corner.

▶ Porthcurno

The paradise beach at Porthcurno is for many the main reason to visit: white sand underfoot created from seashells, plus towering cliffs and crystal-clear sea make it a special place to be. But there's more to Porthcurno than that: this beautiful spot 3 miles from Land's End was at the centre of telegraph technology during World War I, at one time with undersea telegraph cables connecting it with the rest of the world. The Cable and Wireless Company ran a training college in the Porthcurno Valley, and tunnels and chambers were built in the cliffs to protect the technology from harm in 1941, during World War II. Today a visit to the Telegraph Museum tells you more, and gives access to those hidden caves.

The visitor to Porthcurno is really spoiled for choice. The main beach is marvellously persuasive for wriggling the toes; but to either side lie lovely coastal walks. Eastward is the famous Logan Rock, a vast monolith that once rocked at the touch of a finger but is less responsive now, and westward you'll find the Minack Theatre, Porthchapel Beach and the little Church of St Levan. St Levan can also be reached along the narrow road that climbs steeply uphill from Porthcurno. There is a car park by the church. All around Porthcurno Bay you will find sheltered coves, such as Penberth, and exquisite tidal beaches, and the eastern side is flanked by the magnificent headland of Treryn Dinas.

VISIT THE MUSEUM
Porthcurno
Telegraph Museum
porthcurno.org.uk
Eastern House,
TR19 6JX | 01736 810966
Reopening summer 2014
This remarkable museum is all about the history of Porthcurno Valley, which was at the centre of international cable communications from 1870–1970 and was a training college until 1992. Cornish miners dug tunnels to house the entire telegraph operations during World War II and they can be visited here today. New facilities including a cafe and new exhibitions were being developed at time of writing prior to a reopening in summer 2014. Check the website for events.

GO TO THE THEATRE
Minack Theatre
See highlight panel opposite

HIT THE BEACH
Porthcurno Beach is beautiful, popular and safe for bathing, with a river running through it popular with paddling toddlers. There is a lifeguard presence in the summer, when dogs aren't welcome. Some of the beaches nearby are only visible at low tide and have rips, so take care.

▶ Minack Theatre

minack.com
TR19 6JU | 01736 810181

Cornwall's famous open-air theatre, devised in the 1920s by
visionary Rowena Cade and built in the 1930s, is unmissable.
Surrounded by sub-tropical gardens, it's a vision itself, open on one
side to the sea. You can clearly see why Ms Cade decided on this
location for a theatre to show *The Tempest*, with raging seas as a
natural backdrop. Visit in the daytime to find out more about her
and her vision, and for children's shows; book well in advance for
an evening show, which could be anything from Shakespeare to the
Proms, opera or family shows. It's a really wonderful experience.

▶ **PLACES NEARBY**

Along the coast from Porthcurno you'll find the cliffs and beach of Porthgwarra, a secluded cove safe for swimming.

Porthgwarra

Porthgwarra lies to the southwest of Porthcurno and is sheltered from the Atlantic winds by high ground leading to the magnificent granite cliff Chair Ladder at Gwennap Head. It is the most southerly extent of the Land's End Peninsula. Tunnels were carved through softer rock to allow access to the beach by donkey and trap in the days when neighbouring farmers collected seaweed to fertilise their fields, and they are the fabulous atmospheric access route to the beach today. The clifftop walks to the west are magnificent, and the area is noted for rare species of birds that often make landfall here during spring and autumn migrations.

The Logan Rock Inn

theloganrock.co.uk
Treen, St Leven, near Penzance, TR19 6LG | 01736 810495
Named after the 80-tonne rock that balances on the cliffs nearby, this traditional pub is just as popular in the winter months for its roaring fire as it is as a pre-theatre spot for those visiting the Minack Theatre in summer. With traditional Cornish ales, seafood dishes and a pub garden, it's an inviting place. Families will enjoy the two gardens, family room and children's menu. The nearby Pedn Vounder beach is popular with naturists.

Visitors should note that this is one of two Treens in Cornwall; the other is near Zennor.

▶ Portreath

This small north coast resort with a sheltered harbour is 5 miles north of Redruth and along the coast from Porthtowan. Looking at it today, it's hard to imagine that the narrow harbour was once a key export port for the area's copper – you can barely believe that a large ship would navigate such a tight space. Today, just a few fishing boats come in and out, and the main attraction is the wide, sandy, family-friendly beach. Bodyboarders flock here when there's a big swell to ride the Vortex around the harbour wall.

Portreath is the start of the Mineral Tramways Trail, a cycling and walking route along the old tram roads used to transport ore from the mines, and there are some lovely walks along the cliffs, including a 5-mile walk to Basset's Cove along slate and sandstone cliffs topped with wildflowers and seabirds.

HIT THE BEACH

Portreath has a popular north-facing beach with lifeguards in season. Like many of the beaches along the north coast, it's a surf beach and also attracts bodyboarders. There's a large car park nearby and plenty of shops, cafes, ice cream stands and surf hire shops.

CYCLE THE MINERAL TRAMWAYS TRAIL

Mineral Tramways Coast-to-Coast route
sustrans.org.uk

Elm Farm Cycle Hire
cornwallcycletrails.co.uk
Cambrose, TR16 5UF
01209 891498

This coast-to-coast route uses the old tram roads once used by miners and runs from Portreath on the Atlantic coast to Devoran on the south coast. Along the way you can see a number of important mine buildings, all linked by trails along the original tram and railway routes. It was specifically created with walkers, cyclists and horse-riders in mind and there are refreshment stops along the way. Hire bikes from Elm Farm Cycle Centre in nearby Cambrose, who have tandems, bikes for all ages, and bike seats, trailers and tagalongs for children.

▸ The Devoran to Portreath Mineral Tramway

EAT AND DRINK

The Basset Arms
bassetarms.com
Tregea Terrace, TR16 4NG
01209 842077

Built as a pub to serve harbour workers, at one time this early 19th-century Cornish stone cottage served as a mortuary for ill-fated seafarers, so there are plenty of ghost stories! Tin-mining and shipwreck paraphernalia adorn the low-beamed interior of the bar where you can wash down a meal with a pint of Skinner's real ale.

Portreath Bakery
portreathbakery.co.uk
Local specialities and a huge range of pasties, savoury and sweet.

▶ Probus

The village of Probus, northeast of Truro, has the tallest church tower in Cornwall. It is more than 123-ft high and is lavishly decorated. The village also has several interesting gardens: Probus Gardens has a varied display of flowers, shrubs, vegetables and fruit, and a short distance along the A390, the 18th-century Trewithen House has extensive gardens open to the public. Tregothnan tea estate (see page 267) is also nearby.

GO ROUND THE GARDENS

Trewithen Gardens

trewithengardens.co.uk
Grampound Road, Truro,
TR2 4DD | 01726 883647
Open Mar–May daily 10–4.30,
Jun–end Sep Mon–Sat 10–4.30

This historic, privately owned estate has beautiful gardens renowned for their plant-hunter origins, red squirrels and a fantastic house dating from 1715 that is open for guided tours and still home to the same family, some 300 years on. The horticultural vision has stood the test of time: woodland paths are bordered by mature trees, rare blooms and incredible colours, with bird hides hidden among them. *Trewithen* is the Cornish for 'house in the spinney'.

George Johnstone inherited the property in 1904 and devoted the rest of his life to creating and maintaining the 28-acre garden, which occupies a level site 250ft above sea level. A great hybridist, he played an important part in the development of the popular *Camellia x williamsii* 'Donation', but his first love was magnolias, and the Royal Horticultural Society published his magisterial work, *Asiatic Magnolias in Cultivation*, in 1955. Many of Johnstone's plants are still to be seen today at Trewithen, and this wonderful garden is now owned by his grandson, Michael Galsworthy.

It is ironic that the Glade, perhaps the most admired part of Trewithen, came about as a result of a government order during World War I to fell 300 trees.

The lawn stretches for more than 200 yards to the south of the house, but the first part of this magnificent amphitheatre is dominated by one of the garden's great trees. Magnolia and camellia are the key species, all of which have an interesting horticultural history. Shrubs, including viburnums, azaleas, potentillas, euonymus and berberis, edge the lawn in front of the house.

The walled garden, which houses many tender plants, surrounds a pool, while a wisteria-draped pergola adds colour to this formal area. Recently planted beds of birch and sorbus, mahonia, dogwoods and roses, heathers and conifers help to make Trewithen not only a garden with an outstanding plant collection, but a place of ever-changing variety and colour.

Visitors to the house should book in advance via the website. The interior hasn't changed significantly since the 18th century, and the Great Saloon or dining room has ionic columns, views of the south lawn and rococo plasterwork. The tea shop serves traditional Cornish cream teas and there is also a plant centre.

EAT AND DRINK
Probus Lamplighter Restaurant
lamplighter-probus.co.uk
Fore Street, TR2 4JL
01726 882453

Chef-patron Robert Vogel used to be head chef on the *QE2*. His family-run restaurant is in a 300-year-old former farmhouse with bags of period features (oak beams, roaring log fires), plus a charming country vibe. The food is unpretentious, seasonal stuff, with top West Country produce put to good use in satisfying modern British dishes.

▶ Rame Head

This headland to the east of Whitsand Bay near the Devon border on the south coast is well known to sailors leaving Plymouth as the last point of land they see on departure. It's a dramatic promontory, with the well preserved remains of an Iron Age fort on the top of it along with heathland grazed by Dartmoor ponies. Until modern times it was considered part of Devon; these days it's better known as the forgotten corner of Cornwall.

Rame Head has been important through history: a medieval chapel and hermitage once stood here and a small 11th-century building survives, its roof mottled with moss and lichen and its walls rough with age. A warning beacon was once maintained on Rame Head as an aid to navigation, but tradition speaks of its more likely use by smugglers.

From Rame Head, the great crescent of Whitsand Bay curves to the west; see page 117, and also Kingsand and Cawsand, two atmospheric villages nearby, page 113. Above Whitsand Bay, in a crook of the coast road, is Tregantle Fort, the most westerly of the line of defences that march from Fort Bovisand on the Devon shore of Plymouth Sound through a series of surviving bulwarks. They were built in the 1860s in response to fears of French invasion.

▶ Redruth

Copper and tin mining created Redruth, and then abandoned it. It's one of Cornwall's poorest areas today, a town that gets missed off the map when it comes to talking about tourism, and one that never makes the posters advertising sun, sand, sea and surf. Many people forget that for all its holiday spirit, Cornwall experiences some of the worst poverty in the UK. Nevertheless, from the early 18th century until the middle of the 19th, Redruth was the true capital of Cornish mining. Redruth, with the mining country that surrounds it, is now recognised for the importance of its industrial archaeology, and has been designated a World Heritage Site.

In the early days, the extraction method was tin streaming, whereby tinners sifted through river sand and gravel for fragments of ore. The process caused disturbance, which released a red stain into rivers and streams, and it was this that gave the town its name, although in an odd reversal from what you would expect: 'red' coming from *rhyd* for ford, and *ruth* meaning red.

The town contains some interesting buildings, including Georgian, Victorian neo-Gothic and art deco architecture. There is a great deal of brickwork and some startling features, such as the Italianate clock tower on the corner of Fore Street and Alma Place. Leading off Fore Street is Cross Street, where there is a house with an external staircase which was once the home of William Murdock, a Scottish engineer and inventor who worked in Redruth during the late 18th century. Among his many achievements, Murdock developed a lighting system using coal gas, and his home in Redruth was the first house in the world to be lit in this way, in 1872.

East Pool Mine (see page 80) and the remains of the Wheal Coates mine (see page 227) can be seen nearby, as can Tehidy and Tuckingmill Parks (see page 80 and page 81). Stithians Lake (see page 101) is a watersports and course fishing lake.

5 born in Cornwall

▶ Mick Fleetwood – Redruth

▶ Kristen Scott Thomas – Redruth

▶ John Nettles – St Austell

▶ Rosamunde Pilcher – Lelant

▶ Rory McGrath – Redruth

GO ROUND THE GARDENS
Tregullow
Scorrier, TR16 5AY
01209 820775 | Open 6 May 12–5; groups by appointment
This beautiful 15-acre private garden is best seen in the spring when bluebells create a colourful carpet under the trees. The current

owners are replanting and clearing the estate, revealing two large walled gardens and a yew walk as they go. Cream teas are also on offer.

▶ Rock

Known variously for being the site of Sloaney teenage parties following GCSE and A-Level results and the holiday spot of choice of Prime Minister David Cameron, Rock is popularly known as 'Kensington-on-Sea' and is very upmarket. Just across the Camel Estuary, a key oyster and mussel farm, from Padstow (see page 189), it's a little village with delis, boutiques, a watersports centre and pubs. Access is best on the Black Tor Ferry from Padstow and there's also a water taxi available. Nathan Outlaw's Michelin-starred restaurant is at the St Enodoc Hotel and is incredibly popular. Look out for celebrities arriving by helicopter. The beach is lovely, great for swimming and very calm. There is no surf in Rock.

LEARN TO WATERSKI
Camel Ski School
camelskischool.com
The Pontoon, PL27 6LD
01208 862727
Waterskiing and wakeboarding lessons are on offer at this watersports school, which suffered a major fire in summer 2013. They also have stand-up paddleboarding lessons, inflatable bananas, and kite-surfing lessons and equipment. Rock's beach is sheltered and traditional surfing isn't usually possible here as the waves aren't big enough.

PLAY A ROUND
St Enodoc Golf Club, Rock
st-enodoc.co.uk
Wadebridge, PL27 6LD
01208 863216 | Open all year
The classic links course at St Enodoc Golf Club with huge sand hills and rolling fairways is ranked in *Golf World's* top 15 courses in England. On the Church course, the 10th is the toughest par 4 on the course, and on the 6th is a truly enormous sand hill known as the Himalayas. The Holywell course is not as exacting as the Church; it is less demanding on stamina but still a real test of skill for golfers of any handicap.

EAT AND DRINK
Restaurant Nathan Outlaw and Outlaw's ⑳⑳⑳
nathan-outlaw.co.uk
St Enodoc Hotel, Rock, Wadebridge, PL27 6LA
01208 863394
Nathan Outlaw's 2 Michelin-starred Restaurant Nathan Outlaw, and his less formal bistro Outlaw's are both to be

found in the St Enodoc Hotel in Rock. Both have fish as the key ingredient: Restaurant Nathan Outlaw offers a single seafood tasting menu to its diners, while Outlaw's is an à la carte restaurant with outdoor seating, Champagne lunches and an all-day menu. Both are dazzling, and represent the finest take on contemporary and local Cornish food.

▶ Roseland Peninsula

This beautiful peninsula jutting out into the sea east of Falmouth seems quietly detached from mainstream Cornwall. It can feel like another country, particularly when you're trying to drive somewhere quickly. There's much local discussion about where the Roseland begins and ends; it's certainly bordered to the west by the Fal River, with Mylor and Feock opposite, and is most famous for St Mawes, St Mawes Church and the Church of St Just-in-Roseland. The very tip of the Roseland Peninsula is pierced by the twisting Percuil River that cuts deeply inland to create even smaller peninsulas.

Driving advice is necessary: instead of taking the A3078 on to the peninsula, consider taking the faster A39 south of Truro, then the B3289 past Trelissick Gardens (see page 264) and cross the Fal by the King Harry Ferry. There's also a neat passenger ferry from Falmouth to St Mawes which gives you the best of the views without any parking headaches.

St Just-in-Roseland is an exquisite place. The church stands on the banks of a small creek, its mellow stonework embedded in a garden of shrubs and graceful trees that include palms as well as indigenous broad-leaved species.

On the promontory of land between Carrick Roads and the Percuil River, St Mawes (see page 243) is deservedly popular and besieged by moored yachts in summer. On Castle Point to the west stands Henry VIII's St Mawes Castle, a quiet triumph of good Tudor design over function and renowned for its symmetry and decoration. The outer arm of the Roseland Peninsula terminates at St Anthony Head, one of the properties on the peninsula cared for by the National Trust, where you'll find a lighthouse and a gun battery with an interesting history. On the east coast, further north, is Portscatho, open to the sea and with excellent sandy beaches nearby. Nare Head (see page 175) is to the west.

VISIT SOME LOCAL VILLAGES
Porthscatho
This small, working fishing village has a sandy and pebbly beach and a special beach restaurant on a nearby cove that runs feast nights (see below). It's better for rock

pooling than swimming and there's no lifeguard cover. Parking is in the village a short walk away, where you'll also find shops, pubs and cafes. A better bet for swimming is to wait until low tide and walk across to Porthcurnick Beach.

St Just-in-Roseland

This pretty village is known for its 13th-century church overlooking the St Just Creek and is surrounded by semi-tropical shrubs and plants. The path from the road to the church is carved with verses from the Bible. The church was recently restored. Next to the church is Pascoe's Boatyard, which has been in operation since the 18th century.

GET OUTDOORS
St Anthony Head
nationaltrust.org.uk

At the southernmost tip of the Roseland Peninsula, this promontory guards the entrance to the Fal estuary with a white 19th-century lighthouse guiding the passage of ocean liners and fishing boats. It's a lovely area for walking, with wildflowers and seabirds, and the peninsula ends with two sandy beaches, Great Molunan and Little Molunan, and grey seals on the rocks. There's a car park by St Anthony Battery, where the former officers' quarters are now holiday homes, and much of the gun battery, which was in operation from the early 19th century to

the late 1950s, is underground. It's open one day a year; consult the National Trust website for details.

EAT AND DRINK
The Hidden Hut
hiddenhut.co.uk
Porthcurnick Beach, Portscatho, Truro TR2 5EW

The Hidden Hut is a small outdoor beach cafe serving fresh local food around half a mile down the coast path from Portscatho. This is the best way to eat out in Cornwall – never mind white tablecloths and fancy awards, this is rustic eating at its best, with a crowd of locals and visitors alike enjoying the same dishes, warming soup in the autumn and spring, cakes and pasties in summer. Sign up to the mailing list to hear about their pop-up feast nights.

Roseland Inn
roselandinn.co.uk
Philleigh, TR2 5NB
01872 580254

A lovely, peaceful setting near the village church, a rose-clad frontage and an unspoiled bar with a homely atmosphere combine with good cooking to make this 17th-century pub a real find. Dine on local farm meats and fish landed at St Mawes in the low-ceilinged bar, with its slate floors, cushioned settles and winter log fires. The stable door leads to a suntrap terrace.

▶ St Agnes (village)

This large village on the surf coast west of Newquay has beaches, independent shops and a legend about a carnivorous giant. The town and area around it have been mined since prehistoric times – Stone Age remains near New Downs and Polberro date from 4000 BC – but today it's known as a great surf spot and family holiday destination. The ruined mining buildings along the cliff tops add a sense of drama; but let's get back to the giant.

Legend has it that a giant called Bolster lived in the cliffs near St Agnes and feasted on children and adults according to his whim. It was said that he was so large he could stand with one foot on St Agnes Beacon and the other on Carn Brea, 6 miles away. He fell in love with a young girl called Agnes, and to spare her, knights and locals gathered on Chapel Porth Beach, challenging him to a fight to the death. Young Agnes herself outwitted the giant by setting him a challenge to fill a hole on Chapel Porth Beach with his blood as proof of his love. This hole, Agnes knew, had a crack in it and could never be filled. The giant bled to death on the beach in front of her.

This story is retold with giant puppets and music on May Day in Chapel Porth each year for the Bolster Festival. It's one of a few festivals that take place here and demonstrate St Agnes' unique community spirit and sense of fun. It's a great place to visit. In September, the World Bellyboard Championships celebrate a simpler age of surfing, where no wetsuits, leashes or fins are allowed and contestants turn up with plain wooden boards and swimming costumes, and retro bathing caps for fun too. It's an enjoyable event, very inclusive, and pokes fun at the more serious surf industry up the coast at Newquay.

In the village itself, there's a small local museum with MP3-guided walks around the village and independent shops, pubs and cafes.

St Agnes has four beaches: Trevaunance Cove, Trevellas Porth, Chapel Porth and Porthtowan, which is known in particular for its surf. With significant mining heritage dotted around the cliffs nearby, cliff walks are particularly interesting. Between St Agnes Head and Porthtowan you'll find one of Cornwall's last surviving ancient heathlands, with heather and spiders that somehow survived despite the soil contamination caused by the mines. Keeping things pollution free is still a big concern here; the environmental charity Surfers Against Sewage was formed in 1990 to improve the water quality of the beach here, along with that of Chapel Porth and Trevaunance

Beaches, at a time when surfers were falling ill because of sewage in the water. Today the water quality is good and is monitored closely.

To the west lies St Agnes Beacon, reached by following Beacon Drive to a National Trust parking area on its north side. A good path leads easily to the summit and to spectacular views along the coast to north and south. The heathland around here is significant, says the National Trust, and represents some of the last remaining ancient heathland in Cornwall, with rare plants and butterflies.

Just to the north of Chapel Porth, reached along the coast path, are the impressive remains of the Towanroath Engine House, restored by the National Trust. Dating from 1872, it housed the massive steam engine used to pump water from the nearby Wheal Coates mine. Some of the industrial buildings around St Agnes have been converted into residential units.

VISIT THE MUSEUM
St Agnes Museum
stagnesmuseum.org.uk
Penwinnick Road,
TR5 0PA | 01872 553228
Open Easter–end Oct daily 10.30–5
This award-winning local history museum covers all aspects of life in St Agnes, from the mines to the sea, with exhibitions on 19th-century mining and painter John Opie, and a large, mounted leatherback turtle. There is a treasure hunt for children and a shop selling local crafts. It also offers an MP3 audio guide pre-programmed with a commentary taking you around St Agnes.

HIT THE BEACH
St Agnes has four beaches: Porthtowan, which is a fine family and surf beach; Chapel Porth, where revellers gather for the Bolster Festival in May; Trevaunance Cove, for surf and rock pools; and Trevellas Porth, a small pebbly cove.

Chapel Porth
This cove near St Agnes, with a dramatic entry point, has a long stretch of sand, reduced greatly at high tide, and is looked after by the National Trust. It has a welcoming cafe and is popular with surfers. Lifeguards are on the beach mid-May–end Sep. No dogs Easter–end Sep. The National Trust car park is on the beach; beware the incoming tide which can be swift.

Porthtowan Beach
Porthtowan Beach is large, busy and beloved of surfers. There's a bar across the road from the beach, and wetsuit and board hire available; lifeguards watch over the beach in high season. There's a car park nearby and at low tide it's possible to walk to Chapel Porth Beach, otherwise

accessible by the coast path. It's a Blue Flag beach.

Trevaunance Cove

Chapel Porth is not the only beach in St Agnes to hold events – this beach holds an Easter dog race (St Agnes is that kind of place) and an RNLI day in August. It's a decent surf beach, with limited sand and mostly pebbles, and is also good for rock pooling. There's lifeguard cover and dogs are allowed all year; have a beer at Driftwood Spars (see right) when the sun is going down to experience it like the locals.

Trevellas Porth

This quieter pebbly cove is popular with snorkellers and local fishermen. It's the only one of St Agnes' beaches to have no lifeguard, and has rock pools to explore at low tide. There are no facilities at the beach. When the tide is out, you can walk to Trevaunance Cove.

EAT AND DRINK

Driftwood Spars
driftwoodspars.co.uk
Trevaunance Cove,
TR5 0RT | 01872 552428
Complete with its own smugglers' tunnel, this family-run pub occupies a 300-year-old tin miners' store, chandlery and sail loft adjacent to the Southwest Coast Path in the stunning Trevaunance Cove. It's a multifaceted

▲ Trevellas Porth

offering today: a pub with rooms, a dining room, two beer gardens, three bars, a microbrewery and a shop. The Sunday roast comes highly recommended.

**Rose-in-Vale
Country House Hotel** ◉
rose-in-vale-hotel.co.uk
Mithian, TR5 0QD
01872 562202
This creeper-clad, stone-built Georgian country house hides in its own little valley, amid highly attractive gardens. The Valley, its

chandeliered dining room, showcases contemporary country-house cooking. Attention to detail extends to canapés and amuse-bouches, and Sundays see a carvery operation spring into action.

The Unicorn
theunicornporthtowan.co.uk
Beach Road, Porthtowan, TR4 8AD
01209 890244
This pub is beside the beach and serves family-pleasing meals such as pizzas, burgers, baked camembert and brunch. Along with food and drink, it also has a small 16-seater cinema screening room and shows free children's films at 5pm during the week and 2pm at the weekend, plus feature films at 8pm. In the evening, it regularly hosts live music, and open-mic and quiz nights.

▶ **PLACES NEARBY**
Wheal Coates mine
nationaltrust.org.uk
Chapel Porth
North of Chapel Porth in the heart of old mining country,

standing on a lonely stretch of coastline, is the engine house of the Wheal Coates mine. It is one of many such distinctive buildings, which are a feature of the Cornish countryside, and once housed the engine that provided the essential services of winding, pumping and ventilation for the mine. Wheal Coates is an important relic of the county's industrial past, and has been restored by the National Trust, which cares for much of this historic coast. The coast path to the south leads to Porthtowan.

Cornish Cyder Farm

thecornishcyderfarm.co.uk
Penhallow, Truro, TR4 9LW
01872 573356

Healey's has been making cider for more than 25 years and offers free tours of its farm. This includes a look around the press house, bottlery and jam kitchen and a little tasting. Children are entertained with a quiz as they look round, and orchard walks can be accompanied with a member of the team for an insider's take on how it's all made.

▶ **St Agnes (island)**
see **Isles of Scilly**, page 248

▼ Towanroath Engine House, Wheal Coates mine

▲ St Austell clay works

▶ St Austell

The St Austell Bay area, which includes Fowey, Mevagissey and the Eden Project, is an area worth exploring for sure. But St Austell itself? Well, it's not as pretty as any of the fishing villages nearby, surrounded by industrial sprawl and modern buildings. When you're elsewhere in Cornwall, do look out for St Austell ales – the town's brewery produces some of the county's most distinctive drinks, from Tribute to Smugglers, Admiral's Ale and Proper Job.

The white peaks of Cornwall's 'alps' dominate the landscape around St Austell: great spoil heaps from the area's successful china clay quarrying industry. Even when it was a mere village, St Austell was the centre of good farming country, open-cast tin extraction and stone quarrying. To the north is Cornwall's most startling industrial landscape, from which clay has been extracted on a massive scale. The clay was once used for making porcelain but is now used mainly in paper-making. About 3 million tonnes are produced in the St Austell area annually. Much waste is generated and the great, snowy tips have created a strangely compelling landscape that now hosts the Eden Project and its biomes. The Wheal Martyn Museum and Country Park in Carthew to the north of St Austell on the B3274 includes a museum all about china clay, with examples of how it's used in our daily lives today.

The modern centre of St Austell itself has mainly modern buildings, with a few exceptions. Fore Street and the area around Holy Trinity have been conserved and the Town Hall is in bold Renaissance style, a granite palazzo incorporating a splendid market hall with its interior still intact. The Church of the Holy Trinity has sculpted figures set within niches in the tower, which itself is faced with Pentewan stone from the coastal quarries to the south. The pearly-grey stone has a warmer tinge when wet.

Further north is the village of Roche, with its adjacent Roche Rock. This remarkable outcrop of quartz schorl, an altered form of granite, is unique in Cornwall and a startling feature in the midst of the industrial landscape. The largest outcrop is crowned by the ruins of the chapel of St Michael, built in 1409.

GET INDUSTRIAL

Wheal Martyn Museum and Country Park

wheal-martyn.com
Carthew, PL26 8XG
01726 850362 | Open Apr–Oct 10–5, Nov–Mar 10–4

Set within 26 acres of woodland, Wheal Martyn provides a fascinating day out. The site includes the UK's only china clay museum, set within a complete 19th-century clay works, telling the story of Cornwall's second most important present-day industry. Key features are Cornwall's largest working waterwheel, spectacular views of a wooden working clay pit with machines at work, nature trails, a children's challenge trail, a play area, indoor interactive displays, a cafe and a gift shop.

Clay country circuit

The best way to appreciate the clay country is to drive through it – explore the area north and west of St Austell between the B3279 and the B3274, which takes in Nanpean, Roche, the Roche Rock, and Wheal Martyn Museum and Country Park at Carthew (see above). The vast spoil tips of the St Austell clay country are composed of feldspar and quartz. The raw clay is stripped from the faces of the pits by high-pressure hoses creating flooded pits,

5 Top Local Brews

Ask for these local ales and ciders to show you're in the know:

▶ Betty Stogs (Skinner's)

▶ Cornish Rattler (Healey's)

▶ Black & Gold Pear (Cornish Orchard)

▶ Tribute (St Austell)

▶ Doom Bar (Sharp's)

their translucent green
and blue waters adding to
the odd surrealism of this
'lunar' landscape.

GET OUTSIDE
Footsteps of Discovery
footstepsofdiscovery.co.uk
Survival courses in St Austell.

TOUR THE BREWERY
St Austell Brewery
staustellbrewery.co.uk
63 Trevarthian Road, PL25 4BY
01726 66022 | Visitor centre
open all year Mon–Fri 10–5.30,
Sat 10–4; tours all year Mon–Sat
11–3 by arrangement
If local ales interest you,
St Austell Brewery's Visitor
Centre offers hour-long
tours of the brewery, including
free samples and two half
pints of beer at the end.
The brewery itself dates from
Victorian times and includes
a museum. Children over 8
only (soft drinks are available),
and book in advance as the
tours take limited numbers
of people.

EXPLORE BY BIKE
Pentewan Valley Cycle Hire
pentewanvalleycyclehire.co.uk
1 West End, Pentewan,
PL26 6BX | 01726 844242
There are lots of routes
in the nearby area that are
suited to two wheels.
The Pentewan Valley is one
place to explore, around
St Austell, and you can also
reach Heligan, Mevagissey
and Charlestown easily.
One thing to note: if you cycle

to the Lost Gardens of Heligan
or the Eden Project, you'll get
a reduction on your entry fee.
Pentewan Valley Cycle Hire in
the nearby village of Pentewan
hires bikes, trailers, tagalongs
and more by the half day,
day or week.

PLAY A ROUND
St Austell Golf Club
staustellgolf.co.uk
Tregongeeves Lane,
PL26 7DS | 01726 74756
Open all year
St Austell's challenging
inland parkland course was
designed by James Braid
and offers glorious views
of the surrounding countryside.
It is undulating, well covered
with tree plantations and well
bunkered. Notable holes
are the 8th (par 4) and 16th
(par 3).

EAT AND DRINK
Austell's ⊚⊚
austells.co.uk
10 Beach Road,
PL25 3PH | 01726 813888
In a small parade of shops on
the road to Carlyon Bay,
Austell's is a restaurant of
cool, uncluttered elegance,
with a wooden floor, artwork
on plain walls and slat-backed
chairs at wooden tables.
Seasonality means the
menus change regularly, and
everything is made in house,
from breads (among them
maybe rosemary and pesto) to
petits fours. Cooking is
contemporary British.

The Cornwall Hotel, Spa and Estate ◉
thecornwall.com
Pentewan Road, Tregorrick,
PL26 7AB | 01726 874050
The Cornwall has a smart restaurant, Arboretum, and a more informal brasserie, Acorns. Arboretum's menu takes a broadly contemporary path, drawing inspiration from far and wide while making good use of regional ingredients: hoisin duck spring rolls with a sweet chilli dip, followed by pan-seared line-caught sea bass with Thai purée, for example.

▶ St Columb Major

St Columb Major is set on high ground 5 miles east of Newquay and has a few interesting places to visit nearby. In the village itself, there are holiday homes and some interesting architectural touches, including an Italianate Gothic building of red and yellow bricks that now houses a bank. Opposite is the attractive Red Lion Inn, and much of the main square dates from the Regency period. Off the A39 east of the village, there's the Devil's Quoit, the remaining capstone of an ancient burial chamber; the supporting stones were removed in 1870, but it's still an impressive slab.

Families and those who particularly like owls and birds of prey may enjoy the two largest attractions nearby, the Screech Owl Sanctuary and the Cornish Birds of Prey Centre.

MEET THE BIRDLIFE
Cornish Birds of Prey Centre
cornishbirdsofprey.co.uk
Winnards Perch, St Columb,
TR9 6DH | 01637 880544
Open daily Apr–end Oct 10–5
This family-run centre cares for injured, rescued and neglected birds of prey and has a play area, ponies and a waterfowl lake. There are more than 50 birds housed here – from kookaburras to hawks, vultures and owls – and with regular flying session, visitors have a chance to see why they're so special. Falconry experiences are on offer too, and there are also three fishing lakes.

Screech Owl Sanctuary
screechowlsanctuary.co.uk
Goss Moor, St Columb,
TR9 6HP | 01726 860182
Open 22 Mar–2 Nov daily 10–5; check the website for other opening times
This sanctuary does not only look after screech owls: expect to see meerkats, emus, ponies and pygmy goats too. It's a fun mini-zoo/farm for families, with a hand-tame area and falconry displays, a children's play area and a tea room.

▶ St Ives

The English traditional nursery rhyme 'As I was going to St Ives, I met a man with seven wives...' has featured in Hollywood movies, including *Die Hard with a Vengeance*; *Sesame Street*, and multiple magazines and books to date. If you're going to St Ives too, you're not alone: according to Tate St Ives, in summer 2010, 9% of all visitors to Cornwall had the express intention of going to this town. It's a wonderful seaside town with a rare quality of air and light that has drawn painters and artists – the sea in the harbour is a pellucid turquoise colour – and it has a unique character and place in Cornish culture. The only negative thing to mention is the parking – do your best to arrive by train on the St Ives line, or park out of town to make your visit a happy one.

St Ives' unique character springs from its fishing traditions, its artistic inheritance and its tourism industry. They might clash at times, but the combination of the three makes it an ever-lively place to visit. As well as being an archetypal Cornish fishing port, it's also got magnificent sandy beaches, top-rated beach cafes, fab boutiques, ice cream parlours and restaurants, and two of the best art galleries in the county, if not the country.

Tate St Ives is perhaps its most famous landmark. The gallery stands above Porthmeor Beach in a former gasworks building; its curves and crests are as white as the waves below. The Barbara Hepworth Museum and Sculpture Garden is an equally important artistic attraction here, celebrating the work of the much-lauded English sculptor.

St Ives is a delight overall whether you like art or not because of its narrow, canyon-like streets, ubiquitous granite cobbles and clear, sea-mirrored light. The parish church of St Ia is one of the finest in Cornwall. St Ives' harbour area, known locally as Downlong, is a maze of exquisite granite buildings where you catch satisfying glimpses of shady courtyards and passageways.

▼ St Ives viewed from Godrevy Point

And there are always those beaches to escape to: Porthminster to the south is sheltered and calm; Porthmeor to the north is a bit more lively and popular with the surfing crowd. There are several smaller beaches at the harbour and in the lee of the Island, the breezy, green promontory that juts out to sea from a low-lying neck of land.

The price of all this is potential overcrowding at the busiest holiday periods. Avoid dawdling through St Ives by car and be prepared for a lot of pedestrian traffic in the narrow Fore Street and along the busy harbour front. There is a park-and-ride scheme at Trenwith above the town and another at Lelant Station, southeast of the town, which uses a little branch line.

Whatever you're doing in St Ives, it will be a pleasure: eating cake in Tate St Ives' cafe with views of slate rooftops, seagulls and the sea; paddling on the beach, slurping cornets of local ice cream; or walking around the coast. The town's restaurants are diverse and of high quality, with the beach cafe on Porthminster Beach regularly judged as one of the best in the UK.

VISIT THE MUSEUMS AND GALLERIES

Barbara Hepworth Museum and Sculpture Garden

tate.org.uk/stives
Barnoon Hill, TR26 1AD
01736 796226 | Open Mar–Oct daily 10–5.20, Jan–Feb daily 10–4.20, Nov–Dec Tue–Sun 10–4.20

Visiting the museum and garden is a unique experience offering a remarkable insight into the work and outlook of one of Britain's most important 20th-century artists, Dame Barbara Hepworth. This is where she worked, in Trewyn Studio, which, along with her beautiful gardens and home, form the museum. Hepworth, her husband, Modernist-Abstract painter Ben Nicholson, and their young children, moved to St Ives in 1939 at the outbreak of the war. Some of her bronze, stone and wood sculptures are on display in the garden which she used for viewings. Inside are paintings, drawings and her archive. A combined Tate St Ives/Barbara Hepworth Museum ticket saves 20%; there are also discounts for those visiting by public transport.

Ben Nicholson walking tours

Tate St Ives and the Barbara Hepworth Museum also offer a Ben Nicholson walking tour, showing the town through the eyes of the artists' colony he and his wife established. St Ives had a huge influence on his work. The multimedia walking tour is available on an iPod

Touch for those who have already paid entry to either museum, and there's a small extra fee. Ask at the desk. The walking tour is downloadable for free from the website for those who already have an iPod, iPhone or similar device.

Penwith Gallery

Back Road West, TR26 1NL
01736 795579 | Open all year Tue–Sat 10–1, 2.30–5

The Penwith Society of Arts was founded by 19 local leading artists in 1949, and still continues today. This small gallery, also founded in 1949, exhibits the work of its members in regular exhibitions and also shows the works of leading contemporary artists with paintings, sculpture and ceramics.

St Ives Museum

Wheal Dream, TR26 1PR
01736 796005 | Open Easter–end Oct Mon–Fri 10–5, Sat 10–4

In St Ives' old fishing village at Downlong, this museum traces the history of the town in a building that used to house its pilchard-curing cellar and the famous Troika pottery. It's an independent museum maintained by volunteers and including items of mining and fishing history, with tiny models of cats and kittens in the display cases for children to seek out, in a nod to the famous nursery rhyme.

Tate St Ives

See highlight panel opposite

▶ Tate St Ives

tate.org.uk/stives

Porthmeor Beach, TR26 1TG | 01736 796226

Open 16 May–end Oct daily 10–5.20, Nov–end Feb Tue–Sun 10–4.20
(1 Jan 11–5.20); closed 27 Jan–16 May 2014

This world-class contemporary art gallery is on the edge of the town in a beautiful building, with swirling white curves and a view out to sea. As the home of post-war British Modernism, it is the natural place for a gallery of this calibre. Tate St Ives is the only Tate gallery without a permanent collection; instead, the three seasons of exhibitions each year embrace the best of modern and contemporary art. Along with paintings by leading artists of the St Ives School including Patrick Heron – who designed a stained-glass window for the entry hall – Peter Lanyon and Terry Frost, you might find works by Turner, Juergen Teller, Barbara Hepworth and more. There are regular changing exhibitions and twice-daily free tours of the collection.

There's also a Tate shop, stocking the very best art books and a selection of top Cornish crafts and goodies, plus a cafe with a view and a great line in cakes and light bites, worth the visit in itself.

GET OUTDOORS

Godrevy Head

The National Trust property of Godrevy Head is at the eastern end of St Ives Bay and is the first of a sequence of high, rugged cliffs of dark slate that run uninterruptedly to the northeast. Offshore from the headland stands Godrevy Island and its crowning lighthouse. There is ample parking at Godrevy Head on grassy downs that are reached along a winding road. Paths lead across and around the headland; the offshore waters attract inquisitive grey seals. To the south lies Gwithian Beach (see page 109), and inland is the village of Gwithian where there is a handsome church and an attractive pub.

HIT THE BEACH

St Ives has four beaches, Porthminster, Porthmeor, Porthgwidden and Harbour Beaches, and the gorgeous white-sand Carbis Bay beach is just a mile to the east.

Harbour Beach

St Ives' Harbour Beach is backed by shops and ice cream parlours right in the centre of the town and is a great place to eat an ice cream or fish and chips, sitting on or beside the harbour walls. The water is clean and fine for swimming. Watch out for seagulls. No parking nearby; no lifeguards.

Porthminster Beach

The second-largest St Ives beach, Porthminster is sandy, north facing and sheltered with great facilities. It's a Blue Flag beach and has views of the town and Godrevy lighthouse. Along with a famous beach cafe (see below) it also has beach huts and mini-golf, and lifeguards patrol May–end Sep.

Porthmeor Beach

St Ives' largest and most popular beach, Porthmeor is the beach under Tate St Ives parallel to Harbour Beach. Safe for families, it's also popular with surfers and there is a summer surf school on the beach. Lifeguards patrol May–end Sep. It's also a Blue Flag beach, and has a beach cafe and shops nearby. The parking situation is tricky – if you can, park out of town and use park-and-pide as there is rarely a space on the narrow streets nearby.

▼ St Ives harbour

Porthgwidden Beach

By St Ives Island a short walk from town, Porthgwidden is a family-friendly stretch of sand with safe swimming and plenty of sun. You can walk to and around St Ives Island to Porthmeor beach, and there is a cafe and beach huts here too. The car park nearby gets very busy in season. There are no lifeguards.

Carbis Bay

A mile to the east of St Ives, and linked to the town of Lelant (see page 125), Carbis Bay beach is one of the finest in Cornwall. Owned by the Carbis Bay Hotel, it has sub-tropical surroundings and no surf to speak of, making it a prime and popular family spot. It's a gorgeous white-sand beach with views to the lighthouse. Nearby Porthkidney Sands is an RSPB bird sanctuary for its seabirds. Walks on the coast path from here take you to St Ives.

TAKE A BOAT TRIP

St Ives Fast Rib Rides
07786 782352
stivesfastribrides.co.uk

St Ives Boats
stivesboats.co.uk
outside the Lifeboat Station,
Wharf Road, TR26 1LF
07773 008000
Sea cruises, seal-watching trips and fast rib rides are all available from St Ives Harbour. Dolphins and basking sharks are apparently regularly sighted. St Ives Boats runs regular hour-long trips 3 miles west to Seal Island where there is a colony of grey seals.

GO SEA FISHING

St Ives Boats
stivesboats.co.uk
outside the Lifeboat Station,
Wharf Road, TR26 1LF
07773 008000 | Fishing trips depart daily, weather permitting
St Ives Bay sees plenty of mackerel May–end Sep and local fishing charters can take you out to catch them with 1.5- and 2-hour trips teaching you the basics of hand-line fishing. Wreck and reef fishing for other fish species, including cod, haddock and pollock, is also available, as are 4-hour fishing trips.

GO SURFING

St Ives Surf School
stivessurfschool.co.uk
Porthmeor Beach | 01736 793938
Porthmeor is the place to head for surf lessons, where the St Ives Surf School also hires out boards and wetsuits. With group and private lessons on offer, they also offer stand-up paddleboard hire, lessons for calm days and sea kayak guided tours.

EAT AND DRINK

Carbis Bay Hotel ®
carbisbayhotel.co.uk
Carbis Bay, TR26 2NP
01736 795311
Dating from the late 19th century, the family-run Carbis Bay Hotel and spa has stunning views over the eponymous bay

from its lofty position. Its Sands Restaurant serves a traditional menu, including the likes of honey-glazed duck breast, fried cod on parmesan mash and Bailey's crème brûlée.

Garrack Hotel and Restaurant ◉
garrack.com
Burthallan Lane, Higher Ayr, TR26 3AA | 01736 796199
The unstuffy, light and airy restaurant's simple design blends traditional and contemporary elements to allow those stunning vistas pride of place, while menus likewise demonstrate a kitchen making the most of Cornwall's natural resources in creative and ambitious modern dishes. Plenty of seafood on the menu; the sea views are killer.

Moomaid of Zennor
moomaidofzennor.com
Wharf Road, TR26 1LG
01736 799285

5 ice cream parlours

▶ Moomaid of Zennor, St Ives
  see above
▶ Roskilly's Farm, Lizard Peninsula
  page 150
▶ Mr B's Ice Cream, Hayle
  page 112
▶ Helsett Farm, Boscastle
  page 69
▶ Jelberts, Newlyn
  page 206

There are many ice cream parlours in St Ives but it's worth walking past them to find this little gem, serving luxury Cornish ices in traditional flavours such as Clotted Cream and Fudge, right through to Orange and Mascarpone, and Almond and Amarena Cherry. There's a small seating area inside but the best thing is to take a cornet to the beach. Watch out for seagulls – they love the ice cream almost as much as we do.

Porthgwidden Cafe
porthgwiddencafe.co.uk
Porthgwidden Beach, TR26 1PL
01736 796791
This is a relaxed and intimate cafe with a notably Moroccan feel on the quietest beach in St Ives. Call in for smoked salmon and scrambled egg, freshly baked muffins or croissants from 8am. Pick a sunny day and head straight for the terrace for cracking views. Afternoon teas on the terrace are an experience to savour.

Porthminster Beach Restaurant ◉
porthminstercafe.co.uk
Porthminster Beach, TR26 2EB | 01736 795352
This renowned beach cafe requires a reservation much of the time, serving a classic contemporary seafood menu on a prime spot on the beach. Lots of fusion thinking comes courtesy of the Australian chef, and vegetarian dishes

are good too. Sit on the decking on a sunny day. Dishes include baked pollock, crisp salt and pepper squid, and crab linguine with Fowey mussels.

The Queens ◉

queenshotelstives.com
2 High Street, TR26 1RR
01736 796468
This local, welcoming pub is a short stroll from the harbour in a granite-fronted Georgian building, with a pleasing ambience of unclothed tables, sofas and bare floorboards inside. The menu might be short and the dishes might sound straightforward, but there's flair on display in the cooking: it's relaxed and friendly but with real skill too.

The Rum and Crab Shack

rumandcrabshack.com
Wharf Road, TR26 1LG
01736 796353
Just as the name suggests, this quirky little place serves rum and crab, as well as lobster, mackerel pâté, crab soup and tempura squid, all with a view of the sea. It's a rustic-chic, trendy spot with lovely staff and it's good for children too. A great, unusual spot for lunch or tea in St Ives.

Seagrass Restaurant ◉

seagrass-stives.com
Fish Street, TR26 1LT
01736 793763
Seagrass has made quite a splash in St Ives with its

5 smuggler's pubs

▶ The Smugglers' Den Inn, Trebellan, near Newquay
page 188

▶ The Admiral Benbow, Penzance
page 204

▶ The Pandora Inn, Mylor
page 175

▶ Jamaica Inn, Bodmin Moor
page 66

▶ Ye Olde Jolly Sailor Inn, Looe
page 155

modern seafood-oriented cooking. Tucked away just off the seafront, a secretive doorway leads up to the cool, stylish first-floor restaurant, where the focus is firmly on top-class seasonal Cornish produce. Order a fruits de mer platter in advance if that's your thing – it's their speciality.

The Sloop Inn

sloop-inn.co.uk
The Wharf, TR26 1LP
01736 796584
A trip to St Ives wouldn't be complete without visiting this 700-year-old pub perched right on the harbourside. Slate floors, beamed ceilings and nautical artefacts dress some of the several bars and dining areas, while the cobbled forecourt is an unbeatable spot for people- and harbour-watching, preferably with a pint of local Doom Bar.

▶ St Just

St-Just-in-Penwith – not to be confused with St-Just-in-Roseland – is a sturdy Cornish town 8 miles west of Penzance, and the closest town to Land's End. Originally the centre of the tin-mining industry in this area, here you'll find weathered granite buildings, a 15th-century parish church and a market square with pubs, cafes and shops. It is the ideal base from which to explore the mining coast of the Land's End Peninsula.

The elegant headland of Cape Cornwall lies to the west, rugged, shapely and crowned with the chimneystack of a long-defunct mine. On the southern edge of the cape, small fishing boats work from Priest's Cove. From the cove, a stony track leads up to the rocky headland of Carn Gloose. The impressive burial chamber of Ballowall lies about 150 yards inland. The cape, and the coastline to either side, is in the care of the National Trust.

To the north lies the remarkable mining area of Kenidjack and the Nancherrow Valley, a historic mining landscape that is being preserved by the Trust. A mile north of the town along the B3306 is the village of Botallack, and the nearby coastal area is particularly rich in old mine buildings.

SEE A LOCAL CHURCH
St Just Church
High Street, TR19 7EZ
Built of large blocks of worked granite, St Just Church is entered through a handsome battlemented porch. It dates from the 14th to the 16th century. There are many exciting features to be found in the church. The oldest is a memorial stone dating from the 5th or 6th century inscribed 'Silus lies here'. Then there is a Saxon cross shaft re-used as a lintel. The church was restored in 1866, when six wall paintings were discovered. Two remain: one of St George and the Dragon, the other a 'Warning to Sabbath Breakers'. There are two medieval crosses in the churchyard, one depicting a crucifixion.

PLAY A ROUND
Cape Cornwall Golf and Leisure Resort
capecornwall.com
Cape Cornwall, TR19 7NL
01736 788611 | Open all year
The walls are an integral part of its design of this, Britain's first and last 18-hole course overlooking the only cape in England, with views of the north Cornwall coast and old fishing coves. The course features a flat front nine followed by a challenging back nine, and has scenic, wild coastal views.

EAT AND DRINK
The Star Inn
TR19 7LL | 01736 788767
John Wesley is believed to have been among the Star's more illustrious guests over the years, but these days the

pub is most likely to be recognised for having featured in several television and film productions due to its immense charm and character. A choice of local St Austell beers is served, but no food.

The Wellington

wellington-hotel.co.uk
Market Square, TR19 7HD
01736 787319

This family-run inn is an ideal base for exploring the spectacular beaches and countryside nearby. Low ceilings, solid stonework and a secluded walled garden add character. St Austell beers and Cornish Rattler cider are served in the bar, while the menu offers traditional pub grub.

▶ PLACES NEARBY

Close to St Just are the historic church of St Credan, in Sancreed, and Carn Euny, the remains of an Iron Age village.

Carn Euny Ancient Village

english-heritage.org.uk
Near Brane, 2 miles from St Just
0870 333 1181
Open at any reasonable time

Carn Euny is the remains of an Iron Age settlement that was occupied until late Roman times. Surviving features include the foundations of stone huts and an intriguing curved underground passage or 'fogou'. Dogs on leads are welcome.

St Credan's Church

Opposite Glebe Farm,
Sancreed, TR20 8QS

The pretty granite church dates from the 15th century, and still has the base of its rood screen with original paint and pictures of a spotted goat, a jester, a triple-headed king (perhaps representing the Trinity), birds and other beasts. The 15th-century font has shield-bearing angels at the corners. In the churchyard here are two very early full-length crosses, both with crucifixions carved into them. They may date from the 10th century. There are three more crossheads in the churchyard.

▶ St Martin's
see **Isles of Scilly**, page 249

▶ St Mary's
see **Isles of Scilly**, page 250

▶ St Mawes

This pretty seaside town on the Roseland Peninsula has a harbour full of yachts in the summer months, thanks in part to Hotel Tresanton, its upscale boutique hotel, which draws a select and wealthy crowd. The town itself is a pleasant place to visit, with a shoreline road, two shingle and sand beaches and the cloverleaf-shaped St Mawes Castle, built by Henry VIII, at the end of it. It's one of the best-preserved military fortresses that he built and is lavishly decorated. There are plenty of beaches nearby to visit if you want sands or secret coves (see Roseland Peninsula, page 222), and there is a ferry from the town across the Fal River to Falmouth. There is a lovely walk from the castle to St Just-in-Roseland, where there is a pretty church surrounded by sub-tropical gardens; see page 223.

TAKE IN SOME HISTORY
St Mawes Castle
english-heritage.org.uk
Castle Drive, TR2 3AA 01326
270526 | Open Apr–Jun and Sep
Sun–Fri 10–5, Jul–Aug Sun–Fri
10–6, Oct daily 10–4, Nov–Mar
Sat–Sun 10–4
This castle was Henry VIII's most picturesque fort, one of a defensive chain built between 1539 and 1545 to counter an invasion threat from Catholic France and Spain. Although it was designed to mount heavy guns, great care was taken with its design, including carved Latin inscriptions in praise of Henry VIII and his son, Edward VI. It fell to Parliamentarian forces in 1646 with only a single shot being fired, which is one reason why it remains in such good condition.

HIT THE BEACH
The two family beaches in St Mawes, Tavern Beach and Summers Beach, are good for swimming and are on either side of St Mawes harbour. Summers has rock pools to explore at low tide.

GO KAYAKING
St Mawes Kayaks
stmaweskayaks.co.uk
The Quay, TR2 5DG
07971 846786
St Mawes Kayaks rents out 1- and 2–3-person kayaks as a great way to see the Roseland Peninsula from the water. From St Mawes you can explore St Anthony's Head, the lighthouse and nearby seals, with a route taking you to Great and Little Molunan beaches on the way back; there's also an option to explore the Upper Fal with a kayak drop-off point at Turnaware Bar.

▼ St Mawes Castle

▲ St Mawes harbour

TRY SAILING

St Mawes Sailing Club

stmawessailing.co.uk

1 The Quay, TR2 5DG

01326 270696

The St Mawes Sailing Club runs events and offers classes in a variety of craft, from dinghies to yachts and cruisers. Children must be aged 8 and above to take part in classes.

EAT AND DRINK

Hotel Tresanton ◉◉◉

www.tresanton.com

27 Lower Castle Road,

TR2 5DR | 01326 270055

St Mawes' uber-chic boutique hotel is one of Cornwall's A-list weekend retreats. Its restaurant is decked out in nautical style and has a modern Mediterranean-influenced menu, using plenty of local goodies. Cornish duck, John Dory plus Fal River scallops, West Country cheeses and the like are on the menu.

The Victory Inn

www.victory-inn.co.uk

Victory Hill, TR2 5DQ

01326 270324

Named after Nelson's flagship, this friendly fishermen's local near the harbour adopts a modern approach to its daily lunch and dinner menus. Eat downstairs in the traditional bar, or in the modern and stylish first-floor Seaview Restaurant with a terrace that looks across the town's rooftops to the harbour and the Fal River. Booking is advisable in the summer.

▶ St Michael's Mount

see **Marazion**, page 159

▲ St Mary's

▶ Isles Of Scilly

Palm trees, clean and clear water, fine white sands and an even more temperate climate make the Isles of Scilly feel much further than 28 miles away from the UK mainland. They are a soothing holiday spot, reached daily between June and September by helicopter, ferry and plane, with sea views, coastal walks, ancient sights, and superb bird and wildlife watching, on both land and sea.

Known as the Fortunate Islands or the Sunshine Islands, a hundred or so islands and islets make up the archipelago. Only five islands are inhabited – St Agnes, Bryher, St Mary's, St Martin's and Tresco – and together they offer a rare combination of seascapes, golden beaches and crystal-clear sea, with quiet, green corners inland.

Scillonians are outstanding seamen, and the tradition of small-boat handling is maintained by the fishermen and by the boatmen who run pleasure trips. These boat trips are an essential part of getting the best from a visit to the Isles of Scilly, whether you're seal watching, puffin spotting or just keen for a pleasure cruise.

The inter-island launches connect daily to St Mary's and also make trips between the islands so you can tour them at your leisure. Some of the finest trips are those to the outlying uninhabited islands and to the marine wildernesses of the Western Rocks, the Norrard Rocks and the Eastern Isles, where seabirds can be seen at close quarters and seals lie at their ease on sea-sucked ledges.

Entertainment on the Isles of Scilly is of a richly traditional nature. There are numerous slide shows and delightful talks in the local community hall of each of the islands. Island boatmen especially are noted for their salty wit. Cricket is a popular sport and every year local festivals take place, from the Walk Scilly walking festival in March to folk festivals, the World Pilot Gig Championships and the Tresco and Bryher Food Festival in September, a feast of local goodies including Bryer crab and lobster, St Martin's wine and wild food foraging walks.

The best time to visit is late spring or early summer, when the wildflowers are in bloom but the peak holiday season has not yet started, for the best chance of a deserted beach to yourself.

Bryher

Bryher is the smallest of the five inhabited islands, less than a mile across at its widest point and about 1.5 miles from top to bottom. A little to the west of Tresco, which looks like a bustling metropolis by comparison, it consists of a gentle undulation of granite hills leading down to sweeping sandy beaches crunchy with seashells. Hell Bay may sound like something out of the Wild West, but the west of Bryher is entirely peaceable, and makes a supremely relaxing location for the Atlantic-facing boutique hotel in its little cove.

Bryher faces Tresco across the narrow channel of New Grimsby Sound, and island life is focused on the beaches that fringe the Sound. Here boats draw up at a granite quay, or at the jetty, built as one of Anneka Rice's famous 1980s television 'challenges' to extend landing times on Bryher and now known fondly as 'Annequay'.

HIT THE BEACH

Bryher's Great Par is an inspirational place. It's featured in several Michael Morpurgo books (ask the children), including *Why the Whales Came*. We'd bet they came for the sands, sun and sea just like the rest of us – it's also a good beach for snorkelling and swimming. Another famous beach spot is Hell Bay, an Atlantic-facing cove that received many a shipwreck in the 18th and 19th centuries. Along the coast, if you can find it, is High Rock Cave, a 30ft-high cave that is one of the island's largest caves, used by smugglers back in the day.

EAT AND DRINK

Hell Bay ⊛⊛⊛
hellbay.co.uk
TR23 0PR | 01720 422947
This luxury hotel and restaurant has a wonderful art collection including works by Barbara Hepworth and Patrick Heron. The kitchen specialises in fine fresh seafood, with Tresco beef, Cornish cheeses and rich desserts sharing the menu. You can either relax at the spa or take a post-prandial walk on the sweeping sandy beaches and enjoy the smallest of the five inhabited islands.

St Agnes

Just over a mile wide, St Agnes has a special atmosphere of serenity. It is the most southerly of the group and is separated from St Mary's by the deep water channel of St Mary's Sound. The Turk's Head Inn and the Post Office are at the hub of the community – which just goes to show how small it is. To the east the main island is linked by a narrow sandbar to the smaller tidal 'island' of Gugh, and off its western shore is the protected bird island of Annet. Beyond Annet lie the dramatic Western Rocks – reefs that end at the Bishop Rock Lighthouse.

EAT AND DRINK
Covean Cottage
01720 422620
In this quiet tea shop you can enjoy clotted cream fresh from the Isles of Scilly's only dairy with local homemade jam on freshly baked scones, served on delicate vintage plates, with English roses in vases on the table. It's a quintessential Isles of Scilly experience.

St Martin's

The most northerly island in the group, St Martin's is 2 miles in length and just over half a mile wide. Landing on St Martin's can be adventurous at certain stages of the tide, when walking the plank to reach the sandy shore from launches is necessary. Walking here is exhilarating, though the lure of magnificent beaches such as Great Bay on St Martin's northern shore tends to distract.

HIT THE BEACH
As if you needed the encouragement, Great Bay in St Martin's is a gorgeous, dramatic swathe of sand and sea on the north side of the island, with rock pools at low tide and gently shelving waters. It's a great swimming spot.

GO WINE-TASTING
St Martin's Vineyard
stmartinsvineyard.co.uk
Higher Town, TR25 0QL
01720 423418 | Tours during the summer daily 11–4
The UK's most southwesterly vineyard produces white wines that go well with seafood, as luck would have it, as well as red and rosé wines. Tours can be either self-guided or guided and include tastings. There's also an apple orchard.

GO DIVING
St Martin's Dive School
scillydiving.com
Higher Town, TR25 0QL
01720 422848
Who wouldn't want to see what's going on in these clear seas? St Martin's Dive School offers lessons, dive charter, single dives and snorkelling with seals. That's an offer you won't find anywhere else. There are shallow reefs, wrecks and beautiful fish to see in the waters all around the islands.

EAT AND DRINK
Adam's Fish and Chips
adamsfishandchips.co.uk
Highertown, TR25 0QN
01720 423082
Locally caught fish and chips made from potatoes from the owner's family farm

feature on the menu of this simple cafe, which has indoor seating and a larger outdoor garden under a canopy. It's really all about the fish

here, with pollock as the star and lobster making an appearance in the salads. If you want a pasty, you have to pre-order.

St Mary's

St Mary's is the largest of the Isles of Scilly. Its main settlement of Hugh Town is the marine metropolis of the islands, and it is from Hugh Town Quay that the passenger launches leave for the exciting sea trips that are an essential part of holidaying on Scilly. There are beaches on the north and south sides of Hugh Town, the southern bay of Porth Cressa being particularly delightful. A footpath follows the coastline for a 9-mile circuit, passing several well preserved prehistoric sites on the way. Early flower growing developed in Scilly from the late 1860s and daffodils and narcissi are still exported from the islands, though the trade has declined in recent years.

TAKE IN SOME HISTORY
Buzza Tower
Buzza Hill

This squat tower and well-known Grade II listed landmark was originally a windmill built in the early 1800s, and was renamed King Edward's Tower in honour of a visit by Edward VII in 1902. It stands on land that is thought to contain the remains of a Bronze Age cairn and there's a great view over Porthcressa Beach. Buzza Hill is an important wildlife area with Hottentot fig among other species growing around the quarry at the base of the hill, a popular picnic area.

VISIT THE MUSEUM
Isles of Scilly Museum
iosmuseum.org
Church Street, Hugh Town,
TR21 0JT | 01720 422337

Open Easter–end Sep Mon–Fri 10–4.30, Sat 10am–12pm, Oct–Easter Mon–Sat 10am–12pm
The mission of this museum is to preserve the traditions and spirit of the islands and help visitors to understand local traditions and their place in history. Items include Romano-Britain finds thrown up during a storm in the 1960s, a summer wildflower display, local art and stuffed birds.

GO BACK IN TIME
Bant's Carn Burial Chamber and Halandy Down Ancient Village
english-heritage.org.uk
North of St Hugh
On a cliff top a mile north of Hugh Town with views of the sea, this Bronze Age burial mound has an entrance passage and inner chamber and makes for a good walk

on a breezy day. On the slopes below it are the remains of an Iron Age settlement that was used for around 500 years until the end of the Roman period. The burial mound was excavated in the 1900s but was found to be almost empty; it's thought that it was originally over 13ft high. The English Heritage website has a short audio tour available for downloading to MP3 players, iPods and iPhones to accompany a walk around these ancient monuments.

HIT THE BEACH

Bar Point is one of St Mary's most scenic beaches, a sandy stretch backed by dunes between McFarland's Down and the Innisidgen Bronze Age tombs with views to St Martin's and Tresco. It's actually the location of a long-eroded causeway between the islands. Porthlaw is another beautiful scenic spot, a white-sand beach with views of Buzza Hill and the tower on the top of it.

EXPLORE BY BIKE

St Mary's Bicycle Hire
scillybikehire.co.uk
The Strand, TR21 0PT
07796 638506

St Mary's is a lovely place to cycle, car-free, of course, and with views of the sea all around. St Mary's Bicycle Hire rents out bikes, tagalongs, child carriers and tandems by cash or cheque (by prior arrangement) by the half day, day or week.

TAKE A BOAT TRIP

Crusader
crusaderboating.co.uk
7 Launceston Close, Old Town, TR21 0NJ | 07917 891962

Sea Quest
St Mary's Harbour
01720 422511

Island Sea Safaris
islandseasafaris.co.uk
Old Town, TR21 0NH
01720 422732

Boat cruises are the thing to do around these beautiful islands. Try Crusader from St Mary's Harbour for daily direct trips to the other islands, scenic cruising and wildlife spotting. Sea Quest also runs from St Mary's with a glass bottomed boat showing the underwater world on an ocean cruise; and Island Sea Safaris runs 1- and 2-hour-long boat trips to see seals and local wildlife around the islands, from the Hugh Town quay.

TAKE A RETRO COACH TOUR

Island Rover
islandrover.co.uk
Holgate's Green, TR21 0JT
01720 422131

Island Rover offers guided coach tours of the island, running at 10.15am and 1.30pm with full commentary on a stylish retro turquoise bus. Note that dogs and children are not allowed; the bus times the tour to allow visitors to catch the midday boat to Tresco, so it's timed well for day trippers.

▲ Bant's carn

SADDLE UP
St Mary's Riding Centre
scillyonline.co.uk/stables
Maypole, TR21 0NU
01720 423855
Saddle up and see St Mary's by horse, riding along the beach in the surf, or inland along the cliffs and on the heathland. St Mary's Riding Centre is the only riding establishment in the Scilly Isles and caters for beginners and experienced riders alike.

PLAY A ROUND
Isles of Scilly Golf Club
islesofscillygolfclub.co.uk
Carn Morval, TR21 0NF
01720 422692
Open all year

The most southwesterly course in England is open all year with an 18-hole course and distractingly good views. The clubhouse, which has views of St Mary's harbour, is open to visitors and serves lunch 12–2. Hell Bay Hotel on Bryher also has a picturesque seven-hole pitch and putt course.

EAT AND DRINK
Nornour Cafe
Hugh Town, TR21 0PS
01720 423773
This small local cafe serves lunch, afternoon tea and traditional cream teas in a small, cosy house in the centre of Hugh Town with a suntrap back garden.

▶ Tresco

Tresco lies at the sheltered heart of the islands. It is more of a show place than the rest of Scilly, a private domain where there is an atmosphere of carefully regulated life and gentle pace. The exquisite sub-tropical gardens surrounding Tresco Abbey House are the main focus of the island. A priory to St Nicholas was established by Benedictine monks during the 12th century; the scant ruins that remain are now incorporated into the Abbey Gardens, where Burmese honeysuckle, Australian scarlet bottlebrush, aloes, dracaenas, mimosa, gigantic ice plants and a host of other exotics line the terraced pathways. Tresco has a heliport from where connections can be made to Penzance. Dogs must be kept on leads on Tresco.

VISIT THE GALLERY

Gallery Tresco
tresco.co.uk
New Grimsby Harbour,
TR24 0QE | 01720 424925
Open from early Feb–Nov
This fine art gallery shows

paintings inspired by Cornwall and the Isles of Scilly in an airy converted boatshed. It's a great place to find a classy souvenir, and holds several exhibitions a year showcasing the work

Abbey Garden and Valhalla Museum

tresco.co.uk

Tresco Abbey, TR24 0QQ | 01720 424108 | Open daily 10–4

These 14-acre gardens, dating from 1834, are home to many exotic plants, including the South African proteus, tender geraniums from Madeira, tall date palms from the Canary Islands and the striking Chilean myrtle, which has orange bark. There are also acacias, eucalyptus and the New Zealand *Metrosideros tomentosa*, which is 80ft tall and produces crimson flowers in summer.

Around St Nicholas's Priory, honeysuckles, the blue-flowering *Convolvulus mauritanicus* and pretty Mexican daisies spill out of cracks in the ancient walls and arches, and there is a magnificent rock garden excavated into a 40ft cliff below. The Middle Terrace has an area known as Mexico, and is covered with the turquoise flowers of *Puya alpestris* from Chile. Further along, a stone summerhouse is overgrown with Burmese honeysuckle.

One of the best sights here is Valhalla, a building open on one side containing some of the figureheads of ships that have tragically foundered on the treacherous rocks around the Isles of Scilly in the course of the last three centuries. The Abbey Gardens also have a cafe serving light snacks and cakes.

of new and established artists. As well as paintings, the gallery stocks local craft items and jewellery.

GO ROUND THE GARDENS
Abbey Garden and Valhalla Museum
See highlight panel opposite

HIT THE BEST BEACH IN BRITAIN
Pentile Bay
Pentile Bay on Tresco was rated as one of Britain's top 20 beaches by the *Daily Telegraph*, a beautifully situated white-sand bay with an emerald sea lapping at its shore and islands leading your eye out to the horizon. Go see what all the fuss is about.

GO WINDSURFING
Isles of Scilly Sailing Centre
sailingscilly.com
Old Grimsby, TR21 0NE
01720 424919
Open Jul–end Aug only
Sailing, windsurfing and powerboating are all on offer at the Isles of Scilly Sailing Centre, along with kayak and boat hire by the day. The Scillys are a watersports paradise and whether you're a beginner or experienced, this watersports centre offers a range of suitable options.

EAT AND DRINK
The New Inn ⊚
tresco.co.uk
TR24 0QQ | 01720 423006
A popular venue for Tresco walkers, the New Inn is

10 Cornish sayings

▶ **Teazy asn adder** – moody
▶ **Rough as rats** – of poor or uncouth upbringing
▶ **Drekly** – later, if at all
▶ **Got feet like half-crown shovels** – got big feet
▶ **Face like a whitewashed wall** – pale
▶ **So daft as a carrot half scraped** – not very clever
▶ **Black as pit** – very dark
▶ **Mazed** – a bit daft
▶ **Thick as a hedge** – a thick mist
▶ **A brave step** – a long walk

reliably full of banter and bonhomie, with eating spread across the main bar, the residents' dining room and a pavilion. It's open every day and serves the likes of Scilly crab and baby leek tart, roast venison, bitter chocolate and pecan brownie, and coffee, tea, cakes and handmade ice cream.

Ruin Beach Cafe
tresco.co.uk
Ravens Porth, Old Grimsby, TR24 0QQ
This beach cafe is open all day and serves breakfast, lunch, afternoon tea and dinner along with fantastic sea views. It has a wood-burning oven – handy for its pizzas – and also has a good children's menu. Views are towards St Martin's and the Eastern Isles.

▲ Sennen Cove

▶ Sennen

Holiday snaps of Sennen Cove can be deceptive, its white sand and clear turquoise water looking more like the Caribbean than Cornwall. It's the most westerly surf spot in the country, renowned for its waves, and is close to the small harbour and fishing village of Sennen. With little fishing boats pulled up to the quay and a 150-year-old lifeboat station to visit in summer, it's a photogenic place. It also has its own legend – the Whooper of Sennen Cove was said to send a whooping mist to prevent fishermen sailing out into incoming storms.

The village proper is on the higher ground alongside the A30, while Sennen Cove has the main attractions of the beaches and fine granite cliffs to the south. A car park at the far end gives access to the cliff path and to Land's End on foot – it's roughly a half-hour walk (1.5 miles) along the cliffs from the beach. This southern end of the cove spills into the ocean and has a laid-back atmosphere. The nearby wood and granite Round House contained the capstan that was used for hauling boats out of the water. It is now a craft shop and gallery.

There are two beaches: as well as Sennen Cove, Gwenver Beach to the north is a serious surfing and bodyboarding beach and a decent suntrap on a good day. It's harder to reach and the smaller of the two. Lifeguards are on hand in the summer months, but do take care as tidal currents can be fierce.

HIT THE BEACH
Gwynver Beach
As mentioned above, this is a great surfing and bodyboarding beach known for having some of the county's best surf. Access is tricky, down steep cliffs, and at the bottom there's sand and rocks. At low tide it joins Sennen Cove. It's a dog-friendly beach all year and has a car park beside it. There are lifeguards on the beach in peak season.

Sennen Cove
This is one of the most beautiful beaches in Cornwall, a curve of white sand with water so clear you can see through it from the cliff tops. The nearby promontory Pedn-men-du is popular with rock climbers, and there's plenty to do at the beach beyond swimming, sunbathing and surfing, with a variety of cafes, chippies and beach restaurants plus a small art gallery. There is also a surf school and surf hire on the beach. Lifeguards patrol in season.

GO SURFING
Smart Surf School
sennensurfschool.com
The Blue Lagoon, TR19 7DF
01736 871817

Sennen Surfing Centre
sennensurfingcentre.com
Churchtown House, TR19 7AD
01736 871227 | Open Apr–end Oct
In the UK's most westerly surf spot, what else? There are two surf schools on the beach offering wetsuit and board hire and lessons, plus surf'n'stay options with the nearby Whitesands Hotel and nearby campsites and cottages, and 1–5 day courses for those bitten by the bug. Teachers here are accomplished and have travelled the world surfing and teaching.

EAT AND DRINK
The Old Success Inn
oldsuccess.co.uk
TR19 7DG
01736 871232
Once the haunt of smugglers and now a focal point for the Sennen lifeboat crew, this 17th-century inn overlooks Cape Cornwall. Its name comes from the days when fishermen gathered here to count their catch and share out their 'successes'. Fresh local seafood is to the fore, and favourites include Tribute-battered catch of the day and Cornish fish pie. The inn also has rooms.

▶ Tintagel
Tintagel, on Cornwall's north coast between Bude and Padstow, can feel like a bit of an Arthurian theme park at times, which is both good and bad. Good because who wouldn't want to visit Tintagel Castle dreaming of King Arthur and the Knights of the Round Table – it's one of England's most enduring stories – but

bad because, seriously, King Arthur-themed fudgeries and fish and chip shops are just pushing it over the edge. Get past the rampant commercial exploitation of the legends and you'll find the incredible ruined castle moulded to the blunt summit of 'the Island' of Tintagel Head a real joy to visit. There's more here than a whiff of ancient legend: the castle is 13th century, but historians suggest it was the site of an Iron Age enclosure, a Celtic monastery and a Roman signal station. The prominence of the Island suggests that it was used as a defensive site from the earliest times; it's all watched over by English Heritage.

Barras Nose to the north and Glebe Cliff to the south are in the care of the National Trust. It's tempting to say that the hinterland is in the care of the King Arthur industry, but Tintagel village offers a little more than that. The antiquated Old Post Office (National Trust) at the heart of the village is a delightful building: a small 14th-century manor house with a central hall rising the full height of the building which became a post office in Victorian times. King Arthur's Great Halls in Fore Street is another remarkable token of dedication to a theme, packed with Arthurian memorabilia and with a light and sound show.

TAKE IN SOME HISTORY
Tintagel Castle
See highlight panel overleaf

VISIT THE MUSEUMS
King Arthur's Great Halls
Fore Street, PL34 0DA
01840 770526
Get inspired for a visit to Tintagel by first stopping at this 1930s building on Fore Street. It contains 72 stained-glass windows illustrating the Arthurian tales by Veronica Whall, a pupil of William Morris, a round table, granite thrones, and a light and music show telling more about the legends.

Tintagel Old Post Office
nationaltrust.org.uk
Fore Street, PL34 0DB
01840 770024
Open daily early Apr–end Sep 10.30–5.30, Mar and Oct 11–4
A rare survival of Cornish domestic medieval architecture, this 14th-century yeoman's farmhouse is well furnished with local oak pieces and has a distinctive undulating slate roof. One room was used during the Victorian era as the letter-receiving office for the district. Inside today are relics from the Victorian era; there's also a peaceful cottage garden.

EAT AND DRINK
Granny Wobbly's Fudge Pantry
grannywobblys.co.uk
Fore Street, PL34 0DB
01840 770595

This jolly shop sells handmade fudge and was visited by the Prince of Wales and the Duchess of Cornwall in summer 2013; it has an ice cream parlour next door and a sister shop in Wadebridge. A great place to buy boxes of fudge by the gramme to take home as gifts or souvenirs.

▶ PLACES NEARBY

It's not all myths and legends; just over 2 miles south of Tintagel the coastal settlement of Trebarwith Strand has a beach and more.

The Mill House Inn

themillhouseinn.co.uk
Trebarwith, PL34 0HD
01840 770200
This converted 18th-century mill house is halfway up the wooded valley from the beach at Trebarwith. The bar is big, with flagged floors and a wood-burning stove, and has Sharp's ales on tap. In the new contemporary restaurant you can sample the likes of salt and pepper squid and local lamb with sautéed kale.

The Port William

theportwilliam.com
Trebarwith Strand,
PL34 0HB | 01840 770230
In one of the best locations in Cornwall, this former harbourmaster's house lies directly on the coastal path,

50 yards from the sea. There is an entrance to a smugglers' tunnel at the rear of the ladies' loo. The daily-changing specials board includes dishes such as artichoke and roast pepper salad, warm smoked trout platter, and spinach and ricotta tortellini.

Trebarwith Strand

This sandy and rocky beach is accessible via the Southwest Coast Path as well as from the car park 5 minutes' walk away, and is a good surf and family beach. The beach is completely covered at high tide and incoming tides can be swift, so check before you turn up; there are local lifeguards on hand in season. The added bonuses are dogs are allowed all year, plus there is a beach shop and a cafe in the village but no surf hire.

▶ Tresco

see **Isles of Scilly**, page 253

Tintagel Castle

english-heritage.org.uk
Castle Road, PL34 0HE | 01840 770328
Open Apr–end Sep daily 10–6, Oct daily 10–5,
Nov–end Mar Sat–Sun 10–4; check website for variations

Overlooking the wild Cornish coast, Tintagel is one of the most spectacular spots in the country. Where to start? Well, as the birthplace of King Arthur, according to popular myth, don't head straight to the ruins but watch the video in the visitor centre about searching for the legend before you start. It's a long walk down to the ruins on the cliff top, and it's well worth it. For those less mobile, a Land Rover does return trips. The castle is closed on exceptionally windy days.

Recent excavations have revealed Dark Age connections between Spain and Cornwall, alongside the discovery of the 'Arthnou' stone suggesting that this was a royal place for the Dark Age rulers of Cornwall, so who knows – perhaps the legends have roots in history.

The 13th-century ruined castle is a magical place to visit, with wooden doors studded with metal, overgrown cottage gardens and stone walls crumbling down the cliff. In the summer, history is brought to life with storytelling sessions, an archaeology week and a family trail. After visiting the castle, wander down to the beach and find Merlin's Cave and a shorter tunnel that opens up in the meadow above the cliffs.

▲ Truro Cathedral

▶ Truro

At the heart of Cornwall, Truro is one of the county's great towns, with cobbled streets, independent shops selling cheese, homemade bread, surf duds and more, and a great cathedral right in the middle. Holidaymakers tend to head to seaside towns and villages but missing Truro would be missing a treat: there's always something going on here, thanks to its year-round programme of events, from fashion shows to hip hop.

It's impossible to miss Truro's great cathedral, which catches the eye from all quarters. It rises from the heart of the city, all honey-coloured stone and lancet windows reflecting the sun, with its great Gothic towers piercing the sky. Long before it was built here in the late 1800s, the site held a Norman castle and a Dominican friary stood near the river, but the cathedral makes up for their loss and is known for its Victorian stained-glass windows, said to be among the best in the UK.

The history of the town of course centres on mining. In the late 18th century, it was the political and cultural centre of

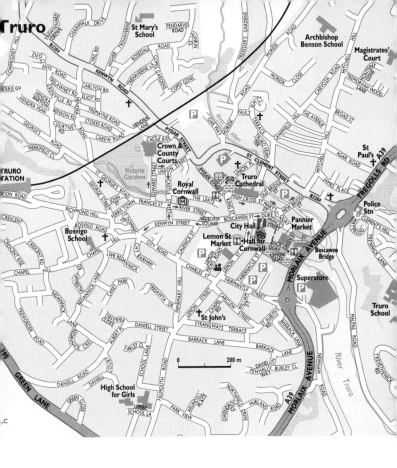

Georgian Cornwall, hence the beautifully proportioned buildings here, and in the last years of the century the striking buildings on Boscawen Street and Lemon Street were built. Today Boscawen Street is a broad, cobbled space, entered at both ends from narrow thoroughfares. The granite facade of the City Hall is on this street, and Lemon Street survives as one of the finest examples of a late Georgian street in Britain, its houses perfectly aligned to either side of a broad avenue that climbs uphill.

There are hidden glories in Truro amid the modern developments which reflect the town's importance today. From the Moorfield car park, a lane leads to Victoria Square, but parallel and to its right is the elegant Georgian crescent of Walsingham Place. Throughout the heart of Truro, the lanes connecting the main streets are lined with attractive shops, cafes and restaurants. From the west end of Boscawen Street, King Street leads up to the pedestrianised area of High Cross in front of the cathedral. The stylish Assembly Rooms, with a facade of Bath stone, stand nearby.

Seen from its forecourt, the cathedral seems crowded in by buildings instead of being the dominating presence that commands the view from outside the city, but the west front with its soaring towers is exhilarating. The foundation stones of the cathedral were laid in 1880 and the western towers were finally dedicated in 1920. Truro's cathedral is a Victorian building, early English Gothic in design but with strong French influences that are seen in the great spires. The interior is glorious, vaulted throughout with pillars and arches in elegant proportion. There are beautiful individual features such as the exquisite baptistery.

Pydar Street runs north from the cathedral as a pleasant pedestrian concourse. A short distance away is the stylish Crown Court, and below here are the Victoria Gardens. Boscawen Park, by the River Truro, is reached along the road to Malpas.

The Royal Cornwall Museum in River Street is worth visiting for a sight of a real Egyptian mummy and a Cornish giant, among its many treasures. The art gallery has works by John Opie, the 18th-century portrait painter, who was born near St Agnes. Truro is an excellent shopping centre with numerous independent and specialist shops in its narrow, characterful streets. The Hall for Cornwall hosts shows, events and touring acts of the calibre you'd expect for the capital of the county: anything from Peppa Pig for the under-7s to breakdancers, touring West End shows and comedians such as Billy Connolly.

Near to Truro you'll find Trelissick Garden, another of Cornwall's key garden estates, and Trewithen Gardens, in the village of Probus (see page 218).

VISIT THE MUSEUM
Royal Cornwall Museum
royalcornwallmuseum.org.uk
River Street, TR1 2SJ
01872 272205 | Open all year
Tue–Sat 10–4.45; library closed
1–2pm, all day Thu & Sat pm;
closed BHs
Cornwall's oldest museum is famed for its internationally important collections. Visitors can see large collections of minerals, a real Egyptian mummy and the Cornish Giant. The art gallery has a fine collection of paintings from the Newlyn and St Ives Schools, and regular temporary exhibitions of local, national and international artists.
The museum runs a range of family activities throughout the year along with a regular programme of lectures; contact them for details of events and activities.

GO ROUND THE GARDENS
Trelissick Garden
nationaltrust.org.uk
Feock, TR3 6QL
01872 862090 | Open mid-Feb–end

Oct daily 10.30–5.30, Jan–mid-Feb & end Oct–Dec daily 11–4

Set amidst more than 500 acres of park and farmland, with panoramic views down Carrick Roads to Falmouth and the sea, Trelissick Garden is well known for its large collection of hydrangeas, camellias, rhododendrons and exotic and tender plants. In the garden's sheltered position many unusual and exotic plants also thrive, including sub-tropical species from South America and Tasmania. The large walled garden has fig trees and climbing plants, and there is a shrub garden. The Cornish apple orchard contains the definitive collection of Cornish apple varieties and is particularly lovely in the spring. Two galleries on the property display Cornish arts and crafts. Check the website for musical and theatrical events.

The grounds were laid out with carriage drives and planted with trees during the 1820s to take full advantage of the picturesque views. The parkland is criss-crossed with pathways, which provide some delightful walks. The beautiful gardens and deciduous woods, which run down to the Fal River, make a particularly delightful place to work up a healthy appetite for, or to walk off the indulgence of, one of the excellent afternoon teas served here. The traditional spread of sandwiches, cakes and scones might include the the Trelissick fruit slice – a speciality – and

▲ Fisherman on the pier at Truro

there are 20 varieties of tea to choose from. Light lunches are also available. Booking is advisable for Sunday lunch and for anyone with any special requirements. One of the best ways to visit is by river on a boat trip from Truro (see Enterprise Boats below).

TAKE A BOAT TRIP
Enterprise Boats
falriver.co.uk
01326 741194

Enterprise's red and turquoise boats sail regularly from Truro to Falmouth and St Mawes along the banks of the Fal River are a pleasant way to travel and explore the AONBs. The regular crossings stop at the National Trust's Trelissick Garden and Malpas. En route, expect to see plenty of other boats, and historic and Tudor houses. Boats run from the town quay.

WATCH A PLAY
Kneehigh
kneehigh.co.uk
01872 267910
Cornwall's most dazzling theatre company knocks the socks off any other creative company in the UK. Its home in the summer months is the Asylum, a purpose-built tent in this beautiful part of the country just outside Truro (check the website for the precise location, as it changes). Magic is in the air as traditional stories – often children's or folk tales – are reworked with drama, song, circus skills and theatricality. Much is talked about seeing shows at the Minack – the Asylum is just as good, if not more inventive, surprising and memorable.

PLAY A ROUND
Truro Golf Club
trurogolfclub.co.uk
Treliske, TR1 3LG | 01872 278684 (manager) | Open all year
This is a picturesque and gently undulating parkland course with lovely views of Truro and the surrounding countryside. The course offers a great challenge to golfers of all standards and ages. The many trees and shrubs offer open invitations for wayward balls, and with many fairways boasting out of bounds markers, play needs to be safe and sensible. Fairways are tight and the greens small and full of character, making it difficult to play to one's handicap.

EAT AND DRINK
Bustophers Bar Bistro ◉
bustophersbarbistro.com
62 Lemon Street, TR1 2PN
01872 279029
This longstanding neighbourhood bistro has a loyal following in Truro and it's easy to see why. With a buzzy atmosphere, a good wine list and modern bistro food on the menu using quality local ingredients, it attracts suits at lunchtime, and couples and friends in the evening. Tables outside are popular in the summertime.

Charlotte's Tea House
Coinage Hall, 1 Boscawen Street, Truro, TR1 2QU | 01872 263706
This tea house on the first floor of the old Coinage Hall presents a sanctuary of Victorian tranquillity just a few steps from the busy main street below. As well as teas from the Tregothnan Estate, they serve an extensive range of homemade cakes plus scones, quiches, soups and light lunches.

Hooked!
hookedcornwall.com/hooked-in-the-city
Tabernacle Street, TR1 2EJ
01872 274700
On a quiet street, Hooked! is a buzzy restaurant with wooden floors and tables, high ceilings, banquettes and brown and cream leather-look seats, and some 'fish shoal' lampshades reflecting the seafood credentials of the place.

Exciting treats include razor clams in ginger, monkfish tail with spicy clams, and prawn and squid escabeche.

The Old Ale House

oahtruro.com
7 Quay Street, TR1 2HD
01872 271122
This traditional city-centre pub right next to the main bus station in Truro offers a large selection of Skinner's real ales and guest beers, as well as live music and various quiz and games nights. The extensive menus include 'huge hands of hot bread' (quarter or half bloomer covered in a topping of your choice and baked).

Tabb's ◉◉

tabbs.co.uk
85 Kenwyn Street, TR1 3BZ
01872 262110
This charming neighbourhood restaurant uses plenty of wonderful local produce in dishes such as ballotine of pork and duck, grilled fillet of hake and venison cuts. Everything served is produced on the premises, from the bread with the starters to the chocolates with the coffees.

The Wig and Pen

wigandpentruro.co.uk
Frances Street, TR1 3DP
01872 273028
This city-centre pub includes Quills Restaurant in the basement, serving modern pub classics and specials on the menu to go with the Trelawny and Tribute beers. Watch the world go by from the sun terraces. There's a ghost of a woman called Claire, apparently, who has haunted the cellars since she was run over by a stagecoach in Victorian times.

▶ **PLACES NEARBY**

Truro is surrounded by lots of foodie attractions, including a cider farm (see page 228) and a tea estate. There's also a golf course for working it all off again.

Killiow Golf Club

killiowgolf.co.uk
Kea, TR3 6AG | 01872 270246
Open all year
This picturesque and testing parkland course in the grounds of Killiow Estate has mature trees, water hazards, small greens and tight fairways, making this a challenge for golfers of all abilities. Five holes are played across or around water. There is a floodlit, all-weather driving range and practice facilities.

Tregothnan

tregothnan.co.uk
The Woodyard, Tresillian,
TR2 4AJ | 01872 520000
Known in particular for having the UK's most successful tea plantation, Tregothnan is a private family garden and has been home to the Boscawen family since the early 14th century. Garden visits are by prior arrangement only (visit the website for full details); among the things to see are

the Diamond Woodland, planted to celebrate the Queen's Diamond Jubilee, 40 hectares of impressive exotics and a tea plantation, whose climate mimics that of the Himalayan foothills.

The estate's restaurant Smugglers closed in 2013 and will reopen in 2014 with exquisite local food and great cream teas; there's also an inviting Wild Escape

accommodation selection, including old school cottages and stone-built creekside houses to rent.

Penrose Water Gardens
penrosewatergardens.co.uk
TR4 9ES | 01872 222307
Open Mon–Sat 9.30–4.30,
Sun 10–4
Delightful gardens in a woodland valley, along with a tea room.

Wadebridge

Wadebridge is perhaps best known as the start of the Camel Trail, a route along the old railway that has been cleared and reworked for walking, cycling and horse-riding. The town itself is charming, with pedestrianised streets, independent shops, cafes and boutiques and a decent deli. Back in the early part of the 20th century, it was a busy town, and today it supports more than just the tourist industry so you'll find more than buckets and spades in the shops.

The old bridge dates from the mid-15th century and it is said that it was built on foundations of woolpacks, the area being noted for its wool production. To the west, modern technology has spanned the wider estuary with a lofty road bridge that has eased much of the town's traffic problem.

Close to the town of Padstow and the village of Rock, there are beaches to explore nearby, along with a family theme park and St Enodoc Church, part-covered by sand, where Sir John Betjeman is buried. If you want to know more about the former Poet Laureate, the Wadebridge Concern for the Aged centre has memorabilia on display.

VISIT THE MUSEUM
John Betjeman Centre
johnbetjeman.org.uk
Wadebridge Concern for the
Aged, Southern Way, PL27 7BX
01208 812392 | Open all year
Mon–Fri 9–4.30
This Concern for the Aged centre is in the main building of the old Wadebridge railway

station. Inside, along with meeting rooms, is a memorabilia room dedicated to Sir John Betjeman with furniture and personal items that belonged to the poet. Betjeman died in 1984 and is buried at St Enodoc Church in Trebetherick; see page 211. His grave is near the south side of the church, which is approached via the 10th fairway of the golf course.

ENTERTAIN THE FAMILY
Cornwall's Crealy Great Adventure Park
crealy.co.uk/cornwall
Tredinnick, PL27 7RA
01841 540276 | Open all year daily 10.30–5.30, with some small seasonal variations

This family theme park has thrill rides, including water flumes, indoor play zones and arcades, as well as a small zoo with pony rides, a reptile house and a farm. It's Cornwall's largest theme park and has masses of indoor attractions for when it's raining. The entry fee is valid for 7 days – so if you go on the first day of your holiday, you can come back every day for the next week, if you want to.

HIT THE BEACH
Daymer Bay
Daymer Bay is a sandy beach backed by dunes and sand hills. It's a little off the beaten track, safe for swimming and has no lifeguard presence or facilities to speak of. Braey Hill to the south of the beach can be climbed, and St Enodoc Church is nearby. Parking and toilets are nearby and dogs are allowed all year.

CYCLE THE CAMEL TRAIL
Bridge Bike Hire
bridgebikehire.co.uk
The Camel Trail, PL27 7AL
01208 813050

Camel Trail Cycle Hire
cameltrailcyclehire.co.uk
Eddystone Road, PL27 7AL
01208 814104

The route of the old Atlantic Coast Express, from Wadebridge to Padstow, is now the main part of the 18-mile Camel Trail, a recreational walking, riding and cycling route that passes through varied countryside alongside the River Camel. This traffic-free trail is ideal for all the family as the surface is mainly smooth and virtually level, with one gentle climb from Wadebridge to Poley's Bridge. It is ideal for wheelchair users, prams and buggys, and those who have difficulty walking on uneven surfaces. There are plenty of benches and picnic tables along the way where you can stop and enjoy the views.

The Camel Trail can be joined at several points: Padstow, Wadebridge and Boscarne Junction to the west of Bodmin, where it swings north to continue through Hellandbridge to terminate at Poley's Bridge.

PLAY A ROUND
St Kew Golf Course
stkewgc.com
St Kew Highway, PL30 3EF
01208 841500 | Open all year

St Kew Golf Course is an interesting, well laid out parkland course with 6 holes with water and 15 bunkers. It's in a picturesque setting with 10 par 4s and 8 par 3s. Nine extra tees have now been provided, allowing a different teeing area for the back nine.

EAT AND DRINK
The Quarryman Inn
thequarryman.co.uk
Edmonton, PL27 7JA
01208 816444
Close to the famous Camel Trail, this friendly 18th-century free house has evolved from cottages that housed slate workers from the nearby quarry. Several bow windows add character to this unusual inn. The pub's menus change daily but their signature dishes are chargrilled steaks served on sizzling platters and fresh local seafood.

The Swan Hotel
staustellbrewery.co.uk
9 Molesworth Street, PL27 7DD
01208 812526
Popular with families, the main bar at this hotel provides a comfortable place to relax and enjoy a drink or a meal. Typical pub food in the Cygnet Restaurant includes locally smoked salmon; Cornish ham, egg and chips; and beer-battered fish and chips. There's a carvery Wed–Sun.

The Tea Shop
6 Polmorla Road, PL27 7ND
01208 813331
Fresh local produce takes pride of place on the menu at this bright and cosy tea shop, and everything served here is homemade. A choice of 40 teas and around 30 cakes, including boiled fruit cake, strawberry pavlova and apple and almond cake, make it something really special. Ice creams and light lunches are also on the menu.

Trehellas House Hotel and Restaurant ⊛
trehellashouse.co.uk
Washaway, PL30 3AD
01208 72700
Trehellas House has an interesting past: initially an inn that also served as the local courthouse in the 18th century, then a farm, and a pub again in the 1970s. It's now a country-house hotel with an appealing restaurant serving punchy modern cooking with Cornish produce at its heart.

▸ PLACES NEARBY
Four miles southwest of Wadebridge, St Breock Downs' monolith is set amid a nature reserve on Rosenannon Downs run by the Cornwall Wildlife Trust.

St Breock Downs Monolith
english-heritage.org.uk
Rosenannon | Open any reasonable time
This, Cornwall's largest and heaviest standing stone, is on the summit of St Breock Downs with fabulous views to the sea. It was originally 16ft tall, weighs nearly 18 tonnes and dates from the Late Neolithic to mid-Bronze Age (around 2500–1500 bc). There are many other Bronze Age relics and monuments in the nearby area. Dogs on leads are welcome.

▶ Watergate Bay
see **Newquay**, page 183

▶ Whitsand Bay
see **Kingsand & Cawsand**, page 117

▶ Zennor

Storm-tumbled cliffs and wheeling gulls guard Penwith's wild, Atlantic shoreline and it's easy to imagine how and why the local legend of the mermaid of Zennor came to mind. The mermaid is said to have seduced a local chorister into the dark waters below Zennor Head, with promises of a life under the sea together. In the local church of St Senara, you can see the mermaid chair, a chair with a mermaid carved on it, where she is said to have sat the first time she saw him. On quiet evenings, the smooth heads of seals pop up in the bay and perpetuate the legend.

The village itself, along the coast from St Ives, is wild and impossibly romantic, with rough, tawny hills sloping down towards the echoing sea cliffs. Between hills and sea lies a narrow coastal plateau of small, irregular fields whose Cornish 'hedges' of rough granite date from the Iron Age. Because of these historic treats, this long-farmed landscape has earned Zennor protected status for ecological and archaeological reasons. It's a great place to walk.

Access to Zennor Head and to the coast path is on foot down a narrow lane that starts behind the Tinners Arms. Zennor Head has a flat top, but its western flank is spectacular. Towering cliffs fall darkly into a narrow gulf, where the sea crashes white against the shoreline far below. If you can tear yourself away from thoughts of mermaids, it is an invigorating 6-mile walk east to St Ives along some of the most remote coastline in Cornwall.

VISIT THE MUSEUM
**Wayside Folk Museum
and Trewey Watermill**
TR26 3DA | 01736 796945
Open daily Easter–Oct 10.30–5.30
This museum and watermill covers every aspect of life in Zennor and the surrounding area from 3000 BC to the 1930s. More than 5,000 items are displayed in 12 workshops and rooms and cover a wide array of interests: wheelwrights, blacksmiths, agriculture, fishing, wrecks, mining, schools, dairy farming, and domestic and archaeological artefacts. The museum also contains a fully working

watermill with original 19th-century machinery restored to working order grinding grain to flour. The flour is for sale in the shop.

GO BACK IN TIME

Zennor Quoit

This megalithic burial chamber is about a mile east of Zennor and dates from 2500–1500 BC. One of the eight remaining quoits on West Penwith Moor, it's in good condition. Archeologists have found Neolithic pottery and cremated bones here and suggest that it was used for burial and/or cremation rituals; originally, it was probably covered by a mound. It can be found by driving along the B3306 between Zennor and St Ives. Sperris Quoit, 330 yards away, is a more tumbledown example of the same.

EAT AND DRINK

The Tinners Arms

tinnersarms.com

TR26 3BY | 01736 796927

This pub was built from granite in 1271 for masons working on ancient St Senara's Church next door, famous for its richly carved mermaid chair. Don't expect a TV, jukebox or fruit machine, much less a mobile phone signal: this place is full of muddy-booted walkers fresh from the coast path, and Cornish ales and locally sourced food.

▶ PLACES NEARBY

A short drive from Zennor takes you to the Gurnard's Head, a promontory with evidence of ancient residents, and a gastro pub named after it.

Gurnard's Head

Just over a mile to the west of Zennor Head outside St Ives lies Gurnard's Head, a long, elegant promontory that rises to a great, gnarled headland ringed with sheer black cliffs. There are remains of embankments across the neck of this Iron Age site and on the flanking slopes are the rough remains of Iron Age houses. Gurnard's Head may be reached from the B3306, but parking is limited. The coast path between Zennor Head and Gurnard's Head makes for a pleasantly rough walk of about 1.5 miles. Both headlands are in the care of the National Trust.

▶ Pendour Cove and Gurnard's Head

Polzeath
Trebetherick
Long Cross
Victoria
St End

Trevone
Bay
Harlyn
Bay
Prideaux
Place
Rock

Constantine Bay
Treyarnon Bay
Padstow
St Merryn

Porthcothan

A389

Wadebridge

A39

Crealy Great
Adventure Park

Camel Valley
Vineyard

276

Bedruthan Steps

St Mawgan

St Breock
Downs Monolith

B

Mawgan
Porth

A389

Watergate Bay

Lanivet

Tolcarne
Beach

A3059

St Columb
Major

Fistral Beach

Newquay

A30

Roche

A391

Holywell Bay
Holywell

Crantock

A392

Bugle

Cubert

Trerice

Dairyland
Farm World

The Ed
Proje

Ligger or
Perran Bay

Lappa Valley
Steam Railway

Summercourt

Wheal Martyn
Museum &
Country Park

Perranporth

A3075

A30

A39

A3058

St
Austell

unance Trevellas
Cove Porth

Penhallow

Marazanvose

Ladock

St
Stephen

A390

Charlestown

el
th

Wheal
Coates
Mine

St Agnes

Grampound

Lost Gardens
of Heligan

ntowan

Probus

Trewithen
Gardens

St Ewe

Mevagissey

A30

Scorrier

Tresillian

Truro

St Day

Kea

River Fal

Tregony

Caerhays
Castle

Gorran
Haven

ruth

Carnon
Downs

Philleigh

A3078

Portloe

Veryan
Bay

The
Dodman

A393

A39

Trelissick
Garden

Roseland
Peninsula

CORNWALL

Stithians
Lake

Penryn

Mylor

St Just-in-
Roseland

Gerrans
Bay

Nare Head

Argal & College
Waterpark

Falmouth

Camel Roads

Portscatho

St Mawes

dark
ne

Penjerrick
Garden

Pendennis
Castle

St Antony
Head

High
Cross

Mawnan
Smith

Falmouth Bay

ek

Trebah

Carwinion Garden

gan

Cornish
Seal
Sanctuary

Glendurgan

Helford

Manaccan

Halliggye
Fogou

Porthallow

The
Lizard

St Keverne

llion

A3083

Coverack

Cadgwith

ynance
ove
Lizard

zard
oint

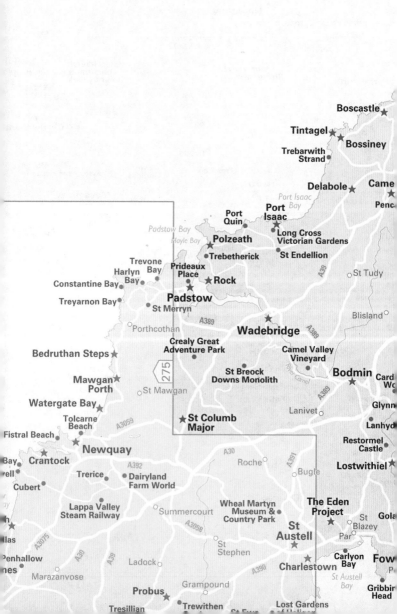

Boscastle ★

Tintagel ★ ● Bossiney

Trebarwith
Strand ●

Delabole ★   Came

Penc

Port Isaac
Bay

Port
Port   Isaac
Quin ●   ●

Long Cross
Victorian Gardens ●

Polzeath ★

Padstow Bay

Hayle Bay

● Trebetherick   St Endellion ●

Trevone
Bay
Harlyn
Bay ●

Prideaux
Place ★

● St Tudy

Constantine Bay ●

★ Rock

Treyarnon Bay ●

Padstow ★

Blisland ○

St Merryn ●

A389

Wadebridge ★

○ Porthcothan

A389

Camel Valley
Vineyard ●

Bedruthan Steps ★

Crealy Great
Adventure Park ●

Mawgan ★
Porth

○ St Mawgan

St Breock
Downs Monolith ●

Bodmin ★

Card
Wo

Watergate Bay ★

★ St Columb
Major

Lanivet ○

Glynn

Tolcarne
Beach ●

A3059

Lanhyd

Restormel
Castle ★

Fistral Beach ●

Newquay ★

A30

Roche ○

Lostwithiel ★

Bay ●

Crantock ★

A392

● Bugle

ell ●

Trerice ●

● Dairyland
Farm World

Cubert ●

Lappa Valley
Steam Railway ★

○ Summercourt

Wheal Martyn
Museum &
Country Park ●

The Eden
Project ★

St Gola
○ Blazey

las ★

A3075

A3058

Par ●

Penhallow ●

A30

A39

Ladock ○

St
Stephen ○

St
Austell ★

Carlyon
Bay ★

Fow

nes ●

Marazanvose ○

Probus ★

Grampound ○

Charlestown ★

St Austell
Bay

P

Tresillian

Trewithen ●

Lost Gardens

Gribbin
Head ★

Morwenstow ★

A39

○ Bradworthy

○ Stibb Cross

Kilkhampton ○

Tamar Lakes

○ Milton Damerel

A388

○ Shebbear

DEVON

Chilsworthy ○

Sheepwash ○

Poughill
Stratton

A3072

Black ○
Torrington

A3072 ○

Bude ★

Bude Bay

Highampton ○

Holsworthy ○

Marhamchurch

Widemouth Bay

Halwill ○
Junction

○ Beaworthy

Poundstock ●

Week
St Mary

○ Clawton

A3079

rackington aven

Penhallam Manor

○ Ashwater

Roadford Reservoir

Bratton Clovelly ○

A388

A38

Tremaine ●

North Petherwin

Tamar Otter & Wildlife Centre

A30

Bridestowe ○

Egloskerry ●

A395

Hidden Valley Discovery Park

Lydford ○

A386

C O R N W A L L

★ **Launceston**

Lifton ○

● **Laneast**

Milton
Abbot ○

Mary Tavy ○

Altarnun ●

19

own illy

Lamerton ○

d m i n

o o r

● **Jamaica Inn**

Tavistock ○

★

Dozmary Pool

Colliford Lake

Upton Cross ●

St Ann's
Chapel

Gunnislake

Siblyback Water Park

Cheesewring ●

Kit Hill Country Park ●

Dupath Well ●

Calstock ★

Horrabridge ○

○ Pensilva

olliford
ke Park

Minions ●

Golitha Falls ●

Trethevy Quoit ●

Cotehele ●

A386

King Doniert's Stone ●

A390

St Dominick

Bere Alston ○

Carnglaze Slate Caverns

Pillaton ○

Bere Ferrers ○

90

★ **Liskeard**

St ○
Keyne

Paul Corin's Magnificent Music Machines ●

Landrake ○

A38

Duloe ●

Widegates ○

Saltash ●

St Germans ●

Polbathic ○

Antony House ●

orfell Animal Land & Wildlife Park

Pelynt ○

Monkey Sanctuary ●

Downderry ○

A374

Torpoint ○

PLYMOUTH

Kilminorth Woods ●

★ **Looe** Seaton ●

Crafthole ○

Millbrook ○

Mount Edgcumbe Country Park ●

Polperro Model Village ★

Looe Bay

Whitsand Bay

Kingsand ★

Polperro

Looe Island ●

Cawsand ★

Heybrook ○
Bay

Rame Head ★

Index, themed

Page numbers in **bold** refer to main entries

Index, places

Page numbers in **bold** refer to main entries; page numbers in *italics* refer to maps

The Automobile Association wishes to thank the following photographers and organisations for their assistance in the preparation of this book.

Abbreviations for the picture credits are as follows – (t) top; (m) middle; (b) bottom; (l) left; (r) right; (c) centre; (AA) AA World Travel Library.

Trade Cover: Helen Dixon/alamy
SS Cover AA/A Burton

4tl AA/A Burton; 4tr AA/A Burton; 4bl AA/A Burton; 5r AA/A Burton; 5bl AA/J Wood; 8-9 AA/J Wood; 11 AA/J Wood; 12t AA/C Jones; 12b AA/R Tenison; 13t AA/A Burton; 13m AA/C Jones; 13b AA/R Moss; 14t Courtesy of National Maritime Museum/Peter Edwards; 14m AA/C Jones; 14b AA/J Wood; 15 AA/R Moss; 16 AA/R Tenison; 18 AA/A Weller; 19 AA/R Tenison; 20 AA/A Burton; 21 AA/J Wood; 22 AA/J Wood; 23 AA/J Wood; 24 digitalunderwater.com/Alamy; 25 AA/J Wood; 26 AA/S&O Mathews; 30-31 AA/A Burton; 32 Jack Sullivan/Alamy; 33 AA/J Love; 34 AA/C Jones; 35 AA/A Mockford & N Bonetti; 36-37 AA/J Love; 38 Chris Lawrence/Alamy; 40 David Pearson/Alamy; 41 AA; 42 AA/A Burton; 43 AA/J Tims; 44 Andrew Ray/Alamy; 45 AF archive/Alamy; 46 AA/J Wood; 49 AA/A Burton; 50 AA/J Wood; 52 AA/A Burton; 54-55 AA/A Burton; 56 AA/C Jones; 60 AA/R Moss; 62 AA/J Wood; 63 AA/R Moss; 64 AA/R Moss; 72 AA/J Wood; 77 AA/J Wood; 80 AA/N Ray; 86 AA/J Wood; 89 AA/J Wood; 91 Michael Willis/Alamy; 92 AA/J Wood; 94 AA/C Jones; 96 Courtesy of National Maritime Museum/Bob Berry; 102-103 Kevin Britland/Alamy; 105 AA/N Ray; 108 AA/N Ray; 111 AA/R Moss; 114 AA/J Wood; 118 AA/R Moss; 120 AA/A Burton; 121 AA/C Jones; 122 AA/R Moss; 129 AA/J Wood; 130 AA/J Wood; 131 AA/J Wood; 132 AA/R Moss; 136-137 Peter Barritt/Alamy; 142 AA/R Moss; 143 David Chapman/Alamy; 148 AA/J Wood; 150 AA/J Wood; 151 AA/N Ray; 157 AA/R Moss; 158 AA/R Moss; 160-161 AA/A Besley; 162 AA/C Jones; 167 AA/R Tenison; 168-169 AA/C Jones; 170 AA/J Wood; 172 AA/A Burton; 176-177 Andrew Ray/Alamy; 178t AA/R Tenison; 178b AA/J Wood; 181 AA/J Wood; 184-185 Kevin Britland/Alamy; 192-193 AA/R Moss; 196 AA/A Burton; 197 AA/C Jones; 202 AA/A Lawson; 205 AA/A Lawson; 207 AA/A Burton; 212 AA/T Teegan; 215 AA/R Moss; 217 AA/J Wood; 226-227 AA/A Burton; 228 AA/A Burton; 229 AA/R Tenison; 234-235 AA/J Wood; 237 AA/J Wood; 238 AA/A Burton; 244 AA/A Lawson; 245 AA/J Wood; 246-247 Peter Barritt/Alamy; 252-253 AA/R Moss; 254 Peter Barritt/Alamy; 256 AA/A Burton; 260 AA/R Moss; 261 AA/C Jones; 262 AA/R Moss; 265 AA/M Lynch; 273 AA/A Burton

Every effort has been made to trace the copyright holders, and we apologise in advance for any unintentional omissions or errors. We would be pleased to apply any corrections in any following edition of this publication.

Series editor: Rebecca Needes | Indexer: Vanessa Bird
Author: Laura Dixon | Designer: Tracey Freestone
Copy editor: Joey Clarke | Digital imaging & repro: Ian Little
Proofreader: Jackie Bates | Art director: James Tims

Additional writing by other AA contributors. *Lore of the Land* feature by Ruth Binney. Some content may appear in other AA books and publications.

Has something changed? Email us at travelguides@theaa.com.

'WE KNOW BRITAIN'

The AA was founded in 1905 as a body initially intended to help motorists avoid police speed traps. As motoring became more popular, so did we, and our activities have continued to expand into a great variety of areas.

The first edition of the AA Members' Handbook appeared in 1908. Due to the difficulty many motorists were having finding reasonable meals and accommodation while on the road, the AA introduced a new scheme to include listings for 'about one thousand of the leading hotels' in the second edition in 1909. As a result the AA has been recommending and assessing establishments for over a century, and each year our professional inspectors anonymously visit and rate thousands of hotels, restaurants, guest accommodations and campsites. We are relied upon for our trustworthy and objective star, Rosette and Pennant ratings systems, which you will see used in this guide to denote AA-inspected restaurants and campsites.

In 1912 we published our first handwritten routes and our atlas of town plans, and in 1925 our classic touring guide, *The AA Road Book of England and Wales* appeared. Together, our accurate mapping and in-depth knowledge of places to visit were to set the benchmark for British travel publishing.

Since the 1990s we have dramatically expanded our publishing activities, producing high quality atlases, maps, walking and travel guides for the UK and the rest of the world. In this new series of regional travel guides we are drawing on over a hundred years of experience to bring you the very best of Britain.